Scenes of the Apple

SUNY series in Feminist Criticism and Theory
Michelle A. Massé, editor

Scenes of the Apple

Food and the Female Body
in
Nineteenth- and Twentieth-Century Women's Writing

Edited by

Tamar Heller
and
Patricia Moran

State University of New York Press

Published by
STATE UNIVERSITY OF NEW YORK PRESS, ALBANY

For information, address State University of New York Press,
90 State Street, Suite 700, Albany, NY 12207

Production by Marilyn P. Semerad
Marketing by Anne M. Valentine

Library of Congress Cataloging-in-Publication Data

Scenes of the apple : food and the female body in nineteenth- and twentieth-century
women's writing / edited by Tamar Heller and Patricia Moran.
    p. cm. — (SUNY series in feminist criticism and theory)
    Includes bibliographical references and index.
    ISBN 0-7914-5783-4 (alk. paper) — ISBN 0-7914-5784-2 (pbk. : alk. paper)
    1. Women in literature. 2. Body, Human, in literature. 3. Food in literature. 4.
Literature—Women authors—History and criticism. 5. Literature, Modern—19th
century—History and criticism. 6. Literature, Modern—20th century—History and
criticism. I. Heller, Tamar, 1959– II. Moran, Patricia. III. Series.

PN56.5.W64 S28 2003
809'.93352042—dc21   2002030971

                    10 9 8 7 6 5 4 3 2 1

Contents

Part 3

FOOD AND COOKING: PATRIARCHAL,
COLONIAL, FAMILIAL STRUCTURES

Illustrations

Acknowledgments

We would like to thank our editors, James Peltz and Michele Massé, for their support and encouragement over the years it took to complete this project. We would also like to thank the readers of the manuscript, who offered invaluable suggestions for improvement. Debra Kalmon deserves our thanks for her expertise in putting the manuscript together.

Tamar Heller would like to acknowledge the support by a Research on Women grant from the University of Louisville. Above all, she would like to thank her coeditor for the wonderful experience she had working with her. Chuck Hatten provided, as usual, fruitful suggestions and moral uplift.

Patricia Moran would like to acknowledge the support of her colleagues at the University of California at Davis, especially Joanne Feit Diehl, Kari Lokke, and David Van Leer. She would also like to acknowledge the support of Dean Elizabeth Langland and Linda Morris, former chair of the department of English, in underwriting some of the costs of preparing this book for publication. She is grateful to Tamar Heller for her initiative in proposing this collaboration and her determination in seeing it through to completion. Michael, David, and Patrick Higgins deserve thanks for their good humor and good company.

Several of these essays have appeared in other publications. Grateful acknowledgment is extended to Taylor & Francis Ltd. for permission to reprint Pamela K. Gilbert's essay, which first appeared in *Literature Interpretation Theory* 8. 1 (Winter 1997): 83–104; and to Gordon and Breach Publishers for permission to reprint Janice A. Jaffe's essay, which first appeared in *Women's Studies: An Interdisciplinary Forum* 22. 2 (1993): 217–30. Adrienne Munich's essay is reprinted by permission of *Victorians Institute Journal*, which first published that essay in volume 28 (2000). Portions of Sue Thomas's essay were first published as "Killing the Hysteric in the Colonised's House: Tsitsi Dangarembga's *Nervous Conditions*" in the *Journal of Commonwealth Literature* 17. 1 (1992): 26–36.

The editors also wish to thank Thomson Publishing Services for permission to quote as an epigraph a passage from Hélène Cixous's essay "Extreme Fidelity," in *The Hélène Cixous Reader,* ed. Susan Sellers (New York: Routledge, 1994), p. 133. The epigraph by Bobbie Ann Mason appears in "The Burden of the Feast," in *We Are What We Ate: Twenty-four Memories of Food,* ed. Mark Winegardner (San Diego: Harvest-

Harcourt, 1998), p. 136. The excerpt from "Breakfast" from *Never Eat Your Heart Out* by Judith Moore, copyright 1997 by Judith Moore, is reprinted by permission of Farrar, Straus and Giroux, LLC, and Absolute Press.

1

Introduction
Scenes of the Apple:
Appetite, Desire, Writing

Tamar Heller and Patricia Moran

> [L]et us take the scene of the apple . . . The first fable of
> our first book is a fable in which what is at stake is the
> relationship to the law . . . It's a struggle between the
> Apple and the discourse of God. . . . [W]hat Eve will
> discover in her relationship to simple reality, is the
> inside of the apple, and that this inside is good. This
> story tells us that the genesis of woman goes through the
> mouth, through a certain oral pleasure . . .
>
> —Hélène Cixous, "Extreme Fidelity"

In the Genesis narrative of the fall, sin and death enter the world when
a woman eats. In "Extreme Fidelity," Hélène Cixous claims that this Eve
story, the "scene of the apple," is the guiding myth of Western culture,
a fable about the subjection of female "oral pleasure" to the regulation
of patriarchal law. An allegory of what she calls "libidinal education"—
the individual's discovery of the body and the cultural prohibitions surrounding it—the Genesis myth is also, according to Cixous, about the
genesis of "artistic being" (15), a *Künstlerroman* in which the writer,
whom she represents as a transgressive woman, encounters not only the
cultural taboos surrounding the body but the realm of language which
encodes them. To "shake [words] like apple trees" (15)—to repeat Eve's

1

transgression, and to question cultural law—is the way the artist can achieve the goal that Cixous, in "The Laugh of the Medusa," calls "writing the body": breaking down the dualism of flesh and spirit that has traditionally devalued and silenced women.

Using Cixous's hungry Eve as our touchstone, these chapters explore how women write about food and oral pleasure, and, in so doing, negotiate their relation to the body as well as to language and culture. We are thus interested in food on two levels, both the literal and the figurative. To discuss how food and cooking are represented in women's writing is on one level to recognize the important role that this quotidian reality has played, and still does play, in women's lives.[1] On a second level, however, we wish to examine the multiple symbolic meanings that food acquires in women's writing.[2] Food can symbolize the realm Cixous calls "libidinal"—bodily and sexual experience—while also signifying, as it does in her version of the scene of the apple, language and voice, a symbolism drawing on the dual association of the mouth with both eating and speaking. As Helena Michie writes, "If Eve's desire for the apple represents the decentering force of women's power, it is also deeply linked with the question of authority and, finally, of authorship" (28). As an example of orality as authorial power, Michie cites Louisa May Alcott's Jo March in *Little Women*, "stuffing apples into her mouth as she writes in her garret," an image that emblematizes how Victorian women writers, in their revisions of the Genesis story, were "transgressing in their hunger to write and to know, and translating trespass into the source of their power" (28). According to Michie, this reappropriation of the Fall myth also animates the work of those contemporary women writers who, "feasting on Eve's apples," celebrate rather than censor "female hunger . . . for sex, authority, creativity, and power" (131).

That Michie's example of orality as authorship is Alcott's Jo March, however, reveals as much about women's anxiety about appetite as it does their vindication of it. In a fit of guilt, Jo will later destroy melodramatic stories of the type she had written while feasting on apples: a containment of creative energy that recalls Alcott's own double life in the 1860s as a pseudonymous writer of sensation fiction and its tales of illicit sexuality and power-hungry women. Like Jo, Alcott shelved this double life to devote herself to domestic fiction like *Little Women*, which she referred to dismissively, in a telling oral metaphor, as "moral pap for the young." The conflict between the transgressive and the domestic in Alcott's own career is another version of what Alcott's biographer Madelon Bedell called "the Drama of the Apple," in which Alcott's father tried to tame his daughter's unruly appetite by shutting her in a room with an apple she was forbidden to eat—a test she promptly failed (81–82), and which, as Elaine Showalter says, is reenacted over and over again in her fiction in scenes of tension between "patriarchal authority" and "female self-assertion" (Introduction to *Little Women*, x). Alcott's ambivalence about female appetite—an advocate of women's suffrage and higher education, she championed women's hunger for power at the same time she often chastened it in her fiction—is emblematic of how the scene of the apple can, for women writers of the twentieth as well as the nineteenth century, express deeply conflicted feelings about appetite and desire, authority and assertion. This collection explores the many, many ways in which women's relationship to food is gendered—as forbidden knowledge, as nurturance, as disordered and symptomatic—even as it also shows that cultural constructions of woman as desiring, self-denying, or nurturing are more complicated than they initially appear.[3] To that end, this collection includes pieces not only on classic and contemporary literary texts, but on memoirs, literary theories, and advertisements—the multiple venues in which women writers have engaged with "scenes of the apple."

Many books have appeared on food, literature, anorexia, disordered eating, and cooking in relation to women in recent years, but our collection is the first to bring together a variety of ways in which literary women have specifically engaged with these topics. Individual chapters resonate with and play off one another, moreover, thereby complicating important conceptualizations that have been developed in the areas of social history, politics, and feminist theory as well as literary and cultural studies. While we are now familiar with the image of the self-effacing anorexic of Victorian literature, for example, that image becomes considerably less ubiquitous when we consider her in relation to the hefty Queen Victoria. Similarly, the stereotypical image of the anorexic as a middle-class white daughter caught in a "golden cage" of her own devising changes when disordered eating is represented as a response to racial or colonial oppressions.[4] Female appetite, so often represented as a continuum—overeaters on one side, bulimics and anorexics on the other—here appears in cannibalistic, grotesque, and ghostly contexts. That "room of one's own," the kitchen, can serve as the locale for female authority, for the preservation of ethnic and religious identities, or for the nostalgic reanimation of the stable "feeding mother" of fifties ideology.[5] In anorexia and other disordered eating, in female consumerism, in cooking and recipe writing, in kitchens, and in political life, female authority and female appetite emerge as related issues.[6]

This collection builds upon several decades of scholarship, a body of work that exists in large part because feminist scholars have insisted that food and eating have been and remain central concerns in women's lives as well as in their literary texts. It arrives, moreover, at the end of a decade that saw the emergence of food studies as a distinct discipline within academia and the publication of a wealth of new scholarship on food and eating.[7] In the following pages, we situate this collection within that body of work; a description of these multiple strands is crucial in order to map out the critical complexity that informs our topic.

EATING AND WRITING IN LITERARY CONTEXTS

Feminist literary scholars first began to study the interrelationships be-tween eating and literary authority in women's literary texts in the late 1970s and early 1980s. In their groundbreaking *The Madwoman in the Attic* (1979), for example, Sandra M. Gilbert and Susan Gubar drew from the fairy tale of Snow White a paradigm of female conflict, embodied in the poisonous "Eve's apple" the wicked Queen offers Snow White (40). Half-red, half-white, half-poisonous, half-pure, the apple represented for Gilbert and Gubar nineteenth-century female choices between plotting and plotlessness, assertion and silence, sexual energy and self-abnegation: "the Queen, adult and demonic, plainly wants a life of 'significant action,' by definition an 'unfeminine' life of stories and story telling. And there-fore, to the extent that Snow White, as her daughter, is a part of herself, she wants to kill the Snow White in *herself*, the angel who would keep deeds and dramas out of her own house" (39). Gilbert and Gubar went on to argue that hunger and starvation on the one hand, speech and story telling on the other, serve as central tropes dramatizing the conflicts of female literary authority in the nineteenth century:

> Rejecting the poisoned apples her culture offers her, the woman writer often becomes in some sense anorexic, resolutely closing her mouth on silence . . . even while she complains of starva-tion. Thus both Charlotte and Emily Brontë depict the travails of starved or starving anorexic heroines, while Emily Dickinson declares in one breath that she "had been hungry, all the Years," and in another opts for "Sumptuous Destitution." Similarly, Christina Rossetti represents her own anxiety of authorship in the split between one heroine who longs to "suck and suck" on goblin fruit and another who locks her lips fiercely together in a gesture of silent and passionate renunciation. (58)

A number of noteworthy studies appeared further elaborating on the connections between anorexia and self-expression in literary women's texts, including important works by Helena Michie, Paula Marantz Cohen, Leslie Heywood, and others. Women writers themselves anticipated this critical work, deliberately making use of tropes of hunger, starvation, and eating to explore complex issues of female identity and expression. From

Margaret Atwood's *The Edible Woman* (1969) and *Lady Oracle* (1976) to Gloria Naylor's multi-generational study of eating disorders in *Linden Hills* (1985) and Toni Morrison's harrowing *Beloved* (1987), women writers relied upon images of feeding and starvation to explore the issues of female voice, identity, and authority.

Although literature both critical and creative of this time foregrounded tropes of hunger and starvation, it is important to remember that work on female pleasure in orality was also taking place. The exuberant and influential "womanifestoes" of Hélène Cixous, for example, urged women to challenge the constraints placed upon female desire and aspiration in images of appetite and ingestion. For Cixous, as we have indicated in the epigraph to this introduction, Eve's defiant eating of the forbidden apple is a paradigmatic moment of female rebellion against the invisible and negative force of patriarchal law: "[W]hat we are told is that knowledge might begin with the mouth, with the discovery of the taste of something, knowledge and taste go together. . . . [T]he apple is, is, is. . . . the apple is visible and it can be held up to the mouth, it is full, it has an *inside*" ("Fidelity" 16). In a similar vein, Patricia Yaeger questioned feminist literary critics' focus on the anorexic and hungering woman writer. Exploring the "pleasurable, powerful aspects of orality," Yaeger celebrated the figure of the "honey-mad woman," an appetitive woman who is "language mad": "A blissful consumer and purveyor of language, the honey-mad writer is a symbol of verbal plenitude, of woman's capacity to rewrite her culture," she charged (28–29). In yet another context, Audre Lorde's 1982 "biomythography" *Zami: A New Spelling of My Name* powerfully celebrated the erotic/poetic bonds among women and more particularly within lesbian relationships in terms of food and eating. Sitting between her mother's legs as a child, Lorde is a "nutmeg nestled inside its covering of mace" (33); later, in an important scene that highlights both Lorde's erotic connection with her mother and her lesbian difference, Lorde contrasts her method of mashing garlic and spices—"[M]y downward thrusts of the pestle grew gentler and gentler, until its velvety surface seemed to caress the liquefying mash at the bottom of the mortar" (79)—with her mother's conventional "heterosexual" mashing—"the thump of wood brought down heavily upon wood. . . . Thump, thump, went the pestle, purposefully, up and down, in the old familiar way" (79–80). This episode, which takes place on the occasion of Lorde's first menstrual period, encapsulates for her the location of her poetic voice in the preverbal space of her mother's womb, Lorde's mythical "home," a Carribean island redolent with spices and "the delicate breadfruit smell, womansmell, warm, shameful, but secretly utterly delicious" (77):

> As I continued to pound the spice, a vital connection seemed
> to establish itself between the muscles of my fingers curved

tightly around the smooth pestle in its insistent downward motion, and the molten core of my body whose source emanated from a new ripe fullness just beneath the pit of my stomach. That invisible thread, taut and sensitive as a clitoris exposed, stretched through my curled fingers up my round brown arm into the moist reality of my armpits, whose warm sharp odor with a strange new overlay mixed with the ripe garlic smells from the mortar and the general sweat-heavy aromas of high summer.

The thread ran over my ribs and along my spine, tingling and singing, into a basin that was poised between my hips, now pressed against the low kitchen counter before which I stood, pounding spice. And within that basin was a tiding ocean of blood beginning to be made real and available to me for strength and information. (78)[8]

Near the end of *Zami* Lorde again merges erotic life and food when she describes a celebratory banquet for lesbians in stunningly rich gastronomic and erotic images: "[T]he centerpiece of the whole table was a huge platter of succulent and thinly sliced roast beef. . . . Upon the beige platter, each slice of rare meat had been lovingly laid out and individually folded into a vulval pattern, with a tiny dab of mayonnaise at the crucial apex" (242).[9]

Cookbooks and culinary memoirs provided yet another venue for feminist inquiry. In the late 1980s, the publication of Susan J. Leonardi's "Recipes for Reading: Summer Pasta, Lobster à la Riseholme, and Key Lime Pie" inaugurated the literary study of cookbooks and food writing. Leonardi argued that recipes were a form of literary production, a "highly embedded discourse akin to literary discourse" (342) and she specifically tied that discourse to women:

In the earlier *Joy*, the establishment of a lively narrator with a circle of enthusiastic and helpful friends reproduces the social context of recipe sharing—a loose community of women that crosses the social barriers of class, race, and generation. Many women can attest to the usefulness and importance of this discourse: mothers and daughters—even those who don't get along well otherwise—old friends who now have little in common, mistresses and their "help," lawyers and their secretaries—all can participate in this almost prototypical activity. (342–43)

While she objected to Leonardi's erasure of cultural difference—the "highly embedded discourse" of cookbooks is not an "archetypally feminine language but rather . . . a form of writing that, if coded feminine, is also a culturally contingent production" (172)—Anne Goldman extended the scope of Leonardi's claims, insisting that "to write about food is to write about the self"(169). Cooking is "a metonym of culture" (169), and hence food writing becomes both "cultural practice and autobiographical assertion": "If it provides an apt metaphor for the reproduction of culture from generation to generation, the act of passing down recipes from mother to daughter works as well to figure a familial space within which self-articulation can begin to take place" (172).[10] Goldman's argument finds ample support, in particular in women's autobiographical and fictional narratives about various types of cultural deracination. Immigrant narratives or postcolonial texts that address the tension between a native and a colonizing culture abound with nostalgic evocations of traditional food, an association strengthened by the role of women (mothers, grandmothers, aunts) in food preparation.[11] "Italy is as near to me as appetite," writes Helen Barolini (228), in a collection of essays, *Through the Kitchen Window: Women Explore the Intimate Meanings of Food and Culture*, that in itself represents an important collection of meditations on women's connections to ethnic cultures through cooking. In an essay from the same collection whose title highlights the issues of belonging and rootlessness, "Food and Belonging: At 'Home' in 'Alien Kitchens,' " Ketu H. Katrak connects the names of foods in her mother tongue to her sense of loss of a motherland: "Clanging sounds from the kitchen enter my waking body as mouth-watering aromas waft in—moist *chapatis, kando-papeto, kheechree-kadhi, papeta ma gosh*. These words in Gujarati, my mother tongue, carry the tastes and aromas that are lost in their English translations" (263). In *The Book of Jewish Food*, Claudia Roden succinctly states the connections between cultural identity and cooking: "Every culture tells a story," she writes. "Jewish food tells the story of an uprooted, migrating people and their vanished worlds" (3). A number of women's books about the recovery or preservation of cultural heritage similarly stress women's role in preserving traditions through cooking, as in Cara De Silva's recently reprinted collection of recipes gathered by starving Jewish women in the Terezin concentration camp, *In Memory's Kitchen*, or the collection of writing by Arab-American and Arab-Canadian feminists, *Food for Our Grandmothers*, edited by Joanna Kadi, which intersperses recipes with poetry and prose in order to "give something back to our grandmothers and to our community" by recalling "the Arabic food that many of them made daily" (xx).

The recent development of a distinct subgenre of autobiography, the culinary memoir, is another indication that women's food-writing is increasingly perceived and cast within more formal, literary conventions. Traci Marie Kelly defines culinary autobiography as a "literary extension of this kitchen storytelling" and describes it as a "complex pastiche of recipes, personal anecdotes, family history, public history, photographs, even family trees":

> These recipes-with-memories are a natural extension of
> storytelling, with the recipes acting as a kind of "cue card"
> giving the memoir a structure and a template to embellish.
> Some women have appreciated the "canvas" of the kitchen,
> using that space to create nourishing meals, memories, and
> art. These works are rich sources for autobiographical asser-
> tion because they present the lives of women through their
> own voices, rendered from a room that has been, truly, a
> room of their own. (252)

The development of this subgenre is significant, since within the field of
food studies it is possible to discern a growing rift between those who
perceive women's primary responsibilities for food making as gender
bound and oppressive and those who argue that it can function as a
crucial means of self-definition.[12] Sherrie A. Inness states "Kitchen culture is a critical way that women are instructed about how to behave like
'correctly' gendered beings" (Introduction, 4), while Sally Cline finds
that acculturation key in women's oppression: "By looking at food we
can get at the kernel of the political relationship between the sexes. For
food is a crucial political area. Women's subordination is locked into
food; an issue even feminists have not yet sufficiently investigated" (3).
While acknowledging that such oppression can exist, Arlene Voski
Avakian urges feminists to remain open-minded about the positive aspects of
women's cooking: "If we delve into the relationship between women and
food we will discover the ways in which women have forged spaces
within that oppression. Cooking becomes a vehicle for artistic expression,
a source of sensual pleasure, an opportunity for resistance and even power"
(6). Barbara Haber has similarly chastised feminists for consistently portraying food preparation as a site "fraught with conflict, coercion, and
frustration". "[D]omestic life can be acknowledged and even celebrated
without buying into an oppressive value system," she declares (68).

Recent culinary memoirs themselves reflect and support both views.
Isabelle Allende wrote her celebratory *Aphrodite: A Memoir of the Senses*
in part to reawaken her corporeal and sensual appetites after the death
of her daughter Paula, while Ruth Reichl's *Tender at the Bone: Growing
Up at the Table* and *Comfort Me with Apples: More Adventures of the Table*
trace her journey to writing and sexual fulfillment through the mediums
of eating and cooking. Judith Moore's *Never Eat Your Heart Out*, on
the other hand, is much more ambivalent about the labor involved in
food preparation; Moore becomes a gourmet cook for her family and
friends during the time in which she takes part in an extramarital affair
that ends her marriage of twenty years, and she writes her memoir while
living alone, writing, and cooking only for herself. Yet another recent
memoir, Elizabeth Ehrlich's *Miriam's Kitchen: A Memoir*, seems to come

down on both sides of the debate: while Ehrlich explicitly chooses to keep kosher and to become a full-time homemaker as a way of preserving ethnic and religious traditions, she also thereby solves seemingly insurmountable difficulties in the gender divisions she experiences both intrapsychically and interrelationally, gender divisions which form an inextricable part of larger cultural, historical, and social contexts (see Moran, this volume). Yet whether women develop critiques or celebrations of food making in their memoirs, they demonstrate the force of Deborah Lupton's observation that "[f]ood and eating habits and preferences are not simply matters of 'fueling' ourselves. . . . Food and eating are central to our subjectivity, or sense of self" (1). "[T]o write about food is to write about the self," Anne Goldman says (169).

THE PRIMAL FEAST: EATING, FEEDING, AND MOTHER-DAUGHTER RELATIONSHIPS

Thus far we have touched only tangentially on a theme that is central to a volume on women's literary authority, their eating and feeding and cooking, their appetites and desires: the role of the mother-daughter relationship within the food nexus as well as within literary representations of that nexus. Significantly, psychoanalysts, therapists, social historians, and feminist scholars have long agreed upon the centrality of the mother-daughter relationship in women's susceptibility to eating disorders.[13] Analyzing the emergence of anorexia nervosa as a modern disease in the nineteenth century, for example, historian Joan Jacob Brumberg charts an increasing possessiveness in the Victorian middle-class family that granted very little "autonomous psychic space" to adolescent girls (137): "Because mothers and daughters were supposed to be especially close, some daughters may have been subjected to socially acceptable (but privately intolerable) forms of possessive behavior that rankled and allowed little room for emotional growth. Since emotional freedom was not a common prerogative of the Victorian adolescent girl, it seems reasonable to assert that unhappiness was likely to be expressed in nonverbal forms of behavior. One such behavior was refusal of food" (138). Women writers in the nineteenth century vividly portray how the ideal Victorian wife and mother modelled self-abnegation and self-denial in a manner conducive to, or even suggestive of, this particular nonverbal response. Turning again to *Little Women*, we see not only Marmee's role as moral guide and confidante to her daughters, sharing (or intuiting) all the girls' most intimate problems and aspirations; we see as well her insistence on self-control and her condemnation of anger or rebellion against duty (insistence usually directed at the would-be writer, the self-assertive, angry, and rebellious Jo). Hence Marmee explains to Jo that, although she herself is angry nearly every day of her life, she has learned not to show it; instead, as Jo observes, "you fold your lips tight together and go out of the room" (79)—a technique Jo learns her mother has acquired through the father's instruction (80). In a chapter particularly relevant to our analysis, Marmee asks her daughters to sacrifice their Christmas breakfast to a needy immigrant family; she "smile[s] as if satisfied" when they eagerly accede, and the girls discover the (here simultaneous) joys of self-abnegation and hunger: "That was a very happy breakfast, though they didn't get any of it; and when they went away, leaving comfort behind, I think there were not in all the city four merrier people than the hungry little girls who gave away their breakfasts and contented themselves with bread and milk on Christmas morning" (15–16). The March girls learn their lessons well: "'That's loving our neighbor better than ourselves, and I like it,' said Meg" (16).

Alcott captures brilliantly in this passage the nonverbal codes embedded in food and tacitly exchanged between mother and daughter(s). Although Alcott represents this sacrifice as a request—"My girls, will you give them your breakfast as a Christmas present?" (14)—it functions as a demand: it is impossible to imagine the girls' refusing to give their breakfast away and Marmee still "smil[ing] as if satisfied." Maternal approval, in other words, depends upon acquiescence to a feminine code of self-abnegation. Virginia Woolf, herself the daughter of a Victorian Angel in the House, similarly represents maternal approval as contingent upon the daughter's effacement of herself and similarly codes that self-effacement in terms of food. In the autobiographical essay "Reminiscences," Woolf imagines Julia Stephen's joy in seeing early maternal impulses in Woolf's sister Vanessa, impulses made evident when Vanessa "giv[es] up her bottle" to her brother: "Her mother would smile silently at this" (28).

If the control of appetite was an important indicator of a girl's ability to control or suppress her libidinal appetites (Brumberg, Michie), then, that control simultaneously functioned as a marker of the mother's ability to instruct her daughter properly: indeed, a girl's sexual lapse was not just evidence of her own fallen nature; it reflected a corrupt genetic inheritance through the maternal line, and one girl's fall could potentially damage the marriageability of her sisters. Katherine Mansfield furnishes tragic evidence of the way in which one rebellious woman writer's libidinal appetites—for food, for sex, for writing—estranged her from her mother. As a young girl, Mansfield established her rebellion against her mother's proper womanhood upon the terrain of her body: Mansfield alone among the four daughters was overweight and unkempt, and biographers have documented her mother's explicit remarks of distaste for Mansfield's body.[14] Later, after several disastrous sexual exploits, Mansfield's mother cut her daughter out of her will and did not see her again, in part as a way of protecting another daughter's engagement and impending marriage. In this context, it is tragic indeed to read Mansfield's later letters to her mother, wherein she celebrates the emaciation consumption has wrought upon her body as proof that her libidinal appetites are (finally) well under control: "Farewell to my portliness. For I who weighed 10 stone 3 at the age of fifteen now weigh 8 stone six. At this rate I will be a midget tooth pick at fifty" (17). Other letters code her eating along conventional cultural lines: for example, Mansfield celebrates her tastes for bland, "feminine" meals like tea and toast, and eschews the libidinal foods of spices and peppers: "I am afraid you took my mention of sausages and stout . . . too much to heart, and have a dreadful fancy that I live almost exclusively upon these highly seasoned comestibles. Nothing could be further from the truth. I am just as simple in my tastes as you. A cup of *good* old-fashioned tea, bread and butter—jam—and eggs plain or in any disguise satisfies me *at* any time and *for* any time" (25).

Mothers' relations to their daughters' appetites changed in the twentieth century, as the ideal of an inner moral purity gave way to an ideal of an external and corporeal norm, a change that made the control of appetite a visible, material emblem of self-discipline and self-control. Both fashion and representations of the normative female body changed dramatically at the turn of the century. Not only did the hourglass figure give way to the ideal of a boyish, prepubescent outline, but the new affordability of and access to ready-made clothing—as opposed to making one's clothing or having it sewn by a dressmaker—meant that middle-class women had to adapt themselves to standard or normal shapes and sizes in order to be fashionable; these new fashions, moreover, did without corsets or other devices that could conceal undesirable flaws. Fashion historian Valerie Steele notes that women now had no choice but to diet or to internalize the constraints of the corset. Some of the most enduring elements of dieting were established during this period: the development of life insurance tables with listings of ideal weights; the development of nutritional science and the counting of calories as a scientific means of reducing; the production of home scales, termed a "materialized conscience" by one 1917 diet manual (Seid 95).

These wide-ranging and powerful changes in fashion and the female form altered the ways in which middle-class mothers related to their own and their daughters' bodies. For, to some extent, the new ideal of a boyish or prepubescent body was a rejection of a mature or overtly maternal outline. As Roberta Pollack Seid explains, "the 'fat' woman . . . symbolized the family; the new slender woman symbolized 'youth' and projected a 'disquieting and alert glamour'" (85). Yet at the same time, the new ideal—and the rise of standardized weights and clothing, of diets and scales and calorie counting—tied a woman's lifelong attractiveness to a slender and youthful outline. "If in the past a young married woman could swell gracefully into matronly contours and not compromise her charms, in the twenties she no longer had this luxury," observes Seid (93). In practice, this meant that many women continued to diet throughout their lives, modeling a very different fear of female appetite for their daughters than that practiced by their Victorian predecessors. For whereas for the Victorians the management of appetite spoke to a woman's moral purity, now the mark of moral purity came increasingly to be the body itself. And the daughter's success or lack of success could be seen as a reflection of a mother's success or lack of success in parenting. As the protagonist of Margaret Atwood's *Lady Oracle* remarks about her mother's determination to control her weight, "If she'd ever gone out and done it, she wouldn't have seen me as a reproach to her, the embodiment of her own failure and depression, a huge endless cloud of inchoate matter which refused to be shaped into anything for which she could get a prize" (64). Instead, "the war between myself and my mother was on in earnest; the disputed territory was my body" (65–6). More recently, in her multiracial study of mother-daughter issues in the etiology of disordered eating, sociologist Becky W. Thompson notes that internalized racism plays an important role in the pressures directed at girls of color; in words that painfully echo Atwood's white, middle-class protagonist, one African American woman felt that "her body became the contested territory onto which her parents' pain was projected" (34). The pressures of assimilation and the desire to rise on the social ladder, Thompson writes, means that cultural ideals of thinness impact all women: the experiences of the women she surveyed "dispel the notion that African American and Latina women—as a group—are less exposed to or influenced by a culturally imposed thinness than white women" (35).

Women writers often portray conflicts in eating and feeding as a way of coming to terms with the symbolic weight of maternity or, less typically, with other family members, such as the father. One such response, exemplified by *Lady Oracle*, is what Adrienne Rich defines as "matrophobia," the fear "not of one's mother or of motherhood but of *becoming one's mother*. . . . Where a mother is hated to the point of matrophobia there may also be a deep underlying pull toward her, a dread that if one relaxes one's guard one will identify with her completely" (236). Matrophobia can then transmute into somatophobia: the rejection of the mother's life becomes a rejection of the body, the flesh, that which symbolically unites the two, or that which comes to stand for the perceived constraints of the mother's role. Other women writers use oral imagery to explore the implications of embracing ambition, depicting how it can symbolically signify the abandonment or rejection of the mother. In her study of Edith Wharton, Ellen Glasgow, and Willa Cather, for example, Josephine Donovan has noted the way in which the Demeter-Persephone story becomes emblematic of the mother-daughter relationships represented in their texts: "Persephone represents the daughters who leave the sphere of the mothers and enter a period of patriarchal captivity, sealed by the eating of the pomegranate seed—which emblematizes the betrayal of the mothers" (3). Echoing the story of the Fall, wherein satisfaction of female appetite is imaged as transgression, Persephone's eating of the pomegranate seed suggests how the desire for the gifts promised by the paternal realm involves the daughter's loyalties: she must choose between the mother and the father. That choice is fraught with difficulty and ambivalence. As Lynda E. Boose has shown, the myth of the Fall "narrates the daughter's desire to acquire the father's knowledge/power through acquiring the sign that has been denied her," since the "seed bearing fruit" initially signified the father's phallus (55). But the betrayal of the mother can generate deep guilt, since in complying with the father the daughter participates in what Kim Chernin calls the "primal feast," the depletion and cannibalization of the mother (*The Hungry Self* 95).

The question of choosing—between maternal and paternal realms, between conventional domesticity and loyalty on the one hand and authority and ambition on the other—is a significant one that resonates with the literature of eating disorders, for as Chernin and a number of other scholars have noted, those disorders become more prevalent during periods in which women must grapple with expanded opportunities and changed expectations—with, that is, different examples of femininity than those experienced and lived by their mothers.[15] Hilde Bruch's anorexic patients often expressed fear of their increased sexual, educational, and professional options: "Growing girls can experience . . . liberation as a demand and feel that they *have* to do something outstanding. Many of my patients have expressed the feeling that they are overwhelmed by the vast number of potential opportunities available to them which they 'ought' to fulfill, that there were too many choices and they had been afraid of not choosing correctly" (37). Sylvia Plath's Esther Greenwood could pass as one of Bruch's patients:

> I saw my life branching out before me like the green fig in the story.
>
> From the tip of every branch, like a fat purple fig, a wonderful future beckoned and winked. One fig was a husband and a happy home and children, and another fig was a famous poet and another fig was a brilliant professor, and another fig was Ee Gee the amazing editor, and another fig

was Europe and Africa and South America, and another fig
was Constantin and Socrates and Attila and a pack of other
lovers with queer names and offbeat professions, and another
fig was an Olympic lady crew champion and beyond and above
these figs were many more figs I couldn't quite make out.
I saw myself in the crotch of this fig tree, starving to
death, just because I couldn't make up my mind which of the
figs I would choose. I wanted each and every one of them, but
choosing one meant losing all the rest, and, as I sat there,
unable to decide, the figs began to wrinkle and go black, and,
one by one, they plopped to the ground at my feet. (62)

The fig tree's crotch is an appropriate place for Plath's heroine to contemplate her dilemma: as if to dramatize her sense of social and cultural
castration, she longs for the testicle-shaped figs; tellingly, she can choose
only one. Starving to death because she can't make up her mind, Esther's
dilemma counterpoints that of her fellow interns at a popular women's
magazine, whose satiation of their appetites at a sumptuous banquet
results in food poisoning, a purgation of forbidden fruits. Female hunger
poses danger; choice may indeed result in self-poisoning. The literature
of eating disorders again supplies a gloss. Joan Jacobs Brumberg writes
that in a climate of bewildering choice—one in which both choices about
eating and the shape of the female body function as statements about the
self—eating disorders might more properly be seen as "consumption
disorders": "In a society where consumption and identity are pervasively
linked, [the anorectic] makes nonconsumption the perverse centerpiece
of her identity" (271). Scenes of the apple, then, can function as crucial
sites that articulate and dramatize the conflicts involved in female ambitions and appetites.

Mothers and daughters can and do figure in more positive contexts
in women's writing, particularly in women's more recent creations of
culinary memoirs and "recipe" novels. As Janice Jaffe's chapter on Laura
Esquivel's *Like Water for Chocolate* points out, for example, the passing
of recipes from one generation of women to another functions as an
example of a mother-daughter plot, or matrilineal narrative. If, in this
sense, the food of an originary culture, and by extension the culture
itself, are a kind of "mother country," so too is the link between food
and language strengthened by this association with the maternal. Ketu
H. Katrak recites the names of Indian dishes her mother cooked, calling
her native dialect of Gujarati her "mother tongue," which conveys "tastes
and aromas that are lost in their English translations" (263), and emphasizing the association of her native food, and language, with maternal
love and nurture: "I love to shake out my half-sleep with a cup of hot
tea, prepared with lemon grass and mint leaves, and it tastes even better

when made by my mother. I keep lingering in that safe space of being held in unspoken love" (264). Similarly, in *Zami*, Audre Lorde associates her original Caribbean home with her mother's mouth, with the orality of both eating and speaking: "Once *home* was a long way off, a place I had never been to but knew well out of my mother's mouth. She breathed exuded hummed the fruit smell of Noel's hill morning fresh and noon hot, and I spun visions of sapadilla and mango as a net over my Harlem tenement cot in the snoring darkness rank with nightmare sweat. . . ." (13) In a sense, the mother who cooks and eats the dishes of the country of origin is also a muse of language, as in Paule Marshall's autobiographical essay "From the Poets in the Kitchen," in which she claims she first fell in love with the poetry of words by listening to her mother and other Barbadian immigrant women speaking in dialect-inflected rhythms in the kitchen—rhythms which incorporated "the few African sounds and words that had survived," such as " 'yam,' meaning to eat" (8).

Such narratives about the association between food, culture, and maternity, however, often contain the kinds of matrophobia or ambivalence about the mother that we have discussed above. In these cases, ambivalence toward the mother's role is complicated yet further by an ambivalence about cultural identity. Often, women's autobiographical and fictional narratives about cultural identity are about the limbo-land of being caught between cultures, and significantly, between differing versions of gender roles in these cultures. The kinds of ideological tensions that we have identified in women's literature—where daughters are caught up in changing beliefs about gender roles—are exacerbated when cultural dislocation is part of the brew. For instance, in ethnic and postcolonial narratives, while women can feel nostalgia for an originary culture threatened by assimilation or colonization, they can also feel alienated from a traditional role for women within the originary culture; such dissatisfaction with traditional gender roles, however, does not mean that they can easily find an alternative substitute in the colonizing or assimilating culture which is obliterating or diluting their cultural heritage.

A classic example of such a plot about food, the mother, and cultural dislocation is Anzia Yezierska's 1925 novel *Bread Givers*, in which the protagonist Sara Smolinsky, a Russian Jewish immigrant, flees the oppressive patriarchy of her orthodox father to become an American—and college-educated—New Woman. Starving as she works and attends night school, she goes to a cafeteria for sustenance and finds that, as in her family where her father got the choicest food, men are given the meat while she only gets watery broth. Such a revelation of the sexism of American culture is ironic, given that the hunger which causes Sara to seek out an American-style cafeteria was awakened by a nostalgia for her mother's cooking and her own cultural heritage:

> One day in the laundry, while busy ironing a shirt, the thought of Mother's cooking came over me. Why was it that Mother's simplest dishes, her plain potato soup, her *gefülte* fish, were so filling? And what was the matter with the cafeteria food that it left me hungrier after eating then before?
>
> For a moment I imagined myself eating Mother's *gefülte* fish. A happy memory floated over me. A feast I was having. What a melting taste in the mouth! (165–66)

At the same time as she yearns for her mother's food, however, Sara feels compelled to flee the example of this self-effacing woman whom neighbors praised at her funeral by claiming that "[n]ever did she allow herself a bite to eat except left-overs" (254). Even when her mother visits her struggling daughter bearing some of the traditional food she had yearned for, Sara is sufficiently threatened by her mother's mixed messages—support of her daughter's rebellion implicit in the visit coupled nonetheless with exhortations to give up her education and marry—that she refuses to visit her family for six years, arriving only when her mother is dying. The conclusion of *Bread Givers* leaves the entwined matrophilic and matrophobic narratives unresolved, as it does Sara's relation to her native culture. When she agrees to take care of her ailing father—the spouse whose vampiric demands had consumed her mother's energy—it is unclear whether Sara will imitate her mother's problematic role or depart from it, just as it is unclear whether she can make her peace with her cultural roots.[16] It is thus not clear which, if any, of her hungers—for love, intellectual fulfillment, autonomy, and community—Sara can finally satisfy.

The representation of gender role confusion in Yezierska's novel, mediated through images of hunger and consumption, demonstrates how some narratives about cultural dislocation represent women's relation to food as a troubled one. In her study of anorexia, *The Obsession*, Kim Chernin compares Sara of *Bread Givers* to Ellen West, an early twentieth-century Jewish woman whose anorexia drove her to suicide. Though Chernin sees Sara as a spiritual sister to West, she does not discuss Sara's own somatophobia, instead seeing Yezierska's heroine, who achieves her dream of a college education, as a woman who succeeded while West failed (182, 184). Yet, even if she is not a classic anorexic, Sara also has an ambivalent attitude to orality and embodiment. Since she cannot afford to eat much while pursuing her education, Sara chooses to starve herself in order to satisfy her intellectual hunger, and to see food as temptation in language strikingly similar to an anorexic's: "I hated my stomach. It was like some clawing wild animal in me that I had to stop to feed always. I hated my eating" (173). Ironically, such somatophobia echoes the dualism of the father she is fleeing, a man who had described women as seductive demons of materiality, "devils and witches" (95) whom the male sage shuns.

A more contemporary example of an ethnic narrative which records a discomfort with food is Ketu H. Katrak's autobiographical essay, which, as we have seen, revels in nostalgic memories of her mother's cooking. Yet, ironically, Katrak claims that, much as she may savor it in retrospect, "[f]ood was not pleasurable to me as a child" (266) because of her awareness of her mother's discontent with her domestic role:

> As a child, I remember that the kitchen was expected to be my mother's domain though she was not happy inhabiting that space. . . . As a child and later as an adolescent, I had observed (though I can only now articulate this) that cooking did not give my mother any authority within the family hierarchy. I recall a deep sense of her powerlessness and invisibility—so much effort and so little acknowledgment. I was stopped short in my sadness for her. I could not enjoy the food, and I could not articulate why I felt distressed. (264, 266–67)

Such ambivalent responses to food as Sara's or Ketu Katrak's indicate how cultural identity can complicate women's attitudes toward orality, and reinforce the insights of recent feminist scholarship that has examined how racism and deracination can affect women's attitude toward orality. Exploding the myth that eating disorders affect only affluent, white, Western women, Becky W. Thompson's compassionate analysis of eating problems among women of diverse racial and ethnic backgrounds shows how "[t]he stresses of acculturation may also lead to eating problems" (88). Similarly, Mervat Nasser's *Culture and Weight Consciousness* documents how eating disorders and distorted body image are on the rise in developing countries due to mixed messages about gender roles, and changing attitudes toward body image[17] in the wake of social change:

> The majority of non-western societies have undergone social changes in the position of their women, with an increase in the number of educated and working women. Feminist movements, similar to those that arose in the West, also arose in some of these societies, and the traditional gender roles were questioned and revised. . . . Now, in the absence of any clear political or social framework, there is a confusion as to what is really expected of women. The higher the degree of societal ambivalence about its own expectations of women, the greater the ambiguity that women experience of their own role. . . . If eating disorders are indeed metaphors . . . it is likely that what they symbolize now encompasses this social disruption and cultural confusion. (95, 97)

As Nasser concludes, "if we accept that eating disorders are expressions of culture, would it not be more appropriate to call them 'culture chaos syndromes'?" (106). It is our contention that, whether they represent actual eating disorders, as in Tsitsi Dangarembga's *Nervous Conditions* and Edwidge Danticat's *Breath, Eyes, Memory*, or some other form of ambivalence about orality and embodiment, women's narratives about food and cultural dislocation are literary refractions of "culture chaos syndrome."

Our overview of the importance of the mother-daughter role in women's representations of orality and desire would be incomplete without some mention of the role of language—and myths of language—in those representations.[18] The psychoanalyst and literary theorist Julia Kristeva, for example, has developed two powerful and influential models of the maternal body's role in the development of language. In the first of these two models, elaborated in *Revolution in Poetic Language* (1974) and *Desire in Language* (1980), Kristeva identified two different modalities in language, one associated with the preoedipal, preverbal period that she labeled the "semiotic," the other associated with the establishment of language and subjectivity, the "symbolic." These two modalities existed in language dialectically, the first inflecting the second with qualities Kristeva assigned to the maternal body and the mother-infant relationship, qualities such as rhythm and sound that derive from the mother's nonsense rhymes, singing, and laughter as well as her body and touch: "Indifferent to language, enigmatic and feminine, this space underlying the written is rhythmic, unfettered, irreducible to its intelligible verbal translation; it is musical, anterior to judgment, but restrained by a single guarantee: syntax" ("The Semiotic and the Symbolic" 50). Hence "the imprint of woman's maternal body is inherent in language itself" (Roman 13).

Kristeva's later work on abjection, however, complicates this first model. In *The Powers of Horror: An Essay on Abjection* (1982), Kristeva argues that the maternal body is the infant's first experience of the abject, an horrific, repudiated, overwhelming sensation of embodiment. The development of language will eventually help the infant demarcate itself from the maternal body, but, significantly, "what [has] been the mother, will turn into an abject" (13). Abjection is, then, primarily a return of the repressed: boundaries fail, what was expelled encroaches, the subject no longer feels secure within a "clean and proper" body. Eating, already a primal event associated with the mother, is also and necessarily an act that involves traversing the body's boundaries: Kristeva claims that "[f]ood loathing is perhaps the most elementary and most archaic form of abjection" (3). And because abjection entails primal sensations, primal events, the subject experiences an overwhelming, uncontrollable, and disgusting return to a nonverbal corporeality: the body engulfs and speaks for the subject.

But there's more. Because abjection has its primal and primary source in the relationship to the maternal body, abjection will always recall its maternal origins. For this reason, in those cultures that develop rigid gender distinctions and that subordinate women to men, women seem to possess irrational and uncontrollable powers that must be contained. Although Kristeva does not say so, her work suggests that female subjects are vulnerable to intensified experiences of abjection: already more like the mother than the son, the daughter's boundaries between her body and her mother's might seem even more tenuous; furthermore, because cultural fears of embodiment are routinely projected upon women, the daughter learns to perceive the female body—her own, her mother's, other women's—as an animalistic force that requires containment. "[T]he threat to autonomy which can come from a woman is felt on a less rational, more helpless level, experienced as more primitively dangerous," writes Dorothy Dinnerstein, for the mother has become the representative of "the one who beckons her loved ones back from selfhood, who wants to engulf, dissolve, drown, suffocate them as autonomous persons" (112). The mother feels like both threat—that which can "swamp the nascent self's own needs and intentions . . . blur its perceptions of its own outlines . . . deflect its inner sense of direction and drown out its inner voice"—and sirenlike solace—"a lure back into non-being," a "temptation . . . to melt back into that from which we have carved ourselves out" (112). From the perspective of these theories, scenes of eating or hungering; representations of the mother's or the daughter's body, or female bodies in general; or passages in which eating and speaking/writing appear as competing activities, can thus encode gendered conflicts between embodiment and speech that Kristeva attributes to the development of language within a distinctly gendered cultural surround.

Another powerful and influential model of language, embodiment, and cultural production emerges in the work of another psychoanalytic theorist, Luce Irigaray. According to her, women inevitably develop symptomatic or corporeal languages of distress because they exist in a state of "dereliction" within a phallogocentric symbolic that leaves woman "too few figurations, images, or representations by which to represent herself" (*This Sex* 162). This state of dereliction grows out of "women's exile" from their bodies, their mothers, and other women: "She has, imposed on her, a language, fantasms, a desire which does not 'belong' to her . . . That kind of *schizo* which every woman experiences, in our sociocultural system, only leaves her with somatizations, corporal pains, mutism, or mimetism with which to express herself: saying and doing 'like men'" ("Women's Exile" 95). The mother-daughter relationship suffers profoundly, for femininity is absorbed into maternity, into a function or use. The mother suffers, cut off from her autonomy, that in her which exceeds her maternal/institutional function ("Women-mothers" 51). In turn, the daughter suffers, cut off from femininity and forced to identify with a function or use: "[H]ow, as daughters, can we have a personal relationship with or construct a personal identity in relation to someone who is no more than a function?" Irigaray asks ("Women-mothers" 50). The relationship becomes fused with anger, ambivalence, and competition, for the daughter can replace the mother, can become her, can, in effect, kill her, without being able to have a relationship with her "in this place" (Whitford 110).

In an essay particularly relevant to a discussion of women's orality and desire, "And the One Doesn't Stir without the Other," Irigaray conveys the painful, impeded, unsymbolized dynamic of the mother-daughter relationship in images of suffocation, choking, smothering, freezing, and hunger. She explores how food and nurturance become the mother's only way of expressing her love for her daughter; this emphasis on nurturance gives rise to the "good" and "bad" mothers of cultural mythology: the one who gives (feeds) too much and prevents separation, the other who gives too little and creates a state of constant need and hunger. In the dyad Irigaray explores, the mother's love seems suffocating and overwhelming, and the daughter must leave if she is to experience her own boundaries, her own sense of self; at the same time, if the daughter leaves, she takes with her her mother's primary source of identity: "You have made me something to eat. You bring me something to eat. But you give yourself too much, as if you wanted to fill me all up with what you bring me. You put yourself into my mouth and I suffocate" (11). As Irigaray elaborates elsewhere, mothers and daughters feed/feed upon one another in the absence of what she terms "a genealogy of women" and a "female symbolic," both of which require deliberate interventions in the symbolic order. The first would trace a female genealogy of descent, entailing "new kinds of language, new systems of nomenclature, new relations of social and economic exchange—in other words, a complete reorganization of the social order" (Grosz 123). The second demands the creation of a set of powerful metaphors and myths with which women can identify, metaphors and myths that reclaim aspects of female corporeality that have simply vanished from public (or even private) discussion. Irigaray's notorious image of "lips that speak together" is one such challenge to "sexual indifference" in that the image restores female specificity to the speaker(s). A contemporary example, Eve Ensler's *The Vagina Monologues*, demonstrates the power of woman-centered interventions into the symbolic: whereas it was once unusual to hear the word "vagina" except in clinical or medical settings, the numerous productions, publicity, and popularity of Ensler's text/ performance piece have brought the word out of its clinical context and restored to it both a female specificity and a polyvocality, the many, many different female stories told through that corporeal focus.

These interventions into the symbolic order necessitate the restructuring of the mother-daughter relationship, Irigaray writes. The mother must question her maternal function, instead of accepting cultural legitimation through it, while daughters must "say good-bye to maternal omnipotence (the last refuge) and establish a woman-to-woman relationship of reciprocity with our mothers, in which they might possibly also feel themselves to be our daughters" ("Women-mothers" 50). Both must turn to language: the mother gives the daughter "words with which to speak and hear," the "gift of language in place of the suffocation and silence imposed by food" (Grosz 124). And the daughter for her part must rewrite the patriarchal myths that necessitate the murder and silencing of the mother:

> We must also find, find anew, invent the words, the sentences that speak the most archaic and most contemporary relationship with the body of the mother, with our bodies, the sentences that translate the bond between her body, ours, and that of our daughters. We have to discover a language (*langage*) which does not replace the bodily encounter, as paternal language (*langue*) attempts to do, but which can go along with it, words which do not bar the corporeal, but which speak corporeal. (Irigaray, "The bodily encounter" 43).

It is arguable, it seems to us, that women writers' developments of recipe novels and culinary memoirs accomplish some of the goals that Irigaray formulates in these writings. In representing the transmission of recipes between mother and daughter, for example, a "familial space within which self-articulation can begin to take place" (Goldman 172), such culinary memoirs as *Miriam's Kitchen* work to preserve the bodily encounter and speak the corporeal even as they literally transmit a written text, the recipe, that itself embodies "some kind of comprehensive, shaping, directing voice" (Bower 8). Barbara Haber describes the French cookbook author Madeleine Kamman's *When French Women Cook* in a way that literalizes Irigaray's notion of a woman-to-woman specificity: "[T]hese recollections are organized in chapters that center on the different women who influenced her life. Kammen communicates her connections to those who lived in various regions of France, meticulously describing the women and providing precise instructions for recreating the regional cooking and baking" (71). Writing of her collection of her mothers' recipes, often embedded within letters, Sharon L. Jansen notes that the recipe her mother is transmitting becomes "part of a larger whole, an occasion for a comment at least, more often for a story into which the recipe has been inserted. If the recipe is the text, it has been submerged in the story of which it is a part. Or it may be that the recipe is only an excuse for the larger narrative, which itself is the text that my mother wants to write" (58). Food writing may be an instance par excellence in which writers "speak corporeal."

INGREDIENTS OF THIS COLLECTION

In devising this collection, we hope not only to contribute to but to complicate some of the prevailing conceptualizations of women, food, and literature. With that goal in mind, we have organized the essays around three main rubrics: Appetite and Consumption in Nineteenth-Century Cultural Politics; Grotesque, Ghostly, and Cannibalistic Hungers in Twentieth-Century Texts; Food and Cooking: Patriarchal, Colonial, Familial Structures. We will comment briefly on each of these rubrics below.

APPETITE AND CONSUMPTION IN NINETEENTH-CENTURY CULTURAL POLITICS

In order to introduce the section of our collection that deals with nineteenth-century women and food, it is necessary to ground this discussion in an historical context that allows us to understand why food and embodiment became such charged issues for women at this moment in history. In her discussion of the "anorexic syndrome" and the domestic novel, Paula Marantz Cohen links the rise of eating disorders to the rise of the nuclear family in the late-eighteenth century ("Anorexic Syndrome," esp. 125–29; *Daughter's Dilemma*). Such a genealogy stresses the important role that domestic ideology plays in determining nineteenth- and twentieth-century women's attitudes toward food and their bodies. An outgrowth of the rise of capitalism, domestic ideology segregated home and workplace to a hitherto unknown extent, justifying its relegation of men and women to separate spheres of the private and public by emphasizing fundamental differences between male and female nature. While the association of women with the private sphere, or with distinctive characteristics, was not new, domesticity deployed these associations to disembody women to a greater extent than ever before, elevating an ideal of womanhood that deemphasized female sexuality even as it emphasized women's spiritual power as moral guide within the home.[19] If this ideal apparently redeemed women from the long-standing misogynist tradition of seeing them all as greedy and lustful Eves, it did so by displacing appetite from the virtuous woman within the home to the fallen women outside it. Maternity, the crucial function of women within domesticity, thus came to be defined through the feeding and nurturing of the family rather than the self; as Laura Fasick writes, the ideal wife and mother "must be a figure for food's bounty": "If a woman's relationship with food is primarily to feed others, then her primary pleasure occurs vicariously through their eating, not through her own" (75, 78). In a famous spoof, Virginia Woolf pointed out the disempowering nature of this ideal of the "Angel in the House": "She sacrificed herself daily. If there was chicken, she took the leg . . . in short she was so constituted that she never had a mind or wish of her own" ("Professions" 59).

Since the ideal domestic woman was middle class, the image of the self-effacing angel was also class coded. What Leonore Davidoff calls the Victorian polarity between "woman and lady" (21) defines the female servant—associated with the dirtier tasks of cleaning, cooking, and childcare—as a more embodied figure than the etherealized lady who superintends her labor.[20] The "lady-like anorexia," with its emphasis on the physical delicacy of the middle- or upper-class lady that Helena Michie identifies as a guiding theme in Victorian discourses about gender, is part of this class discourse that situates the appetitive woman as lower class, either as the stout, buxom servant, or as the fallen woman or prostitute. Such class polarities could also be mapped onto race, distinguishing the white "lady" from the sexually appetitive native or slave.

The messages that Victorian women received about embodiment were far from univocal. While "lady-like anorexia" is one important strand of Victorian discourses about female appetite, there was also cultural anxiety about female slenderness and self-starvation. A number of Victorian sources—articles in popular journals, etiquette books, and cookbooks—criticized an overly delicate appetite and overly thin body in women. (Like similar laments today about women's obsessive pursuit of slenderness, however, such critiques are a tribute not to the absence of competing messages regarding the constraint of female appetite but rather to their successful dissemination.) Victorian medical discourses can be particularly censorious about feminine thinness. Treatments of hysteria (the disease with which anorexia was first associated) stressed the need to fatten up "nervous women," who according to the well-known Silas Weir Mitchell, "as a rule are thin, and lack blood" (7). The book that contains this definition, and which discusses the virtues of Mitchell's rest cure for hysteria—a book tellingly entitled *Fat and Blood: And How to Make Them*—presupposes a plump, robust feminine ideal.[21]

Victorian discourses that criticize female slenderness, however, had different, and indeed opposed, ideological agendas. While Victorian feminists criticized the cult of ladylike weakness and delicacy, attacking such slenderizing devices as corsets, so did many Victorian physicians who claimed that such garments posed dangers to women's reproductive systems—and thus impeded the proper exercise of their domestic function. In the late-nineteenth century, evocations of an unfortunate epidemic of overly thin, debilitated women can also be connected to eugenics, an elitist scientific discourse designed to maintain social hierarchies of classes and race—hierarchies which could be maintained by strong and healthy middle-class, and Anglo-Saxon, mothers. For instance, Edward Clarke, who in *Sex in Education* argued that higher education drained women's energies from their wombs to their brains, inveighed against the social degeneration—the female "palor [sic] and weakness"—caused by this trend: "[O]ur women are a feeble race" who "will give birth to a feeble race"(21). Revealingly, though, Clarke expressed a certain ambivalence about the stout, hearty woman, admiring the "physical force" of "the lower classes of women in Europe" while lamenting their "infamous degradation": "[t]he urgent problem of modern civilization is how to retain this force, and get rid of the degradation" (178). Such an anxiety about the fine line between force and degradation—a term that refers to the lack of refinement of the lower classes, but which also suggests sexual defilement—animates Victorian medical and social discourses about women appetite, which in consequence often give contradictory advice. For instance, Joan Jacobs Brumberg has discussed how nervous Victorian physicians were about women ingesting too much red meat, which in young girls especially was supposed to stimulate sexual passion and encourage masturbation (176–78). One popular cure for anemia, however—an ailment which frequently plagued young girls—had them drink the blood of animals, an image of red-blooded carnality that, as Bram Dijkstra has argued, is nightmarishly echoed in the many late Victorian images of voracious, vampiric women (337–38). The cure of one malady associated with female appetite could, presumably, all too easily lead to another.

Thus the anxiety about sexuality and power in Victorian discourses about female appetite underscores contradictions in domestic ideology, which gave women confusingly mixed messages about food and embodiment. As Helena Michie notes, "[T]he paradoxical demands of nineteenth-century culture are seen most clearly in the ideal of the hourglass figure which, in effect, prescribes that women live in two bodies at the same time: they must have the breasts and hips of a sensuous woman and the waistline of a schoolgirl" (22). This combination of youthful innocence and adult capacity for maternity coalesces in the figure of the girlish, yet nurturing, daughter that Paula Marantz Cohen observes was so popular in the domestic novel (*Daughter's Dilemma* 22), an image that infantilizes women by diminishing their sexuality and appetite. Such reassuringly asexual and maternal daughters are particularly prominent in novels of Dickens such as *Little Dorrit*—whose eponymous heroine, as Gail Turley Houston has argued, is literally "little" because she anorectically denies herself food in order to nurture her needy father (139–53).

Given these contested and frequently competing messages about female appetite in Victorian culture, then, the figures of both the embodied and disembodied woman can be reassuring and threatening in differing ways. The woman who eats can be a good mother capable of feeding others—but she can also easily become a monster of appetite, the greedy or lustful woman. At the same time, the more etherealized of domestic heroines, while appropriately unselfish, can also be worrisomely fragile, potentially unable to assume a reproductive role. Indeed, the most hyperbolically etherealized of domestic heroines, like Richardson's Clarissa—whom Cohen calls "literature's original anorexic" ("Anorexic Syndrome" 132)—die before they can become wives and mothers. Moreover, as some critics have argued, feminine wasting, illness, and death in nineteenth-century texts can register resistance to domesticity, not merely an acquiescence to its restrictions on female power.[22] In the late-nineteenth century, the emergent figure of the anorexic—like her discursive and etiological sister, the hysteric—is apparently on a hunger strike against domesticity and the lack of nourishment it provides for women, the kind of hunger for a sphere outside the domestic that runs as a guiding metaphor through works like Florence Nightingale's *Cassandra* (for example 124–26, 220). Thus, as Linda Schlossberg argues in her chapter in this volume on the actual hunger strikes of female suffragettes, the nonappetitive woman can be a rebel rather than an angel.

Our three chapters on appetite and consumption in nineteenth-century cultural politics expand our understanding of the conflicted and competing messages women received about food and embodiment at this time. This section opens with a piece on the fat queen whose name became synonymous with the period, Adrienne Munich's "Good and Plenty: Queen Victoria Figures the Imperial Body." Munich explores the often contradictory bodily meanings encoded in representations of Queen Victoria: "During the course of her long reign," Munich explains, "Queen Victoria's gustatory appetite functions both as a figure of feminine transgression and as a figure of imperial plenty." While, on the one hand, the queen's appetite and enjoyment of eating were at odds with the Victorian assumption that women should put the nurturance of others before their own needs, her expansive girth finally came to manifest England's prosperity and imperial spread: "By the time of the two Jubilees, in 1887 and 1897, the conjunction of the Queen's body, the nation's fat purse, and the nation's fat empire are implicit."

Pamela K. Gilbert's chapter on Mary Elizabeth Braddon's sensation fiction addresses another aspect of Victorian women's relation to consumption, their place in the literary marketplace. A writer of sensation fiction—melodramatic tales of crime and sexuality—Braddon was an immensely popular yet aesthetically marginal writer in a literary world that increasingly differentiated between "low" and "high" culture. Focusing on the many food images in Braddon's sensation fiction *The Doctor's Wife*, Gilbert offers a provocative reading of how Braddon internalizes the negative assessments of the sensation genre. In its self-reflexive portrayal of sensationalism as unwholesome fare for the female reader, the novel—a revision of Flaubert's *Madame Bovary*—echoes the obsessive alimental metaphors used by reviewers and critics to describe sensation fiction as corrupting and contaminating food for women. In this sense, Gilbert sees Braddon expressing a somatophobia about the body of her work similar to the self-hatred that women often feel about their bodies, a reading that offers an original look at what Sandra M. Gilbert and Susan Gubar call the nineteenth-century woman writer's "anxiety of authorship."

Focusing on the demands by women of this period for political power, Linda Schlossberg's "Consuming Images: Women, Hunger, and the Vote" analyzes a figure of enormous importance in this history, the hunger-striking suffragette. In the case of the hunger striker, Schlossberg argues, the refusal to eat is an explicitly political act: "By refusing food, the suffragettes called attention to the practices of a government that would not let them speak, that refused to honor or nourish their political appetites and ambitions." Yet, even if the Angel in the House has become the Martyr in the Prison, the hunger-striker's renunciation, ironically, also reproduces domestic ideology, reinforcing the idea that women are morally superior to men by transcending appetite and passion. Grounding her analysis in a rich variety of documents—both feminist and antifeminist—about female appetite in the suffrage era, Schlossberg's chapter, which also reads Mrs. Humphrey Ward's novel of the suffrage movement, *Delia Blanchflower*, is a study of ideological debates about female appetite in a period of tumultuous social change.

GROTESQUE, GHOSTLY, AND CANNIBALISTIC
HUNGER IN TWENTIETH-CENTURY TEXTS

Our second section on various metaphorical hungers deployed by women's literary and theoretical texts complicates a number of issues we have explored in the introduction. To begin with, the essays in this section take seriously the concept that appetite can function as a form of voice, an idea popularized by Suzie Orbach's work on eating disorders in the 1980s. Orbach called food and body-image issues "the language of women's inner experience" (*Hunger Strike* 7); she went on to argue, "Food is a metaphor through which women speak of their inner experiences. Until we have a real voice in the body politic, individual women are likely to use their bodies as their mouthpieces to express the forbidden and excluded feelings we carry inside" (*Hunger Strike* 7). Orbach's work, however popular—she became Princess Diana's therapist, and was the impetus for the latter's appearance on network television, where she confessed her "massive bulimia" to interviewer Barbara Walters—did nothing to dispel the notion that disordered eating was solely the province of middle- to upper-middle-class white women who were too mannerly to express their dissatisfaction about their seemingly privileged lives. The chapters in this section, by contrast, show how issues of race, class, and sexual orientation alter considerably women's relation to the "body politic"; women's eating and appetites are emphatically not the same and do not encode the same meanings.

The first two chapters of this section take racial inscriptions on the female body as their focus. In "'The Courage of Her Appetites': The Ambivalent Grotesque in Ellen Glasgow's *The Romantic Comedians*," Debra Beilke explores a southern woman writer's attempts to contest restrictions of female appetite. Creating a character who embodies the sexual appetite usually suppressed in images of the white southern lady, Glasgow challenges the hierarchies of race, class, and gender that maintained southern culture. Yet, by making the character of Edmonia Bredelbane in *Romantic Comedians* a grotesquely comic figure, Beilke argues, Glasgow also diminishes the force of her critique and reveals her own ambivalence about female appetite. Beilke's essay, which examines the ideological construction of the southern lady and argues for the importance of understanding how this stereotype maintained racial stereotypes, also is theoretically important in challenging the Bahktinian notion that the grotesque, carnivalesque body is necessarily subversive of social hierarchies.

Ann Folwell Stanford's chapter on Toni Morrison's acclaimed novel *Beloved* looks at the mother-daughter relationship from a different angle, that of the mother's, rather than the daughter's, perspective. *Beloved* is a novel in which orality is inseparably linked with the protagonist Sethe's experience of maternity, an experience created under and irrevocably scarred by slavery. Focusing on the novel's images of self-starvation, hunger, and compulsive eating, Stanford shows how such imagery figures the trauma of African American history; in particular, Sethe's maternal relationship with the enigmatic ghostly Beloved, troped as a cannibalistic consumption of the mother's body by the daughter figure, reflects Sethe's own somatophobia and self-hatred, her internalization of the racist ideology of slavery, and her resulting sense of lack of love and ownership of her body. Morrison's use of disordered eating radically shifts its popular and common meanings; overeating and starvation function, as Stanford argues, "as tropes for marking historical memory on the bodies, minds, and souls of African-Americans."

The remaining two chapters in this section contest the notion that women's appetites and eating can only function as pathology. As we noted earlier in our introduction, the foregrounding of self-starving behaviors in women's literary and critical texts has obscured the more positive meanings women writers have attached to appetite, desire, and orality. Here, however, both Chris Foss and Suzanne Keen turn to theorist Hélène Cixous and take up her challenge to women writers to "Write your self. Your body must be heard" ("Medusa" 350). Foss's essay, "'There Is No God Who Can Keep Us From Tasting': Good Cannibalism in Hélène Cixous's *The Book of Promethea*" reads Cixous's own text as an example of a good female consumption, "a cannibalism that is not ghastly or ghostly or grotesque, but rather generous and loving and fulfilling." This "good cannibalism," Foss writes, is a "textual embodiment of Cixous's alternative female economy," an economy which establishes as its founding movement Cixous's rewriting of Genesis and Eve's eating of the apple: "[T]he genesis of 'femininity' goes by way of the mouth, through a certain oral pleasure, and through the nonfear of the inside" ("The Author in Truth" 151). Foss analyzes Cixous's commitment to "libidinal education," a female creativity that revisions the self-other relationship through love/writing.

Suzanne Keen also makes use of Cixous's celebration of female orality in her analysis of Jeannette Winterson's fiction. In "'I Cannot Eat My Words but I Do': Food, Body, and Word in the Novels of Jeanette Winterson," Keen shows how scenes of food and eating "contribute to a sacramental theory of authorship organized around metaphors of incorporation, communion, and sexual ecstasy." In particular, Keen argues, Winterson uses food "in a relatively schematic way to figure and explore variations in human sexuality," as well as in less schematic ways, where food—especially fruit—becomes part of a mystical experience linked to language and writing: in a crucial Cixousian moment, a Winterson character finds that "[t]he more we ask of language, the more we shall receive."

FOOD AND COOKING: PATRIARCHAL, COLONIAL, FAMILIAL STRUCTURES

Our final section consists of three chapters that examine the relation of food and food preparation to structures of colonial, familial, or patriarchal power. This section leads off with Sue Thomas's analysis of the powerful novel *Nervous Conditions* by Zimbabwean writer Tsitsi Dangarembga, a classic example of the plot of matrophobia and cultural dislocation in the wake of colonization that we discussed above. In Dangarembga's novel—one of the most important of recent postcolonial fictions by women—the anorexic-bulimic character Nyasha, cousin of the narrator, experiences the dis/ease of colonialism and sexism somatically, inscribing on her emaciated body the confusions regarding her cultural and gender identity. The daughter of two educated Rhodesians, Nyasha literally cannot stomach her father's Anglophilia and erasure of her native Shona heritage, particularly because her father, while expecting his children to become westernized, still expects his daughter to remain a traditionally obedient Shona daughter. Nyasha's model of femininity is her mother Maiguru, a highly educated woman whose subservience to her husband blends the submission of the traditional Shona wife with 1950s-style Western domesticity. The psychic stresses that the daughter experiences about her role illustrate how, as Sartre writes in his preface to Fanon's *Wretched of the Earth*, "[t]he condition of native is a nervous condition."

Janice Jaffe's chapter on Laura Esquivel's *Like Water for Chocolate*, a novel interspersed with and organized through recipes, situates that novel within a type of matrilineal narrative tradition—Chicana women's writing about food. Jaffe argues that the form of Esquivel's novel reflects a tradition of recipes passed down through generations of women, a tradition that preserves cultural and familial heritage, even though the bonding between female characters—particularly the relationship between the protagonist Tita and her biological mother Elena—is not always positive. Indeed, one of the central issues Esquivel's novel addresses is how liberating—and how restricting—traditional domesticity is for women. The title of *Like Water for Chocolate* is a reference to Tita's anger, for her sexuality and autonomy are suppressed by a mother who confines her to the kitchen. Yet, Jaffe argues, the novel does not advocate a return to traditional domesticity, but rather stresses women's need for self-expression outside the domestic realm as well as celebrating the creativity of cooking, which can preserve what is most positive about the bonds between women.

Our collection ends with Patricia Moran's consideration of the emergence of the culinary memoir as an index of contemporary women's anxiety about the loss of an exclusively female kitchen culture. Moran develops in particular an extended analysis of Elizabeth Ehrlich's *Miriam's Kitchen*, a memoir that traces Ehrlich's gradual conversion to kosher cooking and full-time domesticity even as it simultaneously traces Ehrlich's growing intimacy with her mother-in-law Miriam, a Holocaust survivor whose cooking preserves a lost world and history. In the interstices of this explicit narrative, Moran discovers a more muted account of the pressures of the "second shift" identified by sociologists Arlie Hochshild and Anne Machung, wherein women who work full-time also end up shouldering the lion's share of household chores and child care. Sensitive to the very real emotional charge assigned to a hitherto female space, Moran urges women not to abandon the "stalled revolution," but rather to sacrifice their exclusive hold on the kitchen and to fight to keep the doors to the kitchen open to the world beyond home.

INVITATION TO THE FEAST:
THE GENESIS OF FEMINIST FOOD STUDIES

*One day my mother and my grandmother were shelling
beans and talking about the proper method of drying
apples. I was eleven and entirely absorbed with the
March girls in* Little Women. *Drying apples was not in
my dreams. Beth's death was weighing darkly on me at
that moment, and I threw a little tantrum—what
Mama called a hissy fit.*

*"Can't y'all talk about anything but food?" I
screamed.*

*There was a shocked silence. "Well, what else is
there?" Granny asked.*

—Bobbie Ann Mason, "The Burden of the Feast"

Perhaps it is fitting that our meditation on scenes of the apple end with
an anecdote by Bobbie Ann Mason and its allusion both to apples and
Little Women, that fable about female appetite to which we referred at the
beginning of this introduction. Here the youthful Mason's attraction to
Beth, the most ethereal of the March girls, makes her resist the prosaic
reality of preparing and preserving food that has traditionally been the
preoccupation of farm women like her mother and grandmother. Ironically, for the eleven-year-old girl, the scene of the apple is not a site of
delicious temptation or, as Helena Michie says of Jo March's apple-munch-
ing, a sign of successful authorship: the appropriately dried apples of the
story suggest how dessicated—how stifling—her mother's and
grandmother's way of life seems to Mason, and how much of an obstacle
she feels this life is to her love of literature and her hunger for "a kind of
food that didn't grow in the ground" (141). Coming back to retell this
story from the vantage point of adulthood and a successful career as a
writer, though, Mason sees the relation of food to her life differently; her
memories of her mother's meals become an originary source of her own
art, and food itself becomes a metaphor for her own conflict—a conflict
she discovers was shared by her apparently domestic mother as well—
between a working-class farm world and a life outside the boundaries of
its gender roles. In this context, Mason can finally acknowledge that her
grandmother was right: in a sense, there isn't anything else but food to talk
about, because, as so many women writers and feminist critics have discovered, food encompasses and is intertwined with *everything*.

The trajectory of Mason's initial rejection of kitchen talk, followed by her rediscovery of its meaning and power, represents in miniature the kind of larger movement in Women's Studies within the past few decades which we have traced in this introduction. Given, indeed, the recent creative and critical efflorescence of work on women's relation to food, it is surely not premature to speak about the development of feminist food studies as an exciting new field within both the academy and the wider culture. In this sense, women writers and critics have revised the Genesis story of Eve that had for so long been a fable about women's need to avoid forbidden fruit, transforming it instead into a story about another type of genesis—the reclamation of the female body and female appetites. Such a transformation recalls Adrienne Rich's definition of "revision" as "the act of looking back, of seeing with fresh eyes . . . an act of survival" ("When We Dead Awaken" 35). "[B]ooks and food, food and books, both excellent things," Gertrude Stein wrote (qtd. in Pierpont 36). We concur, and wish you good appetite and good reading in the pages to follow.

NOTES

1. A number of recent writers have stressed the need for feminists to rethink the denigration of kitchen culture. For representative arguments, see Arlene Voski Avakian's introduction to *Through the Kitchen Window*, as well as essays by Barbara Haber and Margaret Randall in that volume; see also Mary Field Belenky et. al., *Women's Ways of Knowing* and *Knowledge, Difference, and Power*, and Patricia Moran (this volume). Scholars have also begun to excavate the buried community, familial, and personal narratives within cookbooks and recipes; see especially Anne L. Bower, ed., *Recipes for Reading: Community Cookbooks, Stories, Histories* and Janet Theophano, *Eat My Words: Reading Women's Lives through the Cookbooks They Wrote*. The emergence of food studies as a discipline in the last decade has also forced reexamination of the importance of cooking and food preparation in general; see, for example, recent anthologies such as Sherrie A. Inness, ed., *Kitchen Culture in America*; Carole M. Counihan and Penny Van Esterik, *Food and Culture: A Reader*; and Deane W. Curtin and Lisa M. Heldke, eds., *Cooking, Eating, Thinking* as well as individual studies such as those by Sarah Sceats, *Food, Consumption and the Body in Contemporary Women's Fiction* and Doris Witt, *Black Hunger: Food and the Politics of U.S. Identity*. For a discussion of the emergence of food studies as a discipline, see Jennifer K. Ruark, "A Place at the Table."

2. For a psychoanalytically informed study of the connection between eating and speaking, see Maude Ellmann, *The Hunger Artist: Starving, Writing, and Imprisonment*. See also Patricia Moran, *Word of Mouth: Body Language in Katherine Mansfield and Virginia Woolf*.

3. We are indebted to an anonymous reader for this formulation of our project.

4. The term "golden cage" is from Hilde Bruch's study of anorexia, *The Golden Cage*.

5. See Elizabeth Kamarck Minnich's essay in Avakian, ed., *Through the Kitchen Window* for her development of this concept.

6. Lest our claim that female authority and female appetite form a component of political life seem far-fetched, we point not only to the essays by Munich and Schlossberg in this volume; we point to the infamous "cookie contest" between Barbara Bush and Hillary Clinton in the presidential campaign of 1992. That contest began when Clinton asked in frustration whether she was supposed to stay home and bake cookies after developing a successful law career; the resulting media melee, which forced Clinton to pit her chocolate chip cookie recipe against that of Barbara Bush, clearly demonstrated how much Clinton's public and professional authority violated many people's notions of the First Lady's appropriate sphere, the separate sphere of domesticity, nurturance, and self-effacement. The remarkable vituperation leveled against Clinton has not subsided after ten years; she has become an enduring symbol in American politics of the overreaching woman whose appetite for public and professional authority is too much, too excessive—too masculine.

7. For some important works in the interdisciplinary field of food studies, see Deane W. Curtin and Lisa M. Heldke, eds., *Cooking, Eating, Thinking*; Carole M. Counihan, *The Anthropology of Food and Body: Gender, Meaning, and Power*; John Germov and Lauren Williams, eds., *A Sociology of Food and Nutrition: The Social Appetite*; Sian Griffiths and Jennifer Wallace, eds., *Consuming Passions*; Elspeth Probyn, *Carnal Appetites: FoodSexIdentities*; Mary Anne Schofield, ed., *Cooking by the Book: Food in Literature and Culture*. This list is by no means exhaustive.

8. For representative readings of these scenes in *Zami*, see Barbara Christian, *Black Feminist Criticism* 187–204; and Claudine Raynaud, " 'A Nutmeg Nestled Inside Its Covering of Mace': Audre Lorde's *Zami*."

9. This scene both evokes and comments upon the vulval plates Judy Chicago created to memorialize women's history in her multimedia installation of the late seventies, *The Dinner Party*. That installation provoked harsh criticism from black women, who objected to the fact that the token black woman represented—Sojourner Truth—was the sole woman represented without a vulva (she was represented by three heads "inspired by African art" [Chicago, *The Dinner Party: A Symbol of Our Heritage* 88; see also the commemorative volume by Chicago by the same name, 122]). Sadly, Chicago makes no mention of this controversy in the 1996 commemorative volume on *The Dinner Party*, with the possible exception of an oblique justification that not all women could be represented: "To achieve a truly universal history, we would need a record that included all of humankind, in its full diversity. Until that time comes, I hope that

people will accept the idea that, by implication, a symbol can be inclusive" (12). Chicago does not address the absence of Truth's vulva.

10. For scholarship that explores the familial, personal, cultural, and community narratives embedded in cookbooks, see the essays collected in Anne Bower, ed., *Recipes for Reading: Community Cookbooks, Stories, Histories*, as well as Anne Goldman, " 'I Yam What I Yam': Cooking, Culture, and Colonialism"; Susan J. Leonardi, "Recipes for Reading: Summer Pasta, Lobster à la Riseholme, and Key Lime Pie"; and Janet Theophano, *Eat My Words: Reading Women's Lives through the Cookbooks They Wrote.*

11. We do not mean to suggest that this connection between cultural identity and cuisine is limited to women. In an essay in the *San Francisco Chronicle* of January 30, 2002, "Lahlou Weaves Memories into Aziza's Cuisine," Moroccan chef Mourad Lahlou vividly describes how his cooking recreates his mother's stories. He recalls how his fascination with the kitchen developed not out of a desire to cook but out of a desire to hear "the stories my mom told while she was cooking. She would tell me family secrets and stories that amazed me and made me want to come back for more. And that was how I would spend hours watching her cut meats and vegetables" (F1). Later, a homesick student in the United States, Lahlou used cooking to assuage his longing for his mother's company: "I just had to relive moments I spent with her in the kitchen listening to her stories, but this time trying to remember what she was doing. In a way, I was teaching myself to cook by retelling myself those stories" (F4). Eventually he opened a Moroccan restaurant, vowing "to honor my mom's traditions and share her stories beyond the walls of her small kitchen" (F4). His San Francisco restaurant Aziza is named for his mother, and his cuisine represents a merger of his and his mother's storytelling: "My mom probably wouldn't recognize everything that's on Aziza's menu—they are my stories—but when she tastes the food she would definitely hear some of her own stories and secrets, as told by her son" (F4).

12. For scholarship that connects women's preparation of food with gender acculturation and oppression, see Sarah Fenstermaker Berk, *The Gender Factory: The Apportionment of Work in American Households*; Nickie Charles and Marion Kerr, *Women, Food, and Families*; Sally Cline, *Just Desserts: Women and Food*; Rosalind Coward, *Female Desires: How They are Sought, Bought, and Packaged*; Marjorie L. DeVault, *Feeding the Family: The Social Organization of Caring as Gendered Work*; Sherrie A. Inness, "Introduction" to *Kitchen Culture*; Deborah Lupton, *Food, the Body, and the Self*; Robert B. Schafer and Elisabeth Schafer, "Relationship Between Gender and Food Roles in the Family"; and Susan Strasser, *Never Done: A History of American Housework.*

13. A significant exception here is Roberta Pollack Seid, who dismisses the work of Kim Chernin and others in *Never Too Thin*. It is true that the mother-daughter relationship may have become less central in recent years, as a variety of other factors—American "obesophobia," the omnipresence of thinness and fitness as cultural ideas, the widespread attention given to anorexia nervosa and bulimia—have come into play. Writers on American adolescent girls such as

Naomi Wolf and Peggy Orenstein have pointed to the ways in which disordered eating functions as a form of peer belonging; Wolf has argued that eating disorders function as a form of ritualized behavior among girls that has risen spontaneously in response to the dearth of more meaningful rituals. For work on eating disorders and anorexia, in addition to Brumberg, Chernin, and Seid, see studies by Marilyn Lawrence, ed., *Fed Up and Hungry: Women, Oppression, and Food* as well as her *The Anorexic Experience*; Susie Orbach, *Fat is a Feminist Issue* and *Hunger Strike: The Anorectic's Struggle as a Metaphor for Our Age*; Matra Robertson, *Starving in the Silences: An Exploration of Anorexia Nervosa*; Eve Szekely, *Never Too Thin*; and Becky W. Thompson, *A Hunger So Wide and So Deep: American Women Speak Out on Eating Problems*. For some recent first-hand accounts of eating disorders, see Marianne Apostolides, *Inner Hunger*, and Marya Hornbacher, *Wasted*.

14. See especially Claire Tomalin, *Katherine Mansfield: A Secret Life*, in addition to Antony Alpers, *The Life of Katherine Mansfield*, and Jeffrey Meyers, *Katherine Mansfield: A Biography*.

15. See Susan Bordo, *Unbearable Weight* 157, 161–3; Kim Chernin, *The Obsession*, esp. 96–110; and Susie Orbach, *Hunger Strike*, 13–24.

16. For discussion of Yezierska and images of hunger, see Ellen Golub, "Eat Your Heart Out: The Fiction of Anzia Yezierska," and Tobe Levin, "How to Eat without Eating: Anzia Yezierska's Hunger." Two insightful readings of gender and cultural dislocation in *Bread Givers* include Gay Wilenz, "Cultural Mediation and the Immigrant's Daughter," and Thomas Ferraro, " 'Working Ourselves Up' in America: Anzia Yezierska's *Bread Givers.*"

17. For more on immigrant women's confusion about differing ideals of the female body in their native and adopted culture, see Becky W. Thompson, *A Hunger So Wide and So Deep* (28–45); for an illuminating case study on how attitudes toward fat can vary across cultures, see Elisa J. Sobo, "The Sweetness of Fat: Health, Procreation, and Sociability in Rural Jamaica." For a description of how race plays into the representation of food, eating, and black identity, see Doris Witt, *Black Hunger: Food and the Politics of U.S. Identity*. See also Donna A. Gabaccio, *We Are What We Eat: Ethnic Food and the Making of Americans*.

18. For an excellent overview of the scholarship and debates on language, gender, and literary texts see Camille Roman, Suzanne Juhasz, and Cristanne Miller, eds. *The Women and Language Debate: A Sourcebook*. For other research on women and language, see Deborah Cameron, ed., *The Feminist Critique of Language;* Deborah Cameron and Jennifer Coates, eds. *Women in their Speech Communities: New Perspectives on Language and Sex;* David Graddol and Joan Swann, *Gender Voices;* Sally McConnell-Ginet, Ruth Borkar, and Nelly Furman, eds., *Women and Language in Literature and Society;* Joyce Penfield, ed., *Women and Language in Transition;* and Barrie Thorne, Cheris Kramarae, and Nancy Henley, eds., *Language, Gender, and Society.*

19. On the wealth of sources on domestic ideology, among the most useful are Nancy Cott, *The Bonds of Womanhood;* Elizabeth K. Helsinger,

Robin Lauterbach Sheets, and William Veeder, eds., *The Woman Question*, vol. 1; and Mary Poovey, *The Proper Lady and the Woman Writer*, chap.1. Elizabeth Langland insightfully discusses the tensions between the embodied reality of Victorian women and the domestic ideal in *Nobody's Angels*; see esp. chap. 1.

20. A particularly good example of the distinction between the lady and the servant is the doubled mother figures in *David Copperfield*, the delicate Mrs. Copperfield "with her pretty hair and youthful shape," and the servant Peggotty, "with no shape at all . . . and cheeks and arms so hard and red that I wondered the birds didn't peck her in preference to apples" (18). For more on the lady/ servant polarity, see Leonore Davidoff's discussion of the relationship between the maid Hannah Cullwick and the writer Arthur Munby in "Class and Gender in Victorian England."

21. For more on the rest cure and food, see Ellen L. Bassuk, "The Rest Cure: Repetition or Resolution of Victorian Women's Conflicts?"

22. For readings of the heroine's anorexia as a form of both acquiescence to and critique of feminine ideals, see Cohen on Clarissa ("Anorexic Syndrome" 131–35 and *Daughter's Dilemma* 35–58); Sandra M. Gilbert and Susan Gubar's chapter on Brontë's *Shirley* in *The Madwoman in the Attic* (see esp. 390–92); as well as Deirdre Lashgari, "What Some Women Can't Swallow: Hunger as Protest in Charlotte Brontë's *Shirley*."

WORKS CITED

Alcott, Louisa May. *Little Women*. Ed. Elaine Showalter. New York: Penguin, 1989.

Allende, Isabelle. *Aphrodite: A Memoir of the Senses*. New York: Harper, 1998.

Alpers, Antony. *The Life of Katherine Mansfield*. New York: Penguin, 1982.

Apostolides, Marianne. *Inner Hunger: A Young Woman's Struggle through Anorexia and Bulimia*. New York: Norton, 1998.

Atwood, Margaret. *The Edible Woman*. New York: Warner, 1969.

———. *Lady Oracle*. New York: Simon, 1976.

Avakian, Arlene Voski, ed. *Through the Kitchen Window: Women Explore the Intimate Meanings of Food and Cooking*. Boston: Beacon, 1997.

Barolini, Helen. "Appetite Lost, Appetite Found." Avakian 228–37.

Bassuk, Ellen L. "The Rest Cure: Repetition or Resolution of Victorian Women's Conflicts?" *The Female Body in Western Culture: Contemporary Perspectives*. Ed. Susan Rubin Suleiman. Cambridge: Harvard UP, 1986. 139–51.

Bedell, Madelon. *The Alcotts: Biography of a Family*. New York: Potter, 1980.

Belenky, Mary Field and others. *Knowledge, Difference, and Power: Essays Inspired by Women's Ways of Knowing*. New York: Basic, 1996.

―――. *Women's Ways of Knowing: The Development of Self, Voice, and Mind*. New York: Basic, 1986.

Berk, Sarah Fenstermaker. *The Gender Factory: The Apportionment of Work in American Households*. New York: Plenum, 1985.

Boose, Lynda E. "The Father's House and the Daughter in It: The Structures of Western Culture's Daughter-Father Relationship." *Daughters and Fathers*. Ed. Lynda E. Boose and Betty S. Flowers. Baltimore: Johns Hopkins UP, 1989. 19–74.

Bordo, Susan. *Unbearable Weight: Feminism, Western Culture, and the Body*. Berkeley: U of California P, 1993.

Bower, Anne L. *Recipes for Reading: Community Cookbooks, Stories, Histories*. Amherst: U of Massachusetts P, 1997.

Bruch, Hilde. *The Golden Cage: The Enigma of Anorexia Nervosa*. New York: Vintage, 1979.

Brumberg, Joan Jacobs. *Fasting Girls: The Emergence of Anorexia Nervosa as a Disease*. Cambridge: Harvard UP, 1988.

Cameron, Deborah, ed. *The Feminist Critique of Language: A Reader*. London: Routledge, 1990.

Cameron, Deborah, and Jennifer Coates, eds. *Women in their Speech Communities: New Perspectives on Language and Sex*. London: Longman, 1988.

Charles, Nickie, and Marion Kerr. *Women, Food, and Families*. Manchester: Manchester UP, 1988.

Chernin, Kim. *The Hungry Self: Women, Eating and Identity*. New York: Harper, 1985.

―――. *The Obsession: Reflections on the Tyranny of Slenderness*. New York: Harper, 1981.

Chicago, Judy. *The Dinner Party: A Commemorative Volume Celebrating a Major Monument of Twentieth Century Art*. New York: Penguin, 1996.

―――. *The Dinner Party: A Symbol of Our Heritage*. Garden City, NY: Anchor Doubleday, 1979.

Christian, Barbara. *Black Feminist Criticism: Perspectives on Black Women Writers*. New York: Pergamon, 1985.

Cixous, Hélène. "The Author in Truth." Jenson 136–81.

―――. "Extreme Fidelity." *The Hélène Cixous Reader*. Ed. Susan Sellers. New York: Routledge, 1994. 131–37.

————. "The Laugh of the Medusa." Trans. Keith and Paula Cohen. *Signs* 1. 4 (Summer 1976): 875–93. Rpt. in *Feminisms: An Anthology of Literary Theory and Criticism*. Eds. Robyn R. Warhol and Diane Price Herndl. New Brunswick, N.J.: Rutgers UP, 1997. 347–62.

Clarke, Edward H. *Sex in Education; or, A Fair Chance For The Girls*. Boston: Osgood, 1873. Rpt. New York: Arno, 1972.

Cline, Sally. *Just Desserts: Women and Food*. London: Deutsch, 1990.

Cohen, Paula Marantz. "The Anorexic Syndrome and the Nineteenth-Century Domestic Novel." Furst and Graham 125–39.

————. *The Daughter's Dilemma: Family Process and the Nineteenth-Century Domestic Novel*. Ann Arbor: U of Michigan P, 1993.

Cott, Nancy. *The Bonds of Womanhood: "Woman's Sphere" in New England, 1780–1835*. New Haven: Yale UP, 1977.

Counihan, Carole M. *The Anthropology of Food and Body: Gender, Meaning, and Power*. New York: Routledge, 1999.

Counihan, Carole M., and Penny Van Esterik, eds. *Food and Culture: A Reader*. New York: Routledge, 1997.

Coward, Rosalind. *Female Desires: How They Are Sought, Bought, and Packaged*. New York: Grove, 1985.

Curtin, Deane W., and Lisa M. Heldke, eds. *Cooking, Eating, Thinking*. Bloomington: Indiana UP, 1992.

Dangarembga, Tsitsi. *Nervous Conditions*. Seattle: Seal, 1988.

Danticat, Edwidge. *Breath, Eyes, Memory*. New York: Vintage, 1995.

Davidoff, Leonore. "Class and Gender in Victorian England." *Sex and Class in Women's History*. Ed. Judith L. Newton, Mary P. Ryan, and Judith R. Walkowitz. London: Routledge, 1983. 17–71.

DeSilva, Cara, ed. *In Memory's Kitchen: A Legacy from the Women of Terezin*. Trans. Bianca Steiner Brown. Northvale, N.J.: Aronson, 1996.

De Vault, Marjorie L. *Feeding the Family: The Social Organization of Caring as Gendered Work*. Chicago: U of Chicago P, 1991.

Dickens, Charles. *David Copperfield*. Ed. Jerome H. Buckley. New York: Norton, 1990.

Dijkstra, Bram. *Idols of Perversity: Fantasies of Feminine Evil in Fin-de-Siècle Culture*. New York and Oxford: Oxford UP, 1986.

Dinnerstein, Dorothy. *The Mermaid and the Minotaur: Sexual Arrangements and Human Malaise*. New York: Harper and Row, 1976.

Donovan, Josephine. *After the Fall: The Demeter-Persephone Myth in Wharton, Cather, and Glasgow*. University Park: Pennsylvania State UP, 1989.

Ehrlich, Elizabeth. *Miriam's Kitchen: A Memoir.* New York: Penguin, 1997.

Ellmann, Maude. *The Hunger Artist: Starving, Writing, and Imprisonment.* Cambridge: Harvard UP, 1993.

Ensler, Eve. *The Vagina Monologues.* New York: Villard, 1998.

Fasick, Laura. *Vessels of Meaning: Women's Bodies, Gender Norms, and Class Bias from Richardson to Lawrence.* DeKalb: Northern Illinois UP, 1997.

Ferraro, Thomas. " 'Working Ourselves Up' in America: Anzia Yezierska's *Bread Givers.*" *South Atlantic Quarterly* 89. 3 (Summer 1990): 547–81.

Fraad, Harriet, Stephen Resnick, and Richard Wolff. *Bringing it All Back Home: Class, Gender and Power in the Modern Household.* London: Pluto, 1994.

Furst, Lilian R., and Peter W. Graham, eds. *Disorderly Eaters: Texts in Self-Empowerment.* University Park: Pennsylvania State UP, 1992.

Gabaccio, Donna R. *We Are What We Eat: Ethnic Food and the Making of Americans.* Cambridge: Harvard UP, 1998.

Germov, John, and Lauren Williams, eds. *A Sociology of Food and Nutrition: The Social Appetite.* South Melbourne: Oxford UP, 1999.

Gilbert, Sandra M., and Susan Gubar. *The Madwoman in the Attic: The Woman Writer and the Nineteenth-Century Literary Imagination.* New Haven: Yale UP, 1979.

Goldman, Anne. " 'I Yam What I Yam': Cooking, Culture, and Colonialism." *Decolonizing the Subject: The Politics of Gender in Women's Autobiography.* Ed. Sidonie Smith and Julia Watson. Minneapolis: U of Minnesota P, 1992. 169–95.

Golub, Ellen. "Eat Your Heart Out: The Fiction of Anzia Yezierska." *Studies in American Jewish Literature* 3. Albany: State U of New York P, 1983. 51–61.

Graddol, David, and Joan Swann. *Gender Voices.* New York: Blackwell, 1989.

Griffiths, Sian, and Jennifer Wallace, eds. *Consuming Passions.* Manchester: Mandolin, 1998.

Grosz, Elizabeth. *Sexual Subversions: Three French Feminists.* Sydney: Allen, 1989.

Haber, Barbara. "Follow the Food." Avakian 65–74.

Helsinger, Elizabeth K., Robin Lauterbach Sheets, and William Veeder, eds. *The Woman Question: Defining Voices, 1837–1883.* Vol. 1. New York: Garland, 1983.

Heywood, Leslie. *Dedication to Hunger: The Anorexic Aesthetic in Modern Culture.* Berkeley: U of California P, 1996.

Hornbacher, Marya. *Wasted: A Memoir of Anorexia and Bulimia.* New York: Harper, 1998.

Houston, Gail Turley. *Consuming Fictions: Gender, Class, and Hunger in Dickens's Novels.* Carbondale: Southern Illinois UP, 1994.

Inness, Sherrie A., ed. *Kitchen Culture in America: Popular Representations of Food, Gender, and Race.* Philadelphia: U of Pennsylvania P, 2001.

Irigaray, Luce. "And the One Doesn't Stir Without the Other." Trans. Hélène Vivienne Wenzel. *Signs* 7. 1 (1981): 60–7.

———. "The Bodily Encounter with the Mother." Whitford, 34–46.

———. *This Sex Which Is Not One.* Trans. Catherine Porter. Ithaca, N.Y.: Cornell UP, 1985.

———. "Women-Mothers: The Silent Substratum." Whitford, 47–52.

———. "Women's Exile." Interview with Luce Irigaray. Trans. Couze Venn. *Ideology and Consciousness* 1 (1977).

Jansen, Sharon L. " 'Family Liked 1956': Reading My Mother's Recipes." Avakian 55–64.

Jenson, Deborah, ed. *"Coming to Writing" and Other Essays.* By Hélène Cixous. Trans. Sarah Cornell et. al. Cambridge, MA: Harvard UP, 1991.

Kadi, Joanna, ed. *Food for our Grandmothers: Writings by Arab-American and Arab-Canadian Feminists.* Boston: South End, 1994.

Kelly, Traci Marie. " 'If I Were a Voodoo Priestess': Women's Culinary Autobiographies." Inness 228–51.

Kristeva, Julia. *Desire in Language: A Semiotic Approach to Literature and Art.* Ed. Leon S. Roudiez. Trans. Thomas Gora, Alice Jardine, and Leon S. Roudiez. New York: Columbia UP, 1980.

———. *The Powers of Horror: An Essay on Abjection.* New York: Columbia UP, 1982.

———. "The Semiotic and the Symbolic." Roman, Juhasz, and Miller 45–55.

———. *Revolution in Poetic Language.* Trans. Margaret Waller. New York: Columbia UP, 1984.

Lahlou, Mourad. "Lahlou weaves memories into Aziza's cuisine." *San Francisco Chronicle* 30 January 2002: F1+. Pt. 2 of a series, "A Passion for Cooking," begun January 23, 2002.

Langland, Elizabeth. *Nobody's Angels: Middle-Class Women and Domestic Ideology in Victorian Culture.* Ithaca, N.Y.: Cornell UP, 1995.

Lashgari, Deirdre. "What Some Women Can't Swallow: Hunger as Protest in Charlotte Brontë's *Shirley.*" Furst and Graham 141–52.

Lawrence, Marilyn. *The Anorexic Experience.* London: Women's P, 1984.

———, ed. *Fed Up and Hungry: Women, Oppression and Food.* London: Women's P, 1987.

Leonardi, Susan J. "Recipes for Reading: Summer Pasta, Lobster à la Riseholme, and Key Lime Pie." *PMLA* 104. 3 (May 1989): 340–47.

Levin, Tobe. "How to Eat without Eating: Anzia Yezierska's Hunger." *Cooking by the Book: Food in Literature and Culture.* Ed. Mary Anne Schofield. Bowling Green, OH: Bowling Green State U Popular P, 1989. 27–36.

Lorde, Audre. *Zami: A New Spelling of My Name.* Freedom, CA: Crossing, 1982.

Lupton, Deborah. *Food, the Body, and the Self.* London: Sage, 1996.

Mansfield, Katherine. *The Collected Letters of Katherine Mansfield.* Vol. 2. Ed. Vincent O'Sullivan and Margaret Scott. Oxford: Clarendon, 1987.

Marshall, Paule. *Reena and Other Stories, Including the Novella "Merle" and Commentary by the Author.* New York: Feminist, 1983.

Mason, Bobbie Ann. "The Burden of the Feast." *We Are What We Ate: Twenty-four Memories of Food.* Ed. Mark Winegardner. San Diego: Harvest-Harcourt, 1998. 134–45.

McConnell-Ginet, Sally, Ruth Borker, and Nelly Furman, eds. *Women and Language in Literature and Society.* New York: Praeger, 1980.

Meyers, Jeffrey. *Katherine Mansfield: A Biography.* New York: New Directions, 1972.

Michie, Helena. *The Flesh Made Word: Female Figures and Women's Bodies.* New York: Oxford UP, 1987.

Mitchell, Silas Weir. *Fat and Blood: And How to Make Them.* New York, 1877.

Moore, Judith. *Never Eat Your Heart Out.* New York: Farrar, 1997.

Moran, Patricia. *Word of Mouth: Body Language in Katherine Mansfield and Virginia Woolf.* Charlottesville: U of Virginia P, 1996.

Morrison, Toni. *Beloved.* New York: New American Library, 1987.

Nasser, Mervat. *Culture and Weight Consciousness.* London: Routledge, 1997.

Naylor, Gloria. *Linden Hills.* New York: Penguin, 1986.

Nightingale, Florence. *Cassandra* and Other Selections from *Suggestions for Thought.* Ed. Mary Poovey. New York: New York UP, 1993.

Orbach, Susie. *Fat is a Feminist Issue: The Anti-Diet Guide to Permanent Weight Loss.* New York: Paddington, 1978.

———. *Hunger Strike: The Anorectic's Struggle as a Metaphor for Our Age.* New York: Norton, 1986.

Orenstein, Peggy. *Schoolgirls: Young Women, Self-Esteem and the Confidence Gap.* New York: Doubleday, 1994.

Penfield, Joyce. *Women and Language in Transition.* Albany: State U of New York P, 1987.

Pierpont, Claudia Roth. *Passionate Minds: Women Rewriting the World*. New York: Viking, 2000.

Plath, Sylvia. *The Bell Jar*. New York: Bantam, 1971.

Poovey, Mary. *The Proper Lady and the Woman Writer: Ideology as Style in the Works of Mary Wollstonecraft, Mary Shelley, and Jane Austen*. Chicago: U of Chicago P, 1984.

Probyn, Elspeth. *Carnal Appetites: FoodSexIdentities*. New York: Routledge, 2000.

Raynaud, Claudine. " 'A Nutmeg Nestled Inside Its Covering of Mace': Audre Lorde's *Zami*." *Life/Lines: Theorizing Women's Autobiography*. Ed. Bella Brodzki and Celeste Schenk. Ithaca, N.Y.: Cornell UP, 1988. 221–42.

Reichl, Ruth. *Comfort Me With Apples: More Adventures at the Table*. New York: Random, 2001.

———. *Tender at the Bone: Growing Up at the Table*. New York: Random, 1998.

Rich, Adrienne. *Of Woman Born: Motherhood as Experience and Institution*. New York: Bantam, 1976.

———. "When We Dead Awaken: Writing as Re-vision." *On Lies, Secrets, and Silence: Selected Prose 1966–78*. New York: Norton, 1979. 33–49.

Robertson, Matra. *Starving in the Silences: An Exploration of Anorexia Nervosa*. Washington Square: New York UP, 1992.

Roden, Claudia. *The Book of Jewish Food: An Odyssey from Samarkand to New York*. New York: Knopf, 1996.

Roman, Camille. "Female Sexual Drives, Subjectivity, and Language: The Dialogue with/beyond Freud and Lacan." Roman, Juhasz, and Miller 7–19.

Roman, Camille, Suzanne Juhasz, and Cristanne Miller, eds. *The Women and Language Debate: A Sourcebook*. New Brunswick, NJ: Rutgers UP, 1994.

Ruark, Jennifer K. "A Place at the Table." *Chronicle of Higher Education* 9 (July 1999): A17–A19.

Sartre, Jean Paul. Preface. *The Wretched of the Earth*. By Franz Fanon. Trans. Constance Farrington. Harmondsworth, Eng.: Penguin, 1967.

Sceats, Sarah. *Food, Consumption and the Body in Contemporary Women's Fiction*. Cambridge: Cambridge UP, 2000.

Schafer, Robert B., and Elisabeth Schafer. "Relationship Between Gender and Food Roles in the Family." *Journal of Nutrition Education* 21. 3 (1989): 119–26.

Schofield, Mary Anne, ed. *Cooking by the Book: Food in Literature and Culture*. Bowling Green, OH: Bowling Green State UP, 1989.

Schwartz, Hillel. *Never Satisfied: A Cultural History of Diets, Fantasies, and Fat.* New York: Free Press, 1986.

Seid, Roberta Pollack. *Never Too Thin: Why Women are at War with Their Bodies.* New York: Prentice, 1989.

Shapiro, Laura. *Perfection Salad: Women and Cooking at the Turn of the Century.* New York: North Point, 1995.

Showalter, Elaine. Introduction. Alcott vi–xxviii.

Sobo, Elisa J. "The Sweetness of Fat: Health, Procreation, and Sociability in Rural Jamaica." *Many Mirrors: Body Image and Social Relations.* Ed. Nicole Sault. New Brunswick, NJ: Rutgers UP, 1994. 132–54.

Steele, Valerie. *Fashion and Eroticism: Ideals of Feminine Beauty from the Victorian Era to the Jazz Age.* New York: Oxford UP, 1995.

Strasser, Susan. *Never Done: A History of American Housework.* New York: Pantheon, 1982.

Szekely, Eva. *Never Too Thin.* Toronto: Women's P, 1988.

Theophano, Janet. *Eat My Words: Reading Women's Lives through the Cookbooks They Wrote.* New York: Palgrave, 2002.

Thompson, Becky W. *A Hunger So Wide and So Deep: American Women Speak Out on Eating Problems.* Minneapolis: U of Minnesota P, 1994.

Thorne, Barrie, Cheris Kramarae, and Nancy Henley, eds. *Language, Gender, and Society.* Rowley, MA: Newbury, 1983.

Tomalin, Claire. *Katherine Mansfield: A Secret Life.* New York: Knopf, 1988.

Whitford, Margaret, ed. *The Irigaray Reader.* Cambridge, MA.: Basil Blackwell, 1991.

Wilenz, Gay. "Cultural Mediation and the Immigrant's Daughter: Anzia Yezierska's *Bread Givers.*" *MELUS* 17. 3 (1991–92): 33–41.

Witt, Doris. *Black Hunger: Food and the Politics of U.S. Identity.* Oxford UP, 1999.

Wolf, Naomi. *Promiscuities.* New York: Fawcett, 1999.

Woolf, Virginia. "Professions for Women." 1931. *Women and Writing.* Ed. Michele Barrett. New York: Harcourt, 1979. 57–63.

———. "Reminiscences." *Moments of Being.* Ed. Jeanne Schulkind. 2nd ed. San Diego: Harcourt, 1985. 28–59.

Yaeger, Patricia. *Honey-Mad Women: Emancipatory Strategies in Women's Writing.* New York: Columbia UP, 1988.

Yezierska, Anzia. *Bread Givers.* 1925. Rpt. New York: Persea, 1975.

Part 1

Appetite and Consumption in Nineteenth-Century Cultural Politics

2

Good and Plenty:
Queen Victoria Figures
the Imperial Body

Adrienne Munich

*For it is a jubilee; it shall be holy unto you; ye shall eat
the increase thereof out of the field.*

—Leviticus 25:12

On Friday, October 12, 1838, Queen Victoria, still a girl and under the
tutelage of her charming, worldly, and devoted prime minister, Lord
Melbourne, recorded a dinner party conversation in her diary. In the
course of a conversation about reading, Lord Ashley recounted a lurid
fact from an otherwise proper-sounding tome. The book, by a "Captain
or Mr. Yates," *Account of New Zealand and of the Church Missionary
Society's Mission to the Northern Island* (1835), praises the New Zealanders'
character, with one reservation. "They were such a fine people, with one
single exception—they *eat men*; Lord Ashley says, 'When they have a
certain number of daughters, as many as they want, they eat the rest'"
(Victoria, *Girlhood,* 52).

One detects not only the obvious colonial hauteur in the recounting
of an indigenous people's method of population control but also some
cautionary moral in the Lord's telling and the Queen's committing the
episode to her journal. Too many daughters, warns the story, can lead to
a people consuming its superfluous women. In New Zealand's efficient
economy, a particularly gendered cannibalism disposes of female excess

45

while at the same time it makes concrete women's traditional nurturing role. As a parable, the anecdote tells of the power of eating, and possibly, too, of the danger to the Victorian economy of having a woman in the symbolic position of the one who eats rather than the one who is eaten. Because culture always works in multiple and contradictory ways, Victoria operates both as the cautionary daughter who might be eaten should she assert herself beyond conventional feminine bounds and the authority figure who could potentially eat up whomever she herself might consider excessive.

In addition to those two representations, Queen Victoria eventually comes to be figured as the one whose (maternal) body feeds the empire. Victoria figured herself in all three of these economies of eating at the same time that her culture inscribed her body as a symbol of its imperial power to incorporate the Other. The coincidence of the monarch's gender and the fortuitousness of the Victorian woman's representational authority coalesce in figures of Victoria's appetite, femininity, and plenitude.

During the course of her long reign, Queen Victoria's gustatory appetite functions both as a figure of feminine transgression and a figure of imperial plenty. The concept of the two monarchical bodies, the body natural and the body politic, that subtends the English monarchical institution provides a context for the multiply coded meanings of a commonplace act such as eating when performed by a monarch.[1] With medieval antecedents in the notion of the "abstract King," the two bodies concept developed during the reign of Victoria's great predecessor, Elizabeth I. The concept became foundational to the stability of the English monarchy by enabling a person to embody both mortality and immortality. The two bodies—the body natural subordinate to the body politic—were inextricable until death, when the body politic allied itself with the next anointed monarch. As the Elizabethan Edmund Plowden explained in his *Commentaries or Reports*, "[H]e has not a Body natural distinct and divided by itself from the Office and Dignity royal . . . but a Body natural and a Body politic together indivisible; and these two Bodies are incorporated in one Person, and make one Body and not divers" (Kantorowicz 9).

It is possibly significant that the medieval theory would be elaborated during a powerful queen's reign and reexamined (by Frederic William Maitland) in Victoria's. The gendered body of a female sovereign throws such issues as power and control into problematic relief. At a time when women were theoretically limited to the private sphere, that the queen's body natural is always already subordinate to the body politic provides even more contradictions—and more threats—to any venerable political fiction. Eating, feeding, consumption, when figured in a queen's body, even a celebate one, recurs inevitably to issues of nurturance and maternal power. So much more is the case when the Victorian Queen's body produced nine live children. As such, the ideology of Victorian femininity constantly disrupts the discourse of the monarchical body. Not universally signifying as a king's two bodies, the Queen's two bodies carry gendered inflections associated with women's nurturing role. Her physical maternalized body natural figures material yet sovereign plenitude, but her body politic, because it is corporally female, also associates the political with female capacities in its national, eventually imperial, identity.

Traces of mystical theory notwithstanding, Victoria in her lived reality could not avoid being subject to Victorian gender ideology. Her unconventional eating provoked comment. Her appetite for food, and more importantly, her public enjoyment of it, made of her a transgressive spectacle. Whereas the true Victorian woman derives her power by placing nurturing others before nurturing herself, Victoria displayed an unseemly enjoyment in her own eating.[2] To exhibit such self-referential pleasure in public eating might seem to defy Scripture and the way Scripture underwrote the construction of the Victorian woman.

When considered as a tale about the dire consequences of unruly women, the Genesis chapter where Eve bites the forbidden fruit in defiance of highest patriarchal authority suggests that women transgress when they do not control their appetites. For the Victorian, a robust appetite in women could be a sign of low-class status or a sign of moral degradation. Victorian middle-class woman were enjoined to exhibit restraint in eating. According to Barbara Ehrenreich and Dierdre English in *For Her Own Good* (the word *good* in their title playing a variation on a patriarchal imperative that associates womanly morality with delicate health), the good woman is a person emaciated in her body. Good women of the upper classes tighten their corsets and limit their appetites. The more cultivated the woman, the more sickly her frame. According to Victorian ethnographers, the Anglo-Saxon, highest on the evolutionary ladder, exemplified a gendered paradox embedded in racial superiority: they described the male of the species as the sturdiest of all peoples, whereas they idealized his female counterpart as the sickliest. Good Anglo-Saxon women could not also look too healthy. Feminist literary critics have documented the various signifying functions of the anorexic woman as one deprived of spiritual nourishment and, more recently, of the nurturing woman whose power is derived from her care-giving function.[3] And although this script has been reproduced in some novels by some women novelists, it presents only one version of an ideal feminine body. The culture allowed many women's bodies to be both good and plenty.[4] For instance, the word *slender,* frequent in Victorian descriptions of the heroine, is a relative term. Dimples require some flesh.

Even allowing for a generous interpretation of *slender,* however, the queen's enthusiasm for food falls off the scale of Victorian feminine standards. With only minor exaggeration, one could claim that in the gustatory realm, she, like the Virgin Mary in another realm, weighed in as alone among her sex. Judging from the commentaries on her public eating and from her own journal notations, Victoria ignored strictures—Biblical and social—that might be interpreted as equating a woman's unabashed appetite with all sorts of disobedience. From her earliest appearance on the cultural stage, Victoria was noteworthy for her keen enjoyment of food. Although she was very small, she was always round, and, no matter what she might have been taught, no one could force her to hide her love of eating. From her accession as an adolescent queen, when she enjoyed her dinner in plain view, to the last of her days, Victoria demonstrated the possibilities of virtuous, abundant, and visible appetite. From the beginning to the end of her life, she liked her food, and she ate flagrantly before multitudes. The political diarist, Thomas Creevy, M. P., reported on seeing the eight-year-old princess opening her mouth "as wide as it can go. . . . She eats as heartily as she laughs, I think I may say she gobbles" (Strachey 91). In 1837, the year of Victoria's accession and three years before her marriage, Sallie Coles Stevenson, wife of the American minister to the Court of St. James, wrote to her sister about Victoria's unexpected display of appetite, "The Queen sat midway the table, with her lords-in-waiting at each end. Her little Majesty eat with a good appetite, and did full justice to the rich viands" (83). Stevenson noticed this gustatory behavior, without disapproval it seems, for she admired the queen, but she may have been surprised that the nineteen-year-old monarch did not conform to conventional notions of feminine public behavior, an indication of which emerges in Stevenson's contrast between "her little Majesty" and her big appetite.

Forgiving as the diplomat's wife was in her judgment, the body natural of this particular monarch threatened the very philosophical and theological concepts of ruling itself. For if the sovereign shows power in consuming food, the spectacle of a Victorian female monarch eating had the power to disrupt the neat categories of court and common etiquette alike. What would it mean in behavioral terms to eat like a queen? During that first year of testing such questions, the same year of Stevenson's observations, the queen threw her first ball. She adored dancing, eating, and conversing with guests, and apparently performed all three with a grace appropriate to a young Victorian lady. But her behavior, particularly her eating, struck many as not sufficiently monarchical. Another observer of the queen's feeding habits (and it is interesting how many observations are recorded in women's journals and letters on the subject), Mary Frampton, found the spectacle of the queen's eating too common, too accessible. The queen *"stood"* to eat her supper. "This shocked me dreadfully, and horrifies Grand Mama Ilchester," she reported, "as there is not sufficient *state* in it. Even William IV who was quite Citizen King enough, always supped with the Queen in his private apartments with a select party. . . . At all events," she concluded, "the multitude ought not to be admitted to the supper room until the Queen has herself finished" (qtd. in Charlot 104). Frampton's sense of the monarchical body politic as one which shields "the multitude" (if indeed a highly selective multitude) from the sovereign's commonality with them in such essential activities as eating accords with the shielding of the proper woman from exhibiting similar, ordinary appetites.

Whether she ate privately or informally in public view, no one in fact could curb the queen's appetite. For Frampton the sight (as the sight of a pregnant woman) might conjure images of ordinary but undignified bodily activities. For others, the queen's appetite involved concerns about health. Despite efforts on the part of her doctors to regulate her eating, this habit of public—or semipublic—enjoyment of eating extended to the end of her days. She sometimes suffered from indigestion, but palliatives were finally hopeless. Dr. Reid, her personal physician, prescribed Benger's Food (a Victorian weight-loss preparation) as a substitute for her ample meals, but the queen insisted on taking it in addition to rather than instead of her other food. Victoria knew she was dying when she no longer could eat. The diary entry on January 12, 1901, ten days before her death indicates that she was anticipating the return of her pleasure in eating: "Had a good night and could take some breakfast better" (*Letters and Journals* 349). (fig. 2.1)

Moreover, she focused on her own satiation. In her attention to gratifying her appetite, the queen's writing blends a conscious self-gratification at her own embodiment with an unconscious wielding of eating as power. In controlling rituals around food, as a tyrannical manner of wielding sovereign power, Victoria's personal pleasures inevitably represent the monarchy's authority through the mode of personal appetite. This nexus is dramatized in a dining room scene in the movie *Mrs. Brown* (1997). The widowed Queen Victoria's assembled children and household (the Queen's personal staff) await the arrival of Her Majesty and her retinue of ladies in waiting. No one eats, of course, until the plump, morose queen enters, tucks her napkin in her fichu, and brings the first food to her mouth. From that gesture, the camera records Victoria cleaning her plate in efficient, quick strokes, after which those less adroit watch as servants whisk away their barely touched plates. Underscoring her utterly despotic, yet contradictory control of her dependents' eating, Victoria remarks to the Princess of Wales, as she sweeps unceremoniously from the room, that Alix is not eating enough. "One must not let vanity overrule one's appetite," she warns her statuesque daughter-in-law. The scene chooses eating as the trope to delineate the self-absorbed quality of Queen Victoria's mourning for Prince Albert in

WINDSOR.

HER MAJESTY'S DINNER,

Thursday, 28th June, 1900.

Potages.

Consommé de tortue.　　Potage des Rois.

Poissons.

Saumon sauce roche.　　Eperlans frits sauce ravigotte.

Entrées.

Ris de veau à la Senn.

Chaud-froid de volaille à la Reine.

Relevés.

Bœuf braise à la Richelieu.

Selle d'agneau sauce menthe.　　Petits pois à l'Anglaise.

Rôt.

Cailles aux pommes de terre à l'Indienne.

Entremêts.

Asperges sauce Hollandaise.

Babas au curacao.　　Eclairs aux fraises.

Croûtes de Chantilly.

Glaces.

Crême au chocolat.　　Eau de citron.

Buffet.

Hot and Cold Fowls.　　Tongue.　　Cold Roast Beef.

Fig. 2.1 Queen Victoria's dinner six months before her death. (Author's collection)

the mid 1860s. In the spectacle of regal plenitude, the queen denies others their essential nourishment, finds fault with her fashionable daughter-in-law, and satisfies herself.

The movie dramatizes what apparently was in fact Victoria's eating habit. Regardless of her nearest and dearest, her speed of ingestion circumscribed their eating pleasure. In the context of a private meal, the scene demonstrates the significance of the queen's eating as a mode of exercising power, even abusing it. Feeding herself despite others' hunger, she is neither a good queen nor a good mother.

Since she is monarch, however, Victoria's unrestrained appetite can be considered as representing national plenty. In her act of shameless eating, Victoria performs what Elias Canetti describes as the prerogatives of a king or chief to represent national power and fortitude in his public displays of eating:

> Everything which is eaten is the food of power. . . . The man who can eat more than anyone else lies back satisfied and heavy with food; he is a champion. There are peoples who take such a champion eater for their chief. His full belly seems to them a guarantee that they themselves will never go hungry for long. It is as though he had filled it for all of them. . . . The king in his character of champion eater has never wholly disappeared. Time and again the role is re-enacted for the benefit of delighted subjects. Ruling groups in general are also prone to gluttony; the feats of the later Romans are proverbial, in this respect. (257)

Canetti's evocation of gluttonous Roman emperors resonates with the Victorians' harkening back to imperial Rome as a model of their own colonial ambitions. Victoria's eating inscribes her body politic as a material figure for expansiveness. Her specific body in its rotundity comes to stand for the embodiment of the imperium. An empress rather than an emperor, this embodiment is troped as maternal, the quintessential figure of nurturance. Particularly by the end of the century, beginning in the 1880s, Victoria's consumption often represented her subjects' pleasure in their own plenitude as that striving to incorporate things in general intersects with their nationalist pride in the British Empire. Victoria *Regina et Imperatrice* comes to represent a generosity of plenty. Because of her gender, the ability to feed masses and to consume them centers on a figure of a woman who eats prodigiously and, in her body politic, offers herself to be eaten.

These queenly figures of plenteous consumption come together at the end of the century, most forcefully figured in the years around the jubilees but begin when she became engaged to Prince Albert. In that earlier, less prosperous time (1840), Victoria's unstylish shape was represented in a street ballad as signifying English pride in their relative prosperity during hungry times. When Victoria announced her engagement to Prince Albert of Saxe-Coburg and Gotha, the ballad disrespectfully celebrated the Teutonic union by proclaiming that this Germanic upstart had won "England's fat purse and England's fat queen." Using fatness as a nice link between the queen's body natural and the body politic, the ditty distinguished between the (hungry) German prince and the (full) English queen. Denigrating an overly rotund monarch, yet drawing proud connections between her physical embodiment and national wealth, the ballad demonstrates a relatively early example of how Canetti's precept operates in Victorian figuration. By the time of the two jubilees, in 1887 and 1897, the conjunction of the queen's body, the nation's considerably fatter purse, and the nation's fat empire are implicit. Both incorporating the world as a figure of empire and feeding it, Victoria's public feasts associated with her reign represent Britain's celebration of its own expansive self.

While the figure of Eve represents a rich cultural sign of the repression of womanly appetite, its focus on prohibition rather than celebration limits a vocabulary linking woman's appetite with unimpeded pleasure and unmitigated plenty. In contrast to Eve's isolated—though possibly pleasurable—bite, Leviticus provided license for jubilee celebrations of empire, while feasting became a sign of the queen's nurturance. Leviticus 25:12 sets out the ways of celebrating the land which the Lord lent to the Hebrews: "And ye shall hallow the fiftieth year, and proclaim liberty throughout the land unto all the inhabitants thereof; it shall be a jubilee unto you; and ye shall return every man unto his possession, and ye shall return every man unto his family." The chapter elaborates on the relation of the people to the land as sojourners, not owners, its fruits being their rewards: "For it is a jubilee. . . . ye shall eat the increase thereof out of the field." Not only could the queen's eating in the context of the jubilee perform the people's pleasure in their own riches, but in figurative ways the subjects around the world were invited to partake of her body politic. The metaphors linking the queen's feasts with the queen's eating are extended to the queen's lands by figures of Mother Nature applied to Victoria.

Biblical tradition associates cultivated land with women or a female principle. The Hebrew word for earth, *adamah,* is a feminine noun. Queen Victoria could be troped as that kind of womanly figure for Mother Nature of which the earth is a sign. In this figurative mode, sexual attractiveness is secondary to the fecundity signified by her rotund body.[5] Economic plenty embodied in this body, moreover, provides another equation for calculating a significant role for womanly figures in the imperial consumer economy.

Appropriately enough, an ordinary middle-class Victorian matron who was imbued with biblical meanings of *jubilee* suggested the jubilee celebration as a way of honoring Queen Victoria's fifty years on the throne. The queen had equated herself with this influential class of Victorian woman who was associated with consuming and consumerism.[6] Reversing the original benefit of jubilee in liberating lands and peoples, Victoria's jubilees, rather than returning lands to their colonial inhabitants, celebrate royal tenantry signified by the British Empire. The celebrations drew on biblical example to trumpet Britain's world dominion in the name of a consumer queen. They highlighted the unity of the Empire's fecundity, returning its inhabitants not to themselves but to their rightful possessor, Mother Victoria, Queen of Britain and Empress of India.

Massiveness itself characterizes the jubilee celebrations by proclaiming the Empire first in the world imperial sweepstakes. Such gloating over sheer size, combined with biblical reverence, characterizes many jubilee commemoratives. *A Souvenir of the Queen's Jubilee,* for instance, reflects on the "purity of her life, tenderness of her heart, sympathy to those in affliction," while instantiating this characterization by a blend of imperial Christianity and the vastness of imperial reach. The narrative attributes to the queen a reverential colonial attitude: "To a native prince she sent a superbly bound copy of the Bible with the message, 'This is the secret of England's greatness'"(21). The same souvenir booklet reproduces a speech by the lieutenant governor, Sir Leonard Tilley, in which the secret of her greatness is equated with the empire's size:

> [O]ur beloved Queen's authority extends over one fifth of the habitable globe. . . . [N]early three hundred and ten million, or one-fifth of the whole human race, acknowledge her authority. . . . [T]he area of which the British Empire is composed is five times as large as the Persian Empire was under Darius, four times as large as the Roman Empire under Augustus, larger than all the Russias, three times as large as the United States of America, sixteen times as large as France, and forty times as large as Germany. (41)

Sir Leonard's multiplication tables vanquish England's European rivals.

Two extraordinary phenomena—a woman monarch and the length and extent of her reign—come to be represented in the years of jubilee in tropes of food and feasting. To portray a benevolent monarchy—one whose annexations seem not so much to colonize as to liberate—Victoria's capacious body authorizes groaning boards and invites her global community to partake of its gustatory delights. The crops of the world, the tilling and harvesting of fertile soil, are literally called to service—as if in obeisance to the queen's largesse. The Diamond Jubilee literally consumed global crops. Richard Harding Davis, an American writer, marvels at the scope of such consumption: "So far in advance did people prepare of its [the Diamond Jubilee's] coming that managers of hotels in London bought up whole fields before the green stuffs they would produce later had been planted and while the ground was covered with snow" (262). Food consumption as celebration to Davis figured the new global community:

> An invitation to dine on a certain night in June [the jubilee feast] was sent to the colonial premiers in January, six months before the dinner was cooked; and on account of the expected presence in London of an additional million and a half people, food stuffs to feed them were imported months before, and freight rates from the River Plate and New Zealand rose thirty per cent in consequence. This fact alone suggests how far-reaching were the effects of the Jubilee and also how tightly the world is now knit together, since a street parade in London disturbs traffic in Auckland and on the Bay of Plenty. (262)

The aptly named bay figures the mood of goodness deriving from largesse. Jubilees thus figured celebrate British imperialism in a manner that softens and makes familial its aggressive and acquisitive politics. There seems to be plenty for all, and this is good. Such goodness and largeness reside in the body natural of a queen, inseparable from the body politic. A reporter writing for *Blackwood's Magazine* in the jubilee number, expresses that symbolic figure by conveying his awe at the Diamond Jubilee's sheer magnitude and the centrality of Victoria's role in validating the British Empire:

> [I]n her own sphere there is no factor so great in the unity which binds the empire together as it never was bound before. The most distant settlement of her dominions is proud of her, of her history and her name. The only Queen! No one to compete with her, no other to approach her pre-eminence; the Mother, the Friend, ever watchful, ever sympathetic, never failing in the true word, either for sorrow or for joy. We be the sons of one man, said the children of Jacob. We are the children of one Mother, is the meaning of the shout that will go round the earth on the approaching day of triumph. (615)

The writer for *Blackwood's* indicates how literally the queen could be taken as the mother of the empire. In this maternal embodiment (and Victoria was suited for this kind of idealization for she bore nine live children, all of whom survived into adulthood), Victoria has become the perfect, self-abnegating mother, alert and responsive to all her children. Not only could people imagine her in this idealized role, but they could believe that it was she and not her government who foresaw the wisdom of empire.

W. T. Stead, a liberal journalist with republican leanings, surprised himself in his admiration of Queen Victoria. During the Diamond Jubilee year, he published his meditations on personal meanings for him of

Victoria's reign. Notice in the following quotation from that memoir how he describes the empire's lands in the language of nurturance, protection, and generation, to depict an empire unified as a family under the wing of a caring mother, returned to its rightful tenancy under Victoria's sixty-year vigilance:

> What with protectorates and annexations, we have added to the territory sheltered by the Union Jack in the course of Her Majesty's reign dominions nearly double the area of the whole Indian Empire as it existed in 1837. There is nothing approaching to this record in the history of the world. . . .
>
> It would be, of course, absurd to attribute that mighty impulse which is vitalising whole continents with the seed of Empire to any individual, even the most exalted. A world-movement like this is the visible embodiment and incarnation of the genius, of the instinct, and of the necessities of a race. But it may fairly be claimed that during the last sixty years no one mind has contributed so much helpful guidance, generous stimulus, and sage control to the great expansive impulse of the country as that of Her Majesty. (30)

Both Stead and the *Blackwood's* writer give Queen Victoria great power, not, it is true, the conventional kind of direct power but a kind of power that can be internalized to satisfy primal demands. It is the power harnessed by commodity capitalism, and when it employed Victoria's image, her influence over world events might be conceived as almost magical. While Mother Victoria understands her disparate peoples as if they were her children, Queen and Empress Victoria maintains a steadfast vision of British racial supremacy that overcomes a succession of ministers and enables the British to fulfill a racial destiny in "vitalising whole continents with the seed of Empire."

By the jubilee years the equation of lots of money—indeed, lots of more direct forms of enrichment, such as food—with the queen's fat body celebrate wealth of empire. The ordinary citizenry would eventually be able to locate in the familiar lineaments of Victoria's plumpness its own spectacularly expanded self and wealth. Between jubilees in 1887 and 1897 Victoria had achieved her ultimate girth: fifty-eight inches high, she measured over fifty-five inches around at her widest point; with the almost perfect round of her globally recognizable head, her body stood on earth as a substantial pyramid. Such a solid form could be taken up to represent something positive. Nineteenth-century romantic habits of figuring nature as a nurturing mother (sometimes inadequately nurturant) prepare for Victoria's apotheosis as the very image of British global dominance and the figure of good and plenty—also a symbolic representation of plenty of goods.

With Victoria's accession to the throne, representations reembody the feminine figure of romantic nature. Not only is the feminine principle diffused onto the natural world to teach boys how to live morally (as in Wordsworth), but she is also incarnated as a moral nurturer in the person of the Victorian sovereign. The writer for *Blackwood's* expresses a result of that reembodying process, for he gives Victoria the qualities of the Romantic Mother Nature. Although this figure called "Queen Victoria" is no less an idealized figure than was romantic nature, it becomes specifically political. Nature has been grafted onto a historical figure and carries with it a clear nationalistic ideology. Through this process of figuration Queen Victoria authorizes Victorian exploits in gathering treasure and annexing distant lands. Ever vigilant and caring, she adopts the children of those lands as her own and those children's resources as her province. The land is not only her land, it is her. Here indeed is a refiguring of Leviticus.

In evoking the biblical meanings of jubilee, Victorian celebrations reimagine the return of the land as an affirmation of Victoria's right to preside over the global empire, suggesting that such an empire returns the land to its rightful possessors. In support of this ideology, the jubilees imprinted Victoria's familiar round form on the cultural imagination. Using conventional methods of disseminating a ruler's image on coinage and monuments as a way of representing authority, the queen's image appeared everywhere. In this regard, the practice resembles other imperial eras in circulating images of its ruler, but, by virtue of the ruler's gender, the meaning of the images became more domestic. Unlike Caesar, for instance, the proliferating female image, instead of appearing only on official means of exchange, such as seals and coins, also appeared on household goods, on things ordinarily used for cooking and eating. Filtered through the romantic trope projecting the feminine outward onto the familiar landscape, Victoria came to represent the feminine, her image stamped on ordinary material objects—not onto Wordsworth's rocks and stones and trees but onto pitchers, rolling pins, plates, and tea towels. Such daily acts as pouring cream from a jubilee pitcher, authorized by the queen's seal of approval, bring the queen to the table, in a symbolic ritual of eating her.

Victoria was in the habit of feasting her closest servants in the name of her family. "I give the good people and my servants here a dinner in the servants' hall tonight as I did last week for Bertie's birthday," the queen wrote to Vicky (her eldest daughter), Crown Princess Frederick of Prussia, about a banquet held in honor of the crown princess's birthday (*Darling Child* 117). The "good people" and her servants thus had reason to be grateful for the queen's large family. Counting her own birthday, they could depend on at least ten birthday feasts in addition to special holiday dinners. (fig. 2.2)

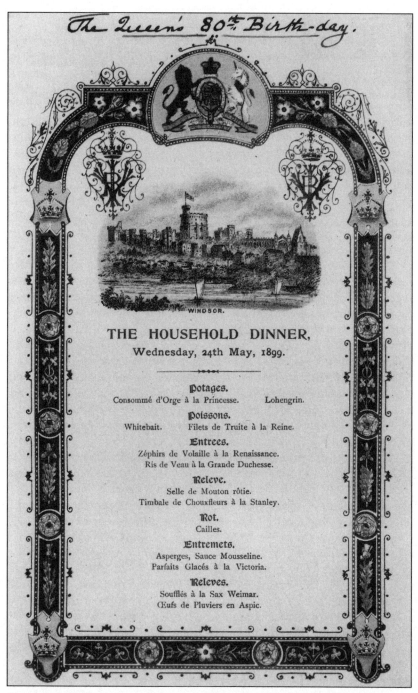

The Queen's 80th Birth-day.

THE HOUSEHOLD DINNER,
Wednesday, 24th May, 1899.

Potages.
Consommé d'Orge à la Princesse.   Lohengrin.

Poissons.
Whitebait.   Filets de Truite à la Reine.

Entrees.
Zéphirs de Volaille à la Renaissance.
Ris de Veau à la Grande Duchesse.

Releve.
Selle de Mouton rôtie.
Timbale de Chouxfleurs à la Stanley.

Rot.
Cailles.

Entremets.
Asperges, Sauce Mousseline.
Parfaits Glacés à la Victoria.

Releves.
Soufflés à la Sax Weimar.
Œufs de Pluviers en Aspic.

Fig. 2.2 Queen Victoria's eightieth birthday menu for her household. (Author's collection)

During the jubilee years, the good people fed in the name of the queen reinforced a figure of benevolent motherhood. Actual feasts of a magnitude exceeding anything comparable in the twentieth century seemed to make Victoria the nurturer of multitudes. But, because her body politic carries mystical meanings, the multitudes feasting in her name symbolically consume her body. Such feasts were held in countless towns and villages throughout her realm. One appreciates the magnitude of such rituals by examining a relatively insignificant English township. Aston Manor published an official record of its Diamond Jubilee celebration, suggesting that its late planning—begun only in April—may have reduced its scope. During the month of June, jubilee hymns and national anthems were sung; 12,600 children were given specially designed jubilee medals and 15,744 children were given "tea and bread and butter, and plain and currant cake, which were provided in abundance" (*Queen Victoria's Diamond Jubilee* 30).

There were concert and fireworks displays, a Thanksgiving service, and dinner for the old people: "roast and boiled joints with the usual vegetables, followed by tarts and puddings. The whole was washed down by a copious supply of nut brown ale and various non-alcoholic beverages. . . . After dinner each aged man was provided with an ounce of tobacco and the women each received a two-ounce packet of tea" (*Queen Victoria's Jubilee* 32). In a manner we have come to associate with Victorian earnestness, the Aston Manor chronicler recounted the numbers of elderly feasters: 317 in Dyson Hall, 283 in Lozells Hall, and 354 in Victoria Hall, for a total of 954, more than two-thirds, he tells us, females. Upwards of 100 people who were too infirm to attend were each presented with a ticket entitling them to receive meat and grocery to the value of two shillings sixpence (*Queen Victoria's Diamond Jubilee* 33). In addition, enough money was raised to purchase a free dispensary. In Aston Manor people are fed and cured in Victoria's name.

If such typical jubilee celebrations seemed to give the queen an unbelievable prominence, it was possible for others to celebrate the accomplishments of the reign while denying the queen any significant role in it. George Gissing's novel *In the Year of Jubilee* replaces the queen's importance with consumable products manufactured for the jubilee as indicating what is important about them. They and their makers and not the aged queen signify a new spirit of the age. What progress some saw as the result of monarchical authority, Gissing portrays as a new bourgeois legal tender. The queen, in this context of imperial expansion and middle-class ascendancy, becomes the spirit of the age, feminine like romantic nature but consumed and absorbed by the culture she, in her person, represents. In the same way as the romantic ideology retained the feminine principle in nature while denying actual women agency, so Gissing's novel denies the queen any significant place in her own celebration. So absorbed has she become by 1893, the year of the novel's publication, that Gissing's characters claim that the Golden Jubilee celebrates themselves, the progress of the middle classes and not Queen Victoria at all. In fact, what one character calls the "Royalties" are expendable: "I don't care for Royalties," he remarks. "Nor do I," agrees another. But "royalties" have their commercial uses that the entrepreneurial classes do not deny: "I know a chap who made a Jubilee Perfume, and he's netting something like a hundred pounds a day." These are royalties in another sense: profits from exploiting royalty. Another character feels he missed the jubilee opportunity: "I had a really big thing,—a Jubilee Drink,—a teetotal beverage; the kind of thing would have sold itself this weather" (57). Royalties have entered the body marketplace in Gissing's novel. By dabbing her as perfume, by drinking her, parts of the monarch could be incorporated into her subjects. Everyone could profit, in one way or another, from the queen's body.

In a literal exemplification of how Victoria's likeness could seem to be reflected in a nature colonized and regulated by the Raj, a Golden Jubilee celebration in Calcutta projected Victoria's image literally onto the stratosphere. The Earl of Dufferin, Viceroy of India, wrote to his queen describing the most dazzling feature of Calcutta's jubilee fireworks: "[T]he outline of your Majesty's head, traced in lines of fire, which unexpectedly burst on the vision of the astonished crowd." That image, emblem of Victoria's way of being translated to another culture, maps her body as a constellation, a formation, a fetish object. We could understand the entire Indian jubilee events as what Anne McClintock refers to in describing nationalism as inhabiting the realm of fetishism (226–231). The Calcutta jubilee celebrations enact what she calls a "commodity spectacle."[7]

It was a spectacle the masses could consume in a ritualistic commodity mass. At the queen's Diamond Jubilee, the cake excelled by its sheer statistical size. According to one diarist, "It was presented to her [the queen] by Gunther, the great man in London for these things, and said to be the grandest cake ever made. It is, I think, fifteen feet high: and the actual *eating part* of it (without all the appendages) weighed over half a ton!!" Rather than a threatening equation between female sexuality and female fat, the queen's body could represent comforting and endless plenitude. This is not the forbidden fruit of Christina Rossetti's poem "Goblin Market," where delicious eating symbolizes the appetites forbidden to women and marketplace abuses of those appetites by domineering yet seductive men.

At the turn of the century, the Victoria Fruit Company of Riverside, California, could equate Victoria's head with their company's delicious produce. (fig. 2.3) Whereas Rossetti's goblin men calling out "Come try our fruits!" echo the devil's seduction of Eve transposed to a market economy, this advertisement encouraged glorious accessibility to regal appetite. On their label, Victoria's round rosy head, wrapped in royal veil, resembles their perfectly round, perfectly ripe, wrapped fruit. The queen's body proclaims her own round juiciness as a sign of abundant good—and goods.[8] Her body offers itself to be eaten in the form of a fruit: permissible, delicious, and against Eve.

Feasting and images of good and plenty impose a solid geometry on global relations, reflecting a culture's multiple ways of making meaning. Opening with an anecdote about the regulatory function of stories about cannibalism from Victoria's first years as queen, this chapter closes with a jubilee story about a sovereign's power to form alliances by means of cannibalism.

Queen Kapiolani of Hawaii attended the Golden Jubilee in 1887, seeming either oblivious to or defiant of her relatively insignificant status among the global potentates. She demanded and received (with Victoria's assent) a full sovereign's escort as well as an invitation to dinner at Buckingham Palace. At one point in the evening, the "Black Queen," as she was known in London, revealed to Victoria what perhaps was the source of her disregard for precedence. She was, she informed a somewhat surprised but ever polite Victoria, a blood relation of the British Queen and Empress of India. "How so?" asked Victoria. "My grandfather ate your Captain Cook," the Hawaiian queen explained (qtd. in Muller and Munson 117).

Turning the tables on the sentiment from *Blackwood's* that Victoria, the Imperial Mother, has no peer, the Black Queen tells her counterpart that all English persons of all classes are alike, related under the skin, in the edible muscle and sinew. Furthermore, they are available to primal colonization. Eating people brings them into the family. Queen Kapiolani's epithet "the Black Queen" represents her as the dark Other to her lighter counterpart. In celebrating the power of eating at its basic level in cannibalism and in visibly consuming as a sign of national colonial appetites, both queens affirm a link between power and eating. And as figures of ample womanhood, they suggest a control allied with motherhood. To inspire fantasies of eating and being eaten, Queen Victoria as a national imperial mother eats her colonies, performs acts of eating as acts of national plenitude, and offers her two bodies to be consumed by a gratified (and obedient) global family.

Fig. 2.3 Victoria brand fruit label. (Author's collection)

NOTES

1. See Munich for a discussion of Victoria's two domestic bodies, one of the private home and the other of the civic life of a nation, and Kantorowicz for a discussion of the Elizabethan elaboration of medieval theory subtending this distinction.

2. Fasick distinguishes between the praiseworthy woman who feeds others as opposed to the woman who deprives herself. Although Fasick's aim is to minimize anorexia as a cultural norm if not an imperative (a point with which I agree), her dichotomy ignores the more transgressive concept of a woman who feeds (rather than starves herself). There is too little room in her scheme for a woman who feeds herself before feeding others or who feeds herself in addition to feeding others. It is this figure of fleshly plenty, of sheer materiality, which has been neglected in a consideration of Victorian culture.

3. In the 1980s, Sandra M. Gilbert and Susan Gubar discussed meanings of the starving women in Victorian women's writing, arguing that they symbolize

the ambitious woman's social oppression. They found that such anorexic images expressed women's cultural silencing: they suffer in Charlotte Brontë's Jane Eyre and Lucy Snow, and in Christina Rossetti's and Emily Dickinson's poetry. The nineteenth-century ambitious woman strives to express herself against social prohibitions but also turns her ambitions against her body by showing it as starved. Expanding upon this argument Helena Michie explores feminine weight-lessness and lack of appetite and refinement, gathered together in what she calls "ladylike anorexia."(21) Michie, like Dierdre English and Barbara Ehrenreich, stresses "the lengths to which nineteenth-century culture was willing to go to deny women's physical need for food." Like them, she shows that the ideal slender woman functioned as well as a marker for class: while women of the lower classes could show their appetites, refined women advertised their position in good society by restraining their public consumption of food. I hope my position in this essay complicates without denying the Victorian trope of starvation.

4. Seid claims that in the nineteenth century "fat was seen as a 'silken layer' that graced the frames of elegant ladies. It was regarded as 'stored-up force,' equated with reserves of energy and strength. Plumpness was deemed a sign of emotional well-being; it was identified with a good temperament, with a clean conscience, with temperate and disciplined habits, and above all, with good health" (5).

5. Fasick argues persuasively that the critical and scholarly emphasis of eating and sexuality mutes the Victorian emphasis on female nurturing and control of appetites.

6. See Richards for uses of Queen Victoria as a consumer queen and Bowlby for the growth of the department store and its uses in literature.

7. It is outside the scope of this essay to illustrate how the jubilees vary McClintock's paradigm, but here is the relevant passage:

> [N]ationalism has been experienced and transmitted primarily through fetishism. . . . More often than not, nationalism takes shape through the visible, ritual organization of fetish objects—flags, uniforms, airplane logos, maps, anthems, national flowers, national cuisines and architectures as well as through the organization of collective fetish spectacle. (374–75)

If we understand the jubilees as organizing a sense of empire as a unified national idea, one can see how all the fetish objects and indeed Victoria herself as a fetishized object create and validate an idea of empire.

8. How this image of royal pleasure remains, yet how much it has been accommodated to a new global economy, can be measured in its commercial capital in our present moment. The former Duchess of York, familiarly known as "Fergie," has been punished for her appetites, both sexual and gustatorial. At one point her weight of 203 pounds earned her the title "Duchess of Pork." Chastened and diminished, she later signed on as an ambassador of Weight Watchers. The Business Section of *The New York Times*, without a

conscious historical imagination, treats the selling of royalty as something new, but drawing on a cultural unconscious for its imagery, portrays Fergie as emerging from a globe. Her avatar, Queen Victoria, might be surprised at the postmodern spin of this globe and probably would not recognize her influence on the image of a fat royal by marriage using her body to sell a product. Victoria Fruit Company inviting Americans to eat is not that distant nor so far in meanings from Fergie's invitation to Americans not to eat so much. Eve's Victorian fruit, it seems, has come full circle. See Claudia H. Deutsch, "A Royal Rebel's Pitch to America" *The New York Times* February 5, 1997, D1.

WORKS CITED

Bowlby, Rachel. *Just Looking: Consumer Culture in Dreiser, Gissing and Zola.* London: Methuen, 1985.

Canetti, Elias. *Crowds and Power.* New York: Penguin, 1962.

Charlot, Monica. *Victoria, The Young Queen.* Oxford: Blackwell, 1992.

Davis, Richard Harding. *A Year from a Reporter's Notebook.* New York, 1898.

Deutsch, Claudia H. "A Royal Rebel's Pitch to America." New York Times (February 5, 1997): D1.

Ehrenreich, Barbara, and Dierdre English. *For Her Own Good: 150 Years of the Experts' Advice to Women.* New York: Anchor, 1978.

Fasick, Laura. *Vessels of Meaning: Women's Bodies, Gender Norms, and Class Bias from Richardson to Lawrence.* DeKalb: Northern Illinois P, 1997.

Gilbert, Sandra M. and Susan Gubar. *The Madwoman in the Attic.* New Haven: Yale UP, 1979.

Gissing, George. *In the Year of Jubilee.* New York: Appleton, 1893.

Kantorowicz, Ernst H. *The King's Two Bodies: A Study in Mediaeval Political Theology.* Princeton: Princeton UP, 1957.

McClintock, Anne. *Imperial Leather: Race, Gender and Sexuality in the Colonial Contest.* New York: Routledge, 1995.

Michie, Helena. *The Flesh Made Word.* Oxford UP, 1987.

Muller, Richard, and James Munson. *Victoria: Portrait of a Queen.* London: BBC, 1987.

Munich, Adrienne. "Empire and Excess." *Tulsa Studies in Women's Literature* 6 (Fall 1987): 265–81.

Queen Victoria's Diamond Jubilee 1897: How it Was Celebrated in Aston Manor. Birmingham, [1899?]

Richards, Thomas. *The Commodity Culture of Victorian England: Advertising and Spectacle, 1851–1914*. Stanford, CA: Stanford UP, 1990.

Seid, Roberta. "Too 'Close to the Bone': The Historical Context for Women's Obsession with Slenderness." *Feminist Perspectives on Eating Disorders*. Ed. Patricia Fallon et al. New York: Guilford, 1994.

Souvenir of the Queen's Jubilee: an account of the celebration at the City of Saint John, New Brunswick in honor of the Jubilee Year of the Reign of Her Most Gracious Majesty Queen Victoria. St. John, NB, 1887.

Stead, W. T. *Studies of the Sovereign and the Reign*. London, Review of Reviews Office, 1897.

Stevenson, Sallie Coles. *Victoria, Albert, and Mrs. Stevenson*. Ed. Edward Boykin. New York: Reinhart, 1957.

Strachey, Lytton. *Queen Victoria*. New York: Harcourt, 1921.

"Tis Sixty Years Since." *Blackwood's Edinburgh Magazine* 161 (May 1897).

Victoria, Queen of Britain. *Darling Child: Private Correspondence of Queen Victoria and the German Crown Princess, 1871–1878*. Ed. Roger Fulford. London: Evans Brothers, 1976.

———. *The Girlhood of Queen Victoria: A Selection from Her Majesty's Diaries Between the Years of 1832 and 1840*. Ed. Viscount Esher. London: Murray, 1912.

———. *Queen Victoria in Her Letters and Journals*. Selected by Christopher Hibbert. New York: Penguin, 1985.

3

Ingestion, Contagion, Seduction: Victorian Metaphors of Reading

Pamela K. Gilbert

The Victorian popular novel market was dominated by women, both as authors and readers. In the context of emerging centralized government, consolidated by public health crises and the entailments of imperialism, a powerful, commodified discourse emerged. This discourse, produced and consumed largely by women and shaped by the demands of an apparently unruly and expanding public, occasioned considerable anxiety for the British social and political elite, expressed in terms which specified the popular novel as a threat to the imperial social body. At the same time, specific anxieties fostered a metaphoric field wherein popular reading became associated with forms of ingestion and bodily invasion.

Many critics have pointed out the tendency of Victorian critics to identify the 1860s sensation novel with disease; the genre's identification with food and drugs has been less noted.[1] Mary Elizabeth Braddon, among the most successful popular novelists of the period, was a primary target of such attacks. In *The Doctor's Wife* (1867), her first attempt to write a nonsensational "novel of character"—what we would now identify as mid-Victorian realism—she both incorporates and critiques these metaphors, using them to distance her novel from the sensational but also to destabilize the very distinction between the middle-class "high" novel and lower-class sensational fiction. In this chapter, I will trace the logic of some of these metaphors, first drawing from a range of typical critical texts from across the latter half of the century, and then through this exemplary Victorian bestseller.

Historian Catherine Sheldrick Ross describes two dominant metaphors of reading, both of which are very much in evidence in the nineteenth century: reading as eating, and reading as a (moral and intellectual) ladder. The morally responsible reader is to "climb the ladder," repudiating "sugary" romances and "highly spiced" fictions and developing the discriminating palate necessary to appreciate "better" imaginative works such as poetry and nonfiction histories and scientific treatises. We should add here two figures not discussed by Ross: reading as sexual intercourse and as the ingestion of drugs—particularly the reading of novels. Books, then, are presented alternately as food and poison, medicine and illicit drugs, erotic and contaminated bodies. In all of these metaphors, the text is a substance that enters the reader and has an effect on him or her. The text is not an inert thing to be merely manipulated, it is active—even opportunistic. In the context of the nineteenth century's twin terrors— epidemic disease and revolution, the disintegration of the physical and social body—these metaphors took on a particular role, one in which they were able to body forth the Victorians' fear of biological and social dissolution. Metaphors of ingression and ingestion rebounded upon the aggressor, emphasizing the reciprocity of the boundary transgression implied. The reader who devours the text is in some sense inhabited by that text.

The metaphor of reading as sexual intercourse is related to the eating metaphor most crucially in that it deals with the transgression of physical boundaries, just as eating itself often is a metaphor for sexual activity. It is convenient in this case to use Ross's example:

> The reader of novels only, especially if he reads many, becomes very soon an intellectual voluptuary, with feeble judgement, a vague memory, and an incessant craving for some new excitement. . . . An inveterate novel-reader speedily becomes a literary roue, and this is possible at a very early period of life. It now and then happens that a youth of seventeen becomes almost an intellectual idiot or an effeminate weakling by living exclusively on the enfeebling swash or the poisoned stimulants that are sold so readily under the title of tales and novels. An apprenticeship at a reform school in literature, with a spare diet of statistics and a hard bed of mathematical problems, is much needed for the recovery of such inane and half-demented mortals. (Noah Porter, 1877, qtd. in Ross 149)

I have excerpted this from a larger quotation in Ross's article to show the mixture of sexual and food-oriented metaphors. Ross uses the excerpt to exemplify the hierarchy of ingestion implied by "poisoned stimulants," "spare diet," and many other food references not shown here. However, she fails to comment on the implications of references such as "intellectual voluptuary," "effeminate weakling" and "hard bed."

Clearly the danger here is not merely that of becoming a gourmand, but of recklessly expending spermatic energy. Effeminacy, loss of intellectual powers, and intellectual and physical enfeeblement all were the hallmarks of the dreaded disease "spermatorrhea," brought on by excessive discharge of semen through masturbation or other sexual activity. (Youths of seventeen, needless to say, were among the principal victims of this complaint.) Hard beds, exercise, and study were the prescriptions then, antecedents of the cold shower, hard work, and exercise regimen even now recommended as a defense against the temptation to illicit sexual activity. Of course, there were those who took a different point of view. In an 1887 *Blackwood's* article we are told:

> Perhaps the greatest pleasure in life is an ill-regulated passion for reading. Books are the best of friends, the most complacent of companions. In that silent, though eloquent and vivacious company, there can be no monotony as there are no jealousies and indeed inconstancy becomes a duty and a virtue, as with the sage King Solomon among his hundreds of wives. ("Literary Voluptuaries" 805)

Although the moral argument is precisely the opposite of the previous passage, the metaphors are identical: reading is equal to sexual activity, and reading for pleasure is equal to illicit and promiscuous sexual activity.

Eating, as Maggie Kilgour has noted in a different context, is, psychoanalytically speaking, an aggressive move, but one not without certain dangers in that eating is the activity which first demarcates the boundaries between inside and outside, and yet perennially destabilizes them. The child first becomes aware of the nonsufficiency of the self when the child cries for the breast and it does not appear. One eats to incorporate that which one lacks into oneself, to become sufficient to oneself, unified once more, but what one eats then is not only changed into one's own substance, but in fact changes that substance in turn. With every attempt to make ourselves whole, therefore, we make ourselves other, not self-identical, and therefore merely succeed in affirming our neediness as we satisfy our desire. As Kilgour puts it:

> To imagine knowledge as tasting or eating is to set up an epistemology in which subject and object are strictly differentiated and yet finally totally identified. As it seems most people would rather be a subject than an object . . . such total identification is seen with a great deal of ambivalence. . . . Intellectual taste is associated with choice and control, the mastery of what is eaten by the eater. (9)

Using Kilgour's insight as a point of departure, we may see that in the case of the nineteenth-century popular fiction market, the expression of that mastery is the intellectualizing discourse surrounding the body of culture. Food is primarily associated with the female body and breast; in this case, desire for an uncomplicated gratification is mediated by fear of subjectivity of the text, the capacity of the female body to transform its consumer. A hierarchy of literary taste emerges in which the most female identified is considered the most dangerous and degraded. This marginalizing strategy is deployed through a veritable *cordon sanitaire* of critical discourse in journals, reviews, and the like which surrounds and contains the body of popular literature, and which defined literary "food" as healthy, unhealthy, sweet, highly spiced, and so on.

In the mid-nineteenth century in particular, the concern with ingestion became central to British Victorians as the food adulteration issue took center stage in the popular press. Food and water contamination became an even more central issue as the terrifying and inexplicable outbreaks of epidemic disease were traced to such contamination as well as to waste disposal. In this way, the desirable, socially acceptable, commercially and culturally reified substance of food was brought both literally and figuratively into proximity with the undesirable, socially unacceptable end product of consumption. The primary concerns of the food adulteration investigations were two: foodstuffs adulterated with additives for gain (poisonous colorings added to tea, for example) and filth-ridden substances added either for gain (to add bulk) or inadvertently, through carelessness. One principal focus of the parliamentary investigations in this matter was the domestic production of milk and its adulteration with water, the condition of which would depend on its source. Several engravings in *Punch* target bakeshops, particularly in terms of bread and sweets. Bread, milk, and tea were staples, of course, which is one reason they received so much attention, but the connection of the adulteration of foods and the image of women unknowingly poisoning their young children with adulterated milk and sweets is very strong in much of the journalistic treatment of the subject. The juxtaposition of mother love/nurturance with the threat of harm was particularly poignant because it hinged upon the fascinated fear of what was lurking beneath the smooth surface of angel-in-the-house-ism—an interest which Braddon would parlay into a fortune with *Lady Audley's Secret*. In any case, food became the focus of anxieties about the invasion of the body by dangerous substances through the wife and mother, the principal food preparer/overseer of the household. These associations became negative entailments of references to food, just as pleasure, community, domesticity, and wealth were positive entailments.

The metaphor of reading as eating or ingestion has a special significance in this era of preoccupation with the boundaries of the body and their violation. The *Temple Bar* asserts, "[P]eople are not satisfied even with reading worthless novels; they must then read still more worthless notices of them in the papers. It is the drunkard, not only draining his glass, but *licking it out*" ("Vice of Reading" 256). Not only is the text here to be devoured, it is a drug (alcohol) which has a specific negative moral effect—that of rendering the consumer bestial, like an animal in his or her consumption. A common opener for articles on literature in general or review articles about particular books or authors was to bemoan the proliferation of "worthless" literature, following the disclaimer with a statement of this sort: "But, for good or evil, the novels we read are becoming as important to us as the water we drink or the food we eat. It is as desirable that we should be supplied with the best possible quality, and protected, by all legitimate means, from the danger of adulteration" ("Literary Exhaustion" 290). In 1870, when this particular essay was published, the food adulteration scare was at its height; the author's reference to it once more invokes the anxiety of poisonous physical invasion in which an unwitting consumer gets more than s/he, literally, bargained for. The apparent mismatch in the analogy is, of course, that one sees what one is getting in a text in a way that one might not be able to see arsenic in a cake; however, the repeated use of similar images makes quite clear that these writers (and presumably their readers) saw texts as potentially deceptive, slippery substances which could affect the reader without the reader's knowledge or consent, like a poison—or a disease.

As the health of the body could be infected by contagion, the health of the mind could be harmed by negative impressions or moral contagion. Indeed, the connection between the tangible and intangible, the mental impression and the physical, was not so neglected as we, in our rediscovery of holistic healing, would like to believe. Benjamin Ward Richardson, one of Britain's most prolific health writers for popular journals, articulates this connection forcefully in his essay "The Health of the Mind":

> We are conscious that the food of the body influences the health of the mind. . . . But we do not recognize with like readiness and in the same way the effect of the foods of the mind on the mind and its health; nor is this remarkable, for the body feeds perceptibly, and by one stomach alone, whilst the mind feeds imperceptibly, by five stomachs, by every sense. . . . Common foods and drinks must be healthy in order that the material of the body may be good; and the impressions which enter the body by the senses, the foods and drinks of the mind, must also be healthy in order that the mind may be good. . . . [T]he coming school of sanitarians will take up a new sanitation . . . as uncleanliness of mind is the most obvious cause of mental disease, and cleanliness the surest indication of mental health. (148–149)

Further, he warns the reader, the mental food taken in repeatedly or in youth will permanently shape the mental tastes of the individual. The mind must be trained to only pure and rational discourse, in order that it may detect and avoid "false and foolish" words that make for mental uncleanliness. Many writers of the period, medical and otherwise, comment on the liability of the body to disease engendered by "mental shocks" and any reader of Victorian fiction will recognize the familiar disease of "brain fever"—a disease not to be found in any modern medical book—which often attacks a character after a severe emotional shock of any kind. Books, of course, comprise this mental food in very large part.

Reading "bad" texts thus consists of a self-poisoning which can become addictive. In "The Vice of Reading," a *Temple Bar* essayist compares indiscriminate reading with dram drinking and condemns it in terms of strongest opprobrium:

> Reading, so long a virtue, a grace, an education, and, in its effects, an accomplishment, has become a downright vice,— a vulgar, detrimental habit, like dram drinking; an excuse for idleness; . . . a cloak thrown over ignorance; a softening, demoralizing, relaxing practice, which, if persisted in, will end by enfeebling the minds of men and women, making flabby the fibre of their bodies, and undermining the vigor of nations. (251)

A number of shallowly submerged concerns collide (and collude) in this passage. Reading is "vulgar," that is, common, plebeian, like dram drinking, a habit principally associated with the lower classes. Like dram drinking, it is addictive, and has a degenerative effect upon the organism. It also softens and relaxes—that is, feminizes and even castrates. Finally, it enfeebles both mind and body of men and women, making them unfit for the business of production and reproduction, lastly undermining the readers at a national level—reference here perhaps both to Darwin's theory of degeneration and Britain's uneasy consolidation of power over her empire. In the reading process, then, the text is seen as actually entering the body (like alcohol) and corrupting it from within ("relaxing the fibers") causing a sort of decomposition in the reader as the text is digested or decomposed by the reader. It also may contaminate the class characteristics of the reader, causing him or her to revert to lower-class, degenerate practices. It also excites and stimulates the body, appealing, even in the intellectual pursuit of reading, to our bestial selves. A *Quarterly Review* essayist advises against reading "trash" such as H. Rider Haggard, warning that,

> [although] the 'aboriginal democratic old monster,' not by any means extinct in the classes which wear silks and broad-

cloth . . . likes sensation; strong waters, not diluted, to warm his digestive apparatus and make his eyes blink, [be warned that] Plato has observed that every man keeps a wolf within him. It is advisable to hold that sanguinary beast by the ears, but not to charm and excite him until his teeth begin to glisten. ("English Realism and Romance" 486–488)

Of romances, the reviewer's opinion is harsher still:

The 'everlasting pantomime' of rose-pink virtue squinting across the pages of its Prayer book at vice, while it gambols within the measure of police-morality, is very laughable. . . . [S]hould we not send for the 'common hangman' if his hand be not entirely out, and bid him make an auto da fe in front of Mudie's, with the feminine public looking on, agonized and much sobbing, but learning in this wholesome manner their first profitable reading lesson? (470)

This pits an image of masculine light reading as something that excites the beast within—a beast, the author implies, unworthy of the upper classes—to hunger, against an image of feminine light reading as associated with sexual vice, vice unnatural enough to warrant burning as a witch or a heretic. The critic collapses eating and sex metaphors into the larger metaphor of reading as consumption. In each case, the text becomes a (female) body, either to be devoured by the wolfish reader or by the purifying flames.

In addition to the fear of contamination and the attempt to legislate against the diseased erotic body that marked the latter portion of the nineteenth century, gender issues surrounding the interaction of author, text, and reader must be considered. The excerpts above display a relatively uncomplicated scenario including a male reader and a female text. This posits a masterful and exploitive reader who need only be careful not to allow the wanton text to drain his virility through overindulgence. However, the typical novel reader was female. So was the typical novel writer. Indeed, as Catherine Gallagher argues, two principal competing metaphors for authorship in this period are those of the male inseminating the text with his ideas, and the woman who prostitutes herself. The female reader on the other hand, complementing the lascivious male, is the passive reader who is drugged or seduced by literature—literature which can figuratively enter her imagination and corrupt her.

Gilbert and Gubar have certainly amply demonstrated the association of authorship with paternity, of the pen with the penis. Gallagher points out, however, that this metaphor coexisted with many competing ones; one in particular with which female authors struggled in the nineteenth century was the metaphor of the author as whore. Gallagher notes that this metaphor was particularly debilitating to women precisely because prostitution was female identified, therefore allowing male authors to remain personally untouched even when defined by this metaphor, whereas women were, both as authors and as individuals, essentially defined thereby:

> The whole sphere to which usury belongs, the sphere of exchange as opposed to that of production, is traditionally associated with women. Women are items of exchange, a form of currency and also a type of commodity. . . . [T]he prostitute never makes this transition from exchange to production [as wife and mother]; she retains her commodity form at all times. Like money, the prostitute, according to ancient accounts, is incapable of natural procreation. For all her sexual activity, indeed because of all her sexual activity, she fails to bring new substances, children, into the world. Her womb, it seems, is too slippery. And yet she is a source of proliferation. What multiplies through her is not a substance but a sign: money. Prostitution, then, like usury, is a metaphor for one of the ancient models of linguistic production: the unnatural multiplication of interchangeable signs. (40–41)

Thus, explains Gallagher, the paternity metaphor involves itself in the production of worthwhile substance, the privileged text, and the whore metaphor with the proliferation of useless signs.

The question remains, how can literature as food be reconciled to an image of the male author, since food and nourishment are traditionally the purview of the female breast rather than the penis? However, just as parenthood is appropriated to the male and the name of the father, and the mother becomes merely a "midwife" to the child, nurturing and giving rebirth to the male's substance, food is provided (produced), in the patriarchal family structure, by the male "breadwinner" and then prepared (reproduced) by the mother. We may speculate, then, that the good mother and bad mother who provide good food and poisonous food (or withheld food) are split, the role of the good mother being usurped by either the patriarch as the artist who generates literary children/nourishment or by the "domestic" female author who (re)produces ideologically correct, family-oriented literature, often for children, leaving the bad mother to be the prostituted author of the commercial novel, who produces only filth and falsehood. The male imagination produces true ideas, the female fancy reshapes those ideas and impressions as the housewife reshapes the substance that the male brings home, nourishing her family with male substance through her female artifice. Naturally, as we move away from the privileged origin of thought and imagination and into the sphere of replication and reproduction, there is an increasing potential for contamination and distortion. Further, the capacity for minute description of everyday detail which was requisite in the mid-Victorian novel was supposed to be the particular strength of the woman, grounded in the body and in the concern with the ordering and reproduction of the physical world, while the male imagination was better suited to the abstract, the conceptual. Thus, male writing produces the world of ideas in history, philosophy, and the like, whereas female writing reproduces the physical world, more or less accurately, through meticulous recording of sense impressions.

Obviously, this is only a simple and schematic explanation of a much more complex issue. The interaction of the specific gendered text, reader, and author is rarely straightforward; when competing gendered cultural icons of the Text, Reader, and Author intrude themselves, it becomes evident that categorical analyses must be viewed skeptically. Yet, there are discernible consequences to particular constellations. As Susan Stanford Friedman notes of the metaphor "writing is giving birth," the gender of the writer using this metaphor—one which has been used by authors of both sexes throughout literary history—does affect the use to which the metaphor is put. Friedman notes that men use the "female" metaphor of childbirth to express the "ethos of their times" whereas women use it to reflect their personal experiences and concerns. Extending this analysis, we can see precisely why the image of the author-prostitute was so crippling to women, and why the concept of paternity excluded them so effectively. In either case the text is an extension of the woman's body—either the prostitute's or the nameless mother's. In either case it is the physical substance of a woman that is exposed in the marketplace. Thus, when Frederic Harrison cautions, "[W]e forget the other side to . . . literature:—the misuse of books, the debilitating waste of life in aimless promiscuous vapid reading, or even, it may be, in the poisonous inhalation of mere literary garbage and bad men's worst thoughts. For what can a book be more than the man who wrote it?" (491), we might substitute "bad women's worst sensations" for "bad men's worst thoughts" and gain a good sense of the subtle difference in audience perceptions of the gendered author. The authority of the woman is based on her feelings, her intuitions, her connection with the earth and nature (see Griffin), in short, on her reproductive body; the authority of man is based on his will, his reason, his name which both identifies him with the patriarchal god and distinguishes him from other men, in short, his productive mind. Note that the thoughts of bad men are "poisonous inhalations," miasma, and morally contagious. In both cases, it is important to note the equation of the book with the author; here, the male author's mind, and by extension, the female author's body.

Novels, as the popular mass market literary form, fall into this metaphor of literary production—authorship as prostitution, the text as commodified body—almost automatically, and as Gallagher notes, "Silly Novels by Lady Novelists" are almost sure to be devalued as illegitimate—often with particular severity by the women authors struggling to distance themselves from the commercial metaphor, like Eliot. (Oliphant has perhaps the most troubled relationship with this metaphor, alternately railing at women authors like Eliot, whom she perceives (erroneously) to have been free of financial need as "kept" women, for their freedom, and money hungry "hacks" like Braddon, for catering to "low" public tastes.) Both Oliphant and Braddon are examples of authors who were frequently told that their immense production disallowed them from writing any truly great work, and both apparently accepted this verdict while excusing themselves from greater efforts by stating that they had to value quantity over quality to support their families, thus both emphasizing the financial nature of their authorship, and deprecating their desire for it in favor of a domestic, noncompetitive image.

Gallagher does not, however, mention the other substance that prostitutes are charged with the proliferation of in the nineteenth century, another intangible sign multiplying itself into infinity and attacking and contaminating the sacredness of paternity and the social body: disease. The disease enters the body through intercourse, sexual and economic, multiplying itself inexplicably and invisibly. The intangible substance of syphilis eventually yields the sign of its presence upon the body of the consumer of the adulterated and adulterous body of the prostitute—and upon those of his wife and children. The danger of diseased text—the apparently innocent book carrying a hidden dose of "moral contagion"—bears vigilant scrutiny. Of all the harsh criticisms Braddon's work received, none stung her so as the charge, levied by an anonymous assailant later identified as Mrs. Oliphant, of indecency. Through all the murders, bigamous unions, and forged identities of her sensation novels, she indignantly claimed, there could not be found one hint of an *illicit* passion. Charles Mudie based his considerable fortune on his claim that, as patrons of a select circulating library, his readers could feel safe from the exposure to immorality usually associated with such libraries since the eighteenth century. In Colman's Polly Honeycombe (1760), a character states that he would rather expose his daughter to Covent Garden, a gathering place of prostitutes, than to a circulating library (in Erickson). Even in the late-nineteenth century, the faint scent of impropriety lingered on; in Braddon's *Joshua Haggard*, a minister states his belief that only married ladies and elderly spinsters could safely read novels. Sometimes, also, the precise nature of the transgression is vague; it is a discriminating critic indeed who can safely diagnose the problem. Nineteenth-century critic A. Strahan quotes a story from a "family paper" to illustrate the subtlety of the symptom:

> "While Lutie and the young trustee were together in the little parlour, they had no end of fun about something—laughed till Madame, in desperation, opened the door and found them confronting each other so gravely, that she apologized and went away."
>
> We do not know anything more ingeniously prurient than this, and yet where is an indecent word? The last few sentences are very vulgar, and that is all. The pruriency is to be felt, rather than defined. (981)

The critic-as-doctor or critic-as-policeman here indicates his superior sense of what is wholesome and what is prurient—itchy, unhealthy. A pruriency such as this one is very dangerous precisely because it cannot be defined or diagnosed through reason; it must be felt, experienced—contacted or contracted directly to be noticed at all. By that time, the damage is done. The critic sets him- or herself up as a buffer between the law-abiding, healthy, but vulnerable public and the subtly adulterated goods of the criminal, diseased vendor of popular fiction.

In all of the discourse surrounding the popular novel, whether savagely denunciatory or ruefully indulgent, there is a strong sense of critical surveillance, a need to categorize, to name and contain. Since the rhetoric of literary surveillance and reform was motivated by precisely the same terrified fascination with transgression as that of sanitary surveillance and reform, it is not surprising that we find the two discourses becoming confluent. Fiction, like contagion, might become the vehicle by which important physical boundaries were breached: distinctions between subject and object, upper and lower bodily strata, upper and lower class, masculine and feminine, food and filth, mother and whore.

Certain kinds of fiction were naturally targeted for more surveillance than others; much of this was class based and perhaps the strongest censure was reserved for morally unacceptable literature with blatantly "lower-class" properties which had yet infiltrated middle class markets. The sensation novel controversy is the most dramatic example, the sensation story having existed for years in broadsheets and penny papers as a lower-class amusement before Braddon was credited with introducing it in *Lady Audley's Secret*. Just as the genre's name derives from the physical sensation of excitement that the story was to produce, the condemnations of the genre are set in extremely physical language: sensation would "breed a pestilence so foul as to poison the very lifeblood of our nation" (Murray 935). Earlier (1863) the *Quarterly Review* wound down a lengthy and generally hostile analysis of sensation novels with this dark observation:

> Regarding these works merely as an efflorescence, as an eruption indicative of the state of health in the body in which they appear, the existence of an impure and silly crop of novels, and

the fact that they are read, are by no means favorable symptoms of the conditions of the body of society. But it is easier to detect the disease than to suggest the remedy. ("Sensation Novels" 512)

Lower-class literature, in particular, was associated with both vice and the incitement to criminal behavior (which, in turn, was often figured forth in terms of disease, as readers of Samuel Butler's 1871 *Erewhon* will doubtless recall). A. Strahan of the *Contemporary Review* writes:

Many a time have we heard a shopkeeper declare "Hard as it is to have an errand boy who cannot receipt a bill, or even read one, I would rather mine could not read at all." . . . "Here is a girl of twenty, who has learnt to read at Sunday School, talks good Evangelical, and yet reads the vilest penny trash, steals in order that she may dress like a prostitute, gets into the company of young roughs who have fed full fat upon just the same kind of reading, and before she has had time to learn what household decency is, she is gone to the bad." (986)

The two types of stories offered in the penny magazines for young people were primarily "highwayman stories"—descendants of the Newgate broadsheets—and romances, usually of the *Pamela* type, but often of "high life." The *Quarterly Review* laments the existence of the "penny dreadfuls," giving voice once more to the apparently general conviction that such stories were turning their young readers into criminals: "When it is remembered that this foul and filthy trash circulates by thousands and tens of thousands week by week amongst lads who are at the most impressionable period of their lives, . . . it is not surprising that the authorities have to lament the prevalence of juvenile crime" ("Penny Fiction" 154). Here we have the suggestion, with "foul and filthy trash," of a reference to the corruption of the body through improper cultural sanitation. But the *Edinburgh Review* makes the most heartrending plea against "penny dreadfuls." In "The Literature of the Streets" (1887), the reviewer apologizes to readers, promising not to make them "wade through such a nauseous mass" of penny literature, but "to select from the whole heap a few specimens" to illustrate the "mental diet" of poor children. The writer singles out for particular opprobrium the "small but pestiferous class of weekly publications which pander to the worst tastes of readers . . . the so-called 'Society journals' . . . all relying on the same poisonous condiments to season every dish. . . . No one scavenger could alone and single-handed contrive to amass such a wealth of unsavory refuse" (55–57). Although somewhat confusingly conceding being able to remember finding in all these pages "no one single indecent phrase or illusion (sic)" (63), the reviewer declares that

> the feast spread for them (poor readers) is ready and abundant; but every dish is poisoned, unclean, and shameful. Every flavour is a false one, every condiment vile. Every morsel of food is doctored, every draught of wine is drugged; no true hunger is satisfied, no true thirst quenched; and the hapless guests depart with a depraved appetite, and a palate more than ever dead to every pure taste, and every perception of what is good and true. (65)

The author asks, once again, for better penny fiction: "They ask for bread of some kind; it will not do to give them a stone. That which they now eat is of adulterate, poisoned flour, and no other is within their reach. . . . To do this is no less than to deliberately poison the springs of a nation's life" (61). Once again the metaphor of reading as ingestion is in play, with its contemporary reference to the adulteration issue. Significantly, adulteration is linked, through subtle imagery, to the sanitary issue of nuisance abatement, an issue of established and perennial interest to journal readers since the 1850s. (The "scavenger" that amasses a "wealth of refuse" must indeed garner his specimens from the "nauseous mass" of the dungheap: Mayhew's pure finders come to mind.) The suggestion is that the children are literally being fed excrement—like the waste which was often found to have leached through the soil and into the springs, wells, and other water sources which supplied drinking water and incidentally cholera—a theory which, even as early as the 1850s, had begun to find an interested, if skeptical audience. The nuisance abatement issue highlighted middle-class ambivalence about the poor: the poor evoked pity and guilt, since they were depicted as the victims of the collected wastes and lusts (for commodities, in the case of sweated tailors and seamstresses, and for sex, in the case of prostitutes); they also evoked fear and aversion, because they were seen both as potentially violent and as vectors for disease which would infect the middle classes. It was also unclear to what extent their condition was the result of victimization or natural tendencies. Hence, literature like sensational novels, which were seen as crossover genres, read by middle classes and working classes alike, was classifiable as a kind of illicit contact or circulation of commodities between the classes, in the same way prostitution was.

M. E. Braddon's 1864 novel *The Doctor's Wife* provides an interesting example of how one author both internalizes these judgments and critiques them. Identified as the paradigmatic sensation novelist after the success of *Lady Audley's Secret*, Braddon conceived of *The Doctor's Wife* as her break with sensationalism. She states that she wanted to write a "novel of character," "something good": "[I am] especially anxious about this novel; as it seems to me a kind of turning point in my life, on the issue of which it must depend whether I sink or swim. . . . I am always divided between a noble desire to attain something like excellence—and a very ignoble wish to earn plenty of money" (qtd. in Wolff 165). Knowing that any novel by her would be typecast as sensational, Braddon took great pains to articulate the novel in opposition to sensation. She uses a sensation novelist, Sigismund Smith, as a character in the novel who both comments on sensational writing and on the events in the novel as a contrasting narrative; she also resorts to blunt authorial intrusion, stating at a key moment, "This is *not* a sensation novel. I write here what I know to be the truth" (309). Of most interest to us, however, is the way in which Braddon mobilizes metaphors of reading culled from the surrounding critical discourse in her realist novel; Isabel, the protagonist, is addicted to reading romances, which almost leads to her seduction and actually leads to the tragic deaths of the men who love her. Both seduction and reading are emblematized in metaphors and scenes of ingestion.

Having just come from Smith's office in the city, where he has been writing copy with the printer's devil waiting on the stair, George (and the reader) first meets Isabel reading in her back garden. The site of production is prosaic enough: "an untidy chamber in the Temple, with nothing more romantic than a waste paper basket, a litter of old letters and tumbled proofs, and a cracked teapot simmering upon the hob" (13). The scene of consumption, however, is a sadly degenerate Eden; Isabel reads in "an old-fashioned garden, a dear old untidy place, where the odour of distant pigsties mingled faintly with the perfume of the roses; and it was in this neglected place that Isabel Sleaford spent the best part of her idle, useless life" (21). Immediately, their talk turns to her fictions:

> A faint blush trembled over Miss Sleaford's pale face.
> "They are so beautiful!" she said
> "Dangerously beautiful, I'm afraid, Isabel," the young man [Smith] said, gravely; "beautiful sweetmeats, with opium inside the sugar. These books don't make you happy, do they, Izzie?"
> "No, they make me unhappy, but"—she hesitated a little, and then blushed as she said—"I like that sort of unhappiness. It's better than eating and drinking and sleeping, and being happy that way." (22)

Her eyes, after reading, are "soft and sleepy, with very little light in them, and what little light there was, only a dim dreamy glimmer, in the depths of the large pupils" (22). The description is clearly based on symptoms of addiction (Braddon, this time in omniscient narrative voice, again terms it "opium-eating" later in the chapter). The blushes, however, and loss of sleep or desire for food point to sexual awakening (as Michie points out, "greensickness" was widely acknowledged as the symptoms of romantic love and its less acceptable counterpart, emerging sexual awareness in young women). Finally, Isabel's choice of comparisons is telling—reading is better than eating, drinking and sleeping, presumably simply the stuff life is made up of, but with a disproportionate emphasis on ingestion, and reading as a substitute for ingestion. Reading is again and again defined as ingestion and texts as food, often in the context of a comparison between the matter-of-fact production of literature and its reified consumption. A single example will do to demonstrate this theme:

> Miss Sleaford had received that half-and-half education which is popular with the lower middle classes. She left the Albany Road Seminary in her sixteenth year, and set to work to educate herself by means of the nearest circulating library. She did not feed upon garbage, but settled at once upon the highest blossoms in the flower-garden of fiction, and read her favorite novels over and over again, and wrote little extracts of her own choosing in penny-account books, usually employed for the entry of butcher's-meat and grocery. . . . Sigismund wrote romantic fictions by wholesale, and yet was unromantic as the prosiest butcher. . . . He sold his imagination, and Isabel lived upon hers. . . . He slapped his heroes into shape as coolly as a butterman slaps a pat of butter into the semblance of a swan. . . . She wanted to be a heroine,—unhappy perhaps, and dying early. She had an especial desire to die . . . by consumption [and when she fancied she was ill, her brothers would tease her:] "Who ate a plum dumpling yesterday for dinner, and asked for more? That's the only kind of consumption *you've* got, Izzie; two helps of pudding at dinner, and no end of bread and butter for breakfast." (25–26)

The slippage from the rather sexual images of flowers in the Eden of reading to Isabel's own writing in penny account books, a corruption of the original texts and deliberate misprision of the intended use of account books, leads us to the "prosiest butcher" or butterman, the penny novelist, whose understanding of the proper use of account books is apparently very clear. These images are rapidly succeeded by that of disease, a reified, fictionalized disease, set against the healthy but prosaic reality of "two helps of pudding"—being consumed against consuming, unhealthy appetites against healthy ones.

The Doctor's Wife is, like *Pickwick*, a difficult book to read while dieting. Literally, where not reading, Isabel is eating. The first two thirds of the book, including the various courtships, are replete with detailed descriptions of food. Innocent scenes are filled with salads, hearty stews and substantial breads. Morally troubled passages tend to feature hot-house fruits, pastries, and sparkling wines. Everywhere there are tables and picnic baskets laden with banquets worthy of Keat's Porphyro or Rossetti's goblin men. Three key scenes center entirely around food, where food is made to do the hard and delicate work of symbolizing seduction: the initial picnic where George proposes to Isabel; dinner at the Lansdells' where Roland and Isabel experience a mutual attraction; and the second picnic, a parodic mirroring of the first, wherein Lansdell yields to his impulse to, at least orally, seduce the doctor's wife. The first picnic, amid lengthy descriptions of food and eating, offers us this cata-log: "a tongue, then a pair of fowls, a packet of anchovy sandwiches, a great poundcake, . . . delicate caprices in the way of pastry, semi-transpar-ent biscuits, and a little block of Stilton cheese, to say nothing of sundry bottles of Madeira and sparkling Burgundy" (76). Although tempting, this can hardly compare with dinner at the Priory:

> This was life. There was a Lance-like group of hothouse grapes
> and peaches, crowned with a pineapple, in a high Dresden basket
> at the center of the table. Isabel had never been in company with
> a pine-apple until today. There were flowers upon the table, and
> a faint odor of orange blossoms and apricots pervaded the
> atmosphere. . . . Mrs. Gilbert had a very vague idea of the nature
> of the viands which were served to her at that wonderul feast.
> Somebody dropped a lump of ice into the shallow glass, and
> filled it afterwards with a yellow bubbling wine, which had a faint
> flavour of Jargonelle pears, and which someone said was Moselle.
> Mr. Lansdell put some creamy white compound on her plate,
> which might or might not have been chicken; and one of the
> servants brought her an edifice of airy pastry, filled with some
> mysterious concoction in which there were little black
> lumps. . . . But all the dishes in that banquet were "of such stuff
> dreams are made on." So may have taste the dew-berries which
> Titania's attendants gave to Bottom. (150–151)

This indeed is a kind of goblin feast, and, lest we miss the sexual impli-cations of the unidentifiable white creamy compound Roland serves Isabel (everything else is served by "somebody" or "one of the servants"), there is the reminder of Titania's inappropriate liaison to drive the point home. By contrast, at home, Isabel is forced to endure the homely cooking of George's housekeeper and his own vulgar tastes: he has a passion for both radishes and spring onions, the crunching of which Isabel contemplates with horror. (Isabel, as a gesture of homage to Roland, picks out all her onions and refuses to eat them.) The food at George's home is plain and healthy; Smith, dining at George's, comments on the portrayal of food in fiction:

[He] ate about half a quarter of dough made up into puffy
Yorkshire cakes, and new-laid eggs and frizzled bacon in proportion. Mr. Smith deprecated the rampant state of his appetite by-and-by, and made a kind of apology. . . . "You see,
the worst of going into society is *that* . . . they see one eat;
and it's apt to tell against one in three volumes. It's a great
pity that fiction is not compatible with a healthy appetite,
but it isn't." (163)

Fiction, of course, creates and represents unhealthy appetites. Lansdell prepares a picnic for Isabel and her friends once he has admitted his attraction:

"Heaven knows I don't want to do any harm," [he thought.]
But, in spite of all this uncertainty and vacillation of mind, Mr.
Lansdell took a great deal of interest in the preparations for
the picnic. He did not trouble himself about the magnificent
game-pie . . . the crust of which was as highly glazed as a piece
of modern Wedgwood. He did not concern himself about the
tender young fowls, nestling in groves of parsley; nor the
tongue, floridly decorated with vegetable productions chis-
elled into the shapes of impossible flowers; nor the York ham,
also in a high state of polish. . . . The comestibles to which Mr.
Lansdell directed his attention were of a more delicate and
fairy-like description, such as women and children are apt to
take delight in. There must be jellies and creams, Mr. Lansdell
said, whatever difficulty there might be in the conveyance of
such compositions. There must be fruit; he attended himself
to the cutting of hothouse grapes and peaches, the noblest
pine-apple . . . and picturesque pears. (174)

This picnic combines both of the earlier meals; however, the innocent
and hearty meats characteristic of the first picnic (both fowls and tongue
reappear) have little interest for him; instead he focuses on the catalog
of the seductive Keatsian dainties which figured in the second meal,
appealing to less healthy appetites: the pastries, grapes, peaches, and
pine-apple reappear, and even the pears evoke the Moselle that so dazed
Isabel earlier.

Roland seduces her first with food and then with books, allowing her
use of the library and using books as an excuse to meet Isabel often. As
the doctor's housekeeper and gardener say of Isabel, knowing she is
headed for disgrace:

"Females whose headaches keep 'em abed when they ought to
be seeing after their husband's meals hadn't ought to marry. . . .

"Them poetry books and such like, as she's allus a-readin,'
has half turned her head long ago, and it only needs a fine
chap like him to turn it altogether." (228–229)

The passage links Isabel's failure to nourish her husband with her seduction by books and then by Roland. Immediately after this passage, Isabel, on her way to meet Roland, attempts to eat an egg and fails. This is among the last references to food in the novel. After Roland declares his intent to make Isabel his mistress and she flees him, food vanishes from the text, except in the unappetizing guise of beef tea for the invalid and occasional, largely untouched dry toast with tea for Isabel, which she is generally unable to do more than toy with.

Braddon does not employ the simple binary of popular versus high literature that the critics use, however; she retains but inverts the conventional dualism. The harmless but highly commercial Smith writes sensation fiction which is not read by Isabel. Smith is exactly the kind of sensation novelist that the critics most loathed, one who is completely satisfied with the notion of text as commodity, and who crosses over from "penny numbers" to the three-volume market. Sensation novels are clearly not as dangerous as romantic novels, and writing, in Smith's view, can be a kind of antidote for the poison of passion— or of too much reading. Suspecting Isabel's problem, Smith advises, "If I were a young lady, and—and had a kind of romantic fancy for a person I ought not to care about, . . . I'd put him into a novel Izzie, and work him out in three volumes" (199). However, Isabel finds that she has no talent for writing, and hence no outlet. Isabel, with all her passion for words, is inarticulate, as a woman should be; she reads and is read as a text, but produces no text herself. Smith, an exemplar of everything wrong about popular authors, is rendered harmlessly comical as a male author. In an important way, however, he is the author of *The Doctor's Wife*; he brings the couple together and witnesses the course of events. It is worth noting that in his reappearance as a successful three-volume novelist in *The Lady's Mile*, he will not allow his wife to read what he writes.

On the other side of the dichotomy, Roland Lansdell, the aristocratic scribbler who falls in love with Isabel, and with whose verse Isabel falls in love before ever meeting its author, does not conform to the degraded commercial image of the popular author. As an aristocrat and dilettante, he stands for the traditional ideal of the artist—one driven by his inspiration and free of the need to sell books or please the rabble. However, it is his writing that is triply dangerous; trite, jaded and cynical, his persona as aristocrat and the style his upper-class education gives his writing meet Isabel's romantic ideal of a "Being," and prevent her from reading his intentions correctly or evaluating his sentiments for what they are worth. Lansdell's close friend Raymond evaluates his poetry and the state of his gastronomic habits in the same terms:

"An alien!" he exclaimed; "why in the name of all the affec-
tations of the present day, should a man with fifteen thousand
a year . . . call himself an alien? 'An Alien's Dreams'—and such
dreams! . . . Surely no alien could have been afflicted with
anything like them, unless he was perpetually eating heavy
suppers of underdone pork, or drinking bad wine." (74)

Unhealthy appetites create unhealthy prose, which, in turn, creates in its
consumers more unhealthy appetites.

Isabel's moral illness results from her seduction by literature; the
fact that she is not physically compromised does not erase her emotional and imaginative unfaithfulness. Like the prostitute, or the lower-
class woman seduced by the upper-class male, her corruption leads to
disease and violence. Her husband dies of typhus, which is linked in the
text to his wife's supposed adultery: " '[Dr. Gilbert] is ill. Low fever—
really in a very dangerous state, . . . *You'll* be sorry to hear it
Gwendoline.' 'I am sorry to hear it. . . . I am sorry he has so very bad
a wife' " (289). Nor does her aristocratic lover fare better; he defines
his passion for Isabel as a "fever," "very foolish, very contemptible to
the solemn-faced doctor who looks on and watches the patient tossing
and writhing, and listens to his delirious ravings" (242). Roland's actual fate blends the two themes of disease and lower-class violence most
dear to critics of popular fiction: Isabel is called from watching over her
husband's corpse to attend the deathbed of Roland Lansdell, whose
attraction to her leads to a fatal confrontation with her criminal father,
who beats "the languid swell" to death.

The themes of the contaminating power of literature, its seductive
and addictive qualities, its ability to mobilize a desire which quickly
becomes murderous drive the realist novel *The Doctor's Wife* purports to
be, and distance it from the fatal fictions which, through Isabel, destroy
the patriarchy of Graybridge, its exemplary young squire and middle-
class professional. At the same time, the novel absolutely depends on
popular fiction and its critiques for its existence; the desire that drives the
plot in *The Doctor's Wife*—the desire of the two men for the doctor's
wife—is propelled by Isabel's desire for fiction and their desire for the
Isabel who is in fact herself a fiction, who "lives in her books," whom
Smith "[do]es for all my dark heroines." The good, high-culture novel
cannot exist without the popular novel, which it must be defined against;
the masculine cannot exist without its corresponding marked term, the
feminine. It is worth noting that for all Braddon's apparent acceptance
of the distinction between good literature and sensation fiction, Isabel
does not confine her reading to popular fiction, and does not read sensational fiction at all; she reads the best fiction from the circulating

library, tends to prefer poetry to fiction (though, admittedly, the dangerous poetry of the late Romantics, and, of course, the "Alien") and is
endangered, not by the grub-street literary butcher Smith, but by the
pastries and hothouse fruits of Romantically inspired Lansdell. On all
levels of structure, theme, and plot, the unmarked term is parodically
inverted and made to demonstrate its dependence on its inferior opposite. And it is Smith's moderate bourgeois appetites that have the last
word in the novel, which ends with his courting his future wife, "whom
he declares to be too good for penny-numbers, and a charming subject
for three volumes of the quiet and domestic school, and he has consulted
Mr. Raymond respecting the investment of his deposit-account, which is
supposed to be something considerable; for a gentleman who lives chiefly
upon bread-and-marmalade and weak tea may amass a very comfortable
independence from the cultivation of sensational literature in penny
numbers" (304).

NOTES

This essay was first published in *LIT: Literature, Interpretation, Theory* 8
(1997): 83–104.

1. This chapter was first written in 1992–3, before I became familiar with
Lyn Pykett's and Kate Flint's excellent work exploring some of these issues.

WORKS CITED

Acton, William. *Prostitution, Considered in its Moral, Social, and Sanitary Aspects,
in London and Other Large Cities and Garrison Towns, with Proposals for the
Control and Prevention of its Attendant Evils.* 2nd ed. London, 1870.

Braddon, Mary Elizabeth, *The Doctor's Wife.* London, 1864.

———. *Joshua Haggard.* London, 1877.

———. *Lady Audley's Secret.* Ed. David Skilton. New York: Oxford UP, 1987.

———. *The Lady's Mile.* London: Simpkin, 1900.

———. *The Trail of the Serpent.* London, 1867.

Eliot, Simon. "Public Libraries and Popular Authors, 1883–1912." *Library* 8
(1986): 322–350.

"English Realism and Romance." *Quarterly Review* 173 (1891): 468–494.

Erickson, Lee. "The Economy of Novel Reading: Jane Austen and the Circulating Library." *Studies in English Literature* 30 (1990): 573–585.

Flint, Kate. *The Woman Reader 1837–1914.* Oxford: Clarendon Press, 1993.

Friedman, Susan Stanford. "Creativity and the Childbirth Metaphor: Gender Difference in Literary Discourse." *Speaking of Gender*. Ed. Elaine Showalter. New York: Routledge, 1989. 73–100.

Gallagher, Catherine. "George Eliot and Daniel Deronda: The Prostitute and the Jewish Question." *Sex, Politics and Science in the Nineteenth-Century Novel. Selected Papers from the English Institute, 1983–1984*. Ed. Ruth Bernard Yeazell. New Series 10. Baltimore: Johns Hopkins UP, 1986.

Gilbert, Sandra M., and Susan Gubar. *The Madwoman in the Attic: The Woman Writer and the Nineteenth Century Literary Imagination*. New Haven: Yale UP, 1979.

Harrison, Frederic. "On the Choice of Books." *Fortnightly Review* 31 (1879): 491–512.

Kilgour, Maggie. *From Communion to Cannibalism: An Anatomy of Metaphors of Incorporation*. Princeton: Princeton UP, 1990.

"Literary Exhaustion." *Cornhill Magazine* 22 (1870): 285–96.

"The Literature of the Streets." *Edinburgh Review* 165 (1887): 40–65.

"Literary Voluptuaries." *Blackwood's* 142 (1887): 805–817.

Mayhew, Henry. *London Labour and the London Poor; Cyclopaedia of the Condition and Earnings of Those That* Will *Work, Those That* Cannot *Work, and Those That* Will Not *Work*. 1861–62. New York: Dover, 1968.

Michie, Helena. *The Flesh Made Word: Female Figures and Women's Bodies*. New York: Oxford UP, 1987.

Murray, Vincent E. H. "Ouida's Novels." *Contemporary Review* 22 (1873): 921–935.

Oliphant, Margaret. "Novels." *Blackwood's* 102 (1867): 257–280.

"On the Reading of Books." *Temple Bar* 72 (1884): 178–186.

"Penny Fiction." *Quarterly Review* 171 (1890): 149–171.

Pykett, Lyn. *The "Improper" Feminine: The Women's Sensation Novel and the New Woman Writing*. London: Routledge, 1992.

Richardson, Benjamin Ward. "The Health of the Mind." *Longman's Magazine* 14 (1889): 145–163.

Ross, Catherine Sheldrick. "Metaphors of Reading." *Journal of Library History, Philosophy and Comparative Librarianship* 22 (1987): 147–163.

"Sensation Novels." *Quarterly Review* 113 (1863): 481–515.

Strahan, A. "Bad Literature for the Young." *Contemporary Review*. 26 (1875): 981–991.

"The Vice of Reading." *Temple Bar* 42 (1874): 251–257.

Wolff, Robert Lee. *Sensational Victorian: The Life and Fiction of Mary Elizabeth Braddon*. New York: Garland, 1979.

4

Consuming Images: Women, Hunger, and the Vote

Linda Schlossberg

In 1910, as part of a fund-raising effort, the Women's Social and Political Union in England published a collection of recipes under the title *The Women's Suffrage Cookery Book,* by Aubrey Dowson (fig. 4.1). The cookbook, apparently marketed for both the middle-class British housewife and the militant suffragette, featured traditional English recipes ("Arrowroot Pudding," "Sweetbreads in Wine Sauce") as well as simpler fare for dedicated, busy campaign workers ("meals that [can] be eaten with impunity at any hour" (73)). On the last page of the cookbook the reader finds Mrs. Bertrand Russell's recipe for "Cooking and Preserving a Good Suffrage Speaker," which suggests "[greasing] the dish by paying all the speaker's expenses . . . [beating] her to a froth with an optimistic spoon . . . [and] avoiding too strong a flavour of apologies" (78). "If this recipe is carefully followed," Russell humorously concludes, the speaker "will preserve her flavour to the last moment" (78). The cookbook, which figures the suffrage speaker as a kind of intellectual nourishment, rhetorically transforms the normally innocuous space of the kitchen into one of militant political activity.

Given the suffragettes' campaign to free women from the tyrannies of domestic routine, the cookbook's language of service and housewifery seems deliciously ironic. Yet the effort to market the women's suffrage movement was largely dependent on transforming ordinary household items (items that might appeal to the female, albeit feminist, consumer) into advertisements for the cause. In addition to postcards, board games, playing cards, jewelry, dolls, soap, and cigarettes, supporters of the campaign could purchase women's suffrage jam, pies, cakes, chocolate, and

The
Women's Suffrage Cookery Book

Fig. 4.1 Front Cover of the *Women's Suffrage Cookery Book*. Sales of this delight-fully irreverent collection of recipes helped raise money for the movement. Courtesy of the Women's Library, London.

tea sets. The competing claims of consumerism, political activism, and domestic responsibility were thus neatly resolved in the WSPU's clever and successful marketing strategies: the suffragette torn between the calls of domestic and political duty could serve a women's suffrage meal on her set of suffrage plates, which bore the slogan "Votes for Women" and were handsomely decorated in the campaign's signature colors of purple, white, and green.[1] In their roles as both rhetorical and functional objects, these items playfully invoke the cult of domesticity the suffragettes were actively working to dismantle, even as they suggest that conspicuous consumption might be one road to political liberation. As such, they are emblematic of the complex and contradictory ways in which images of food and eating function in the rhetoric surrounding the campaign for women's political equality.

It is not surprising that the suffrage movement might try to market itself through household items related to cooking and consumption, given that popular opinions about the right of women to vote were often filtered through debates about the efficacy of two extreme forms of behavior related to the subject of eating: hunger striking and forcible feeding. Imprisoned in Holloway Gaol for a variety of unladylike crimes (window smashing, arson, disrupting parliamentary meetings, vandalism), the suffragettes began their hunger strikes in July of 1909 in response to the British government's refusal to grant them the rights and privileges of political prisoners. Following widespread public debates about the potential consequences of long-term self-starvation on the delicate, middle-class female body, Parliament sanctioned the introduction of forcible feeding in September of the same year. The militant suffragettes' decision to deploy the strategy of starvation, or what Lady Constance Lytton (herself a suffragette) referred to as "the weapon of self-hurt," was a source of fascination for the Edwardian public (42). Political cartoonists and journalists of the period seemed to find in the violent practice of forcible feeding a central metaphor for the struggle for women's political equality itself. The spectacle of male prison wardens holding down suffragettes and forcing tubes into their noses and mouths served as a convenient shorthand for the physical, political, and sometimes sexual cruelty of men towards women. Member of Parliament Keir Hardie, a women's suffrage sympathizer, was shocked at the raucous reception his questions about forcible feeding received at the House of Commons, and begged the readers of the *Daily News* to imagine the cruel ways in which

> women, worn and weak by hunger, are seized upon, held down by brute force, gagged, a tube inserted into the throat, and food poured or pumped into the stomach. Let British men think over the spectacle. . . . Had I not heard it I could not have believed that a body of gentleman could have found reason for mirth and applause in a scene which I venture to say has no parallel in the recent history of our country. (qtd. in MacKenzie 131)

A physician writing for the *Suffragette* also noted that the hunger strikers and the forcible feedings were often the subject of crude humor in both the prison house and the political arena: "Disrespect [for the hunger strikers] shows itself in the prisons, where the medical officers . . . have made stupid jokes about 'stuffing turkeys at Christmas' . . . and in the ribald laughter and obscene jokes with which the so-called gentlemen of the House of Commons received the accounts of these tortures" (Moulilin 6). The obscene jokes, laughter, and applause greeting the graphic descriptions of the forcible feedings serve as a frightening testimony to the ways in which women's political and sexual degradation were mutually constitutive in early-twentieth-century discussions of female political representation.

The violent, spectacular, and apparently titillating nature of what Keir Hardie called the "scene" of forcible feeding was often exploited in the British press. Detailed, unsparing illustrations of forcible feedings were frequently depicted in both prosuffrage and conservative periodicals, highlighted by captions that read, for instance, "Torturing Women in Prison" or "The Government's Methods of Barbarism" (fig. 4.2). The graphic, idealized images of young women being forcibly restrained and orally penetrated suggests that illustrations of the forcible feedings, despite their apparent political intentions, could function as a source of visual pleasure as well as visual horror. Lisa Tickner, in her study of representations of the suffrage movement, identifies "a sado-masochistic element in WSPU [propaganda] posters which was intended to heighten a sense of outrage at women's suffering, but which might equally invite a covert pleasure in its spectacle" (38). I will return to the uncomfortable relationship between martyrdom and pleasure later; for now, it is worth considering that the hunger strikes and forcible feedings, as representational and political acts, were open to a range of interpretive interventions. The meanings or political messages generated by the hunger strikes were never subject to the suffragettes' control; nor were the prison wardens, acting for Parliament, able to control the various meanings attributed to the forcible feedings. These spectacles of eating thus become a contested site over which a battle of interpretation is waged, a struggle for discursive and representational control over what Mervyn Nicholson has called the "power poetics of food" (43).

Despite the violent literalism of such an act, the forcible feedings generally have been read in metaphorical terms, as a way for the British government to literally stop the mouths of the noisy suffragettes with food, or as sites of rape and torture. I want to suggest that the metaphoric capacities of the forcible feedings were, paradoxically enough, suggested by the suffragettes themselves, who, despite the physical indignities they suffered in prison, systematically exploited images of starvation and consumption in their visual and written propaganda. The heated debates around the hunger strikes and forcible feedings could not help but call attention to the vexed space of the female mouth, which the militant suffragettes refused to keep properly, respectfully shut. By refusing food, the suffragettes effectively called attention to the practices of a government that would not let them speak, that refused to honor or

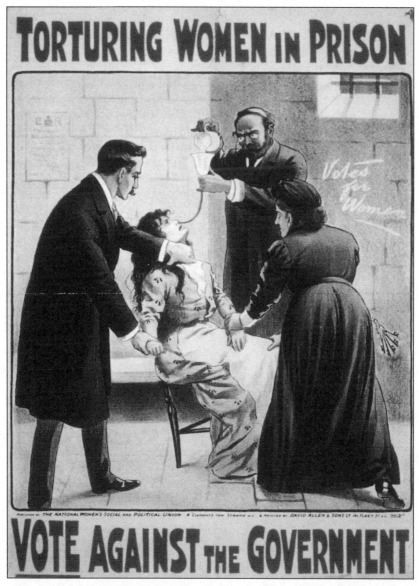

Fig. 4.2 Poster from the National Women's Social and Political Union. Illustrations of forcible feeding often featured female prison guards, to show that the fight for suffrage was a question of politics, not sex. Courtesy of the Women's Library, London.

nourish their political appetites and ambitions. This notion of the starved female political subject is made explicit by an imagery of hunger and eating that repeatedly surfaces in suffrage propaganda and discourse.

It is significant in this respect that the suffrage movement is often read as marking a radical shift in the status of women from embodied object to speaking subject, as being a historical moment "characterized by giving women voice, not only metaphorically through suffrage, but literally in the pervasive speechifying by women on platforms around the world" (Kahane 288). I would suggest, however, that the suffragettes harnessed the trope of embodiment in ways that are at once compelling and problematic: female hunger becomes a recognizable metaphor, in suffrage discourse, for the specific articulation of women's political exclusion. In this light, the WSPU cookbooks, chocolates, and tea sets that are available for consumption seem to function as a temporary way of satisfying these unfulfilled hungers. At the same time, however, hunger striking (as a radical denial of the body and its physical needs) becomes a kind of litmus test, the ultimate signifier, for sustained, militant female political activity. In the remainder of this chapter, I will explore the contradictory implications of this method of political protest by reading the semiotics of hunger in three forms of textual production: the scientific (late-nineteenth-century medical discourses), the political (women's suffrage propaganda), and the fictional (Mrs. Humphry Ward's 1915 novel of the suffrage movement, *Delia Blanchflower*).

If women's political and social needs were increasingly articulated in Edwardian political discourse through an imagery of hunger, such images had a powerful referent in the scientific culture of the preceding century. The noisy suffragettes, despite the highly theatrical nature of their relationship to food, certainly were not the first women whose dietary habits were a matter of anxiety and speculation. Nineteenth-century physicians and health reformers endlessly debated the relationship between women's dietary regimes and racial development, framing the issue as one of national importance: woman's everyday eating practices were imagined to be directly linked to her reproductive capacities, and hence her ability to propagate the race. In a discussion of pregnancy and diet, one author argued:

> If women only knew what foods were requisite to feed the skeleton or bony framework of the living body while that skeleton is in the course of growth, and if she would act upon her knowledge . . . there would hardly be one deformed child left in the land in one or two generations. By a simple application of knowledge she might prevent . . . great national disfigurements and disgraces of ignorance. (Richardson 182–90)

Women are figured here as nurturers not only of children but of the nation as a whole; their bodies operate as a crucial site of sexual and cultural/racial reproduction. Despite this great responsibility to their race, however, women themselves were often imagined, in nineteenth-century medical-scientific discourse, to need less food than men. George Miller Beard, the physician best known for his studies of "American Nervousness," theorized that there was a direct correlation between brain size and diet, and that women, who apparently were less given to intellectual activity than men, needed relatively little food. Teachers, philosophers, politicians, and scientists (the people Beard, like many of his contemporaries, termed "brainworkers") needed more food than those who labored merely with their bodies or hands. Because, as Beard most ungenerously expressed it, "only one-fiftieth of the best work in the world has been done by women," those of the female sex obviously required little food, for "in proportion as woman thinks less than man, in that proportion, so long as she uses her muscles but little, she will need less food than man" (62). Cynthia Eagle Russett notes that an 1882 *Popular Science Monthly* article ("Science and the Woman Question") suggested that men were more active thinkers than women precisely because they ate more (104–5). The confusion over causality here (Are women stupid because they don't eat enough? Do they not eat enough because they're stupid?) is less important than the fact that women are constructed in both of these scenarios as being naturally disposed to a smaller diet.

If scientific treatises of the nineteenth century suggested that contemporary women did not need much food, prescriptive literature was no more generous. The assumed connection between female intellectual (in)activity and dietary practice was far less a source of anxiety than the imagined relationship between seemingly perverse diets and the potential for female sexual proclivity. As Joan Jacobs Brumberg and Helena Michie have demonstrated, Victorian etiquette books and advice manuals, often authored by members of the "delicate" sex, advised women and girls that around the dinner table they should say little and eat less.[2] This advice was coded less as a matter of general physical health than of personal responsibility and sexual morality: many Victorian health reformers suggested that the apparently willful adolescent body, subject to all sorts of bizarre cravings and desires, might unaccountably mature or develop under the influence of exciting and stimulating foods. *Hints Toward Physical Perfection* (1859) went so far as to list "rich and too stimulating food and drink" (along with "feather beds . . . improper books, pictures, and conversation") as one of the causes of early sexual maturity and premature menses, which might, the author warned, "lay the foundation for disease and premature death" (Jacques, 202–3). Michie cites one influential author as suggesting that young women given to masturbation might suddenly "manifest a strange appetite, sometimes desiring mustard, pepper, vinegar, and spices, cloves, clay, salt, chalk, charcoal, etc., which appetites certainly are not natural for little girls" (15). Appetite functions here as a highly readable "barometer of sexuality" (Brumberg 70); these texts, like many of the genre, repeatedly suggest that a delicate, refined appetite and preference for simple foods signifies a decorous and feminine sensibility. Like other physical appetites, hunger is represented in these texts as something to be constrained, ordered, and domesticated, to be indulged only at sanctioned, regularly scheduled times. One author, speaking of the evils of snacking, suggests that "nibblers are great abusers of themselves . . . . Imagine how vexed and fretted the systematic, ordered stomach gets over the messes that nibblers constantly send into it, keeping it always worried, yet never properly at work!" (Dodge 72). Here, the properties of digestion and sexual reproduction are conflated: as with masturbation, that other famously destructive form of self-abuse, nibbling confuses the vulnerable female body, ultimately rendering it unfit for its proper, socially sanctioned duties.

The discourses of physical disgust and moral collapse inspired by the everyday experiences of eating and digestion seem to suggest nothing so much as anorexia nervosa. Though scientific theories about various "wasting" diseases had been circulating for centuries, anorexia—as in the conscious and knowing compulsion to refuse food—was first diagnosed as such by William Withey Gull in 1873. In addition to rest cures and a variety of strange diets (treatments for anorexia were very similar to those for hysteria), late-nineteenth-century medical responses to the disorder included the same kind of violent forcible feeding that would later be used on the suffragettes. As with the suffragettes' seemingly unaccountable decision to refuse food for political ends, the anorectic's self-starvation was perceived as a baseless, nonsensical activity, a disease, as Erin O'Connor has argued, "without an etiology" (535–72). While I would not want to suggest that the suffragettes necessarily were disposed toward anorectic behavior in a clinical sense, it is clear that they may have been responding, in part, to the seductions of a dominant middle-class culture that claimed that women's bodies, as well as political aspirations, should be small and subject to regulatory control. The combined discourses of etiquette and morality, along with codes of fashion that called for tiny waists, wrists, and feet, helped to produce a culture of consumption strangely fixated on the subject of hunger and body size.

Regardless of how we diagnose the scientific and cultural obsession with the bodies and appetites of Victorian middle-class women, the suffragettes' decision to deliberately weaken their bodies through acts of self-starvation becomes particularly suggestive and troubling when we consider the fact that such discourses were still common at the beginning of the twentieth century, and were central to the rhetoric of the antisuffrage movement. The suffragettes were campaigning, in part, against Victorian fantasies of a female body that was too weak to bear the responsibility of making weighty political or intellectual decisions. As historians of the movement have noted, it was precisely woman's delicate and often nervous constitution that was thought to render her unable to participate in the rigors of political debate. William Gladstone, for instance, argued that "the differences of social office rest mainly upon causes, not flexible and elastic like most mental qualities, but physical and in their nature unchangeable" (443). Similarly, a letter sent to the *Nineteenth Century* in June of 1899 stated quite confidently that "women's direct participation [in government] is made impossible . . . by strong formations of custom and habit resting ultimately upon physical difference against which it is useless to contend" (Lewis 409). This letter, signed by 104 prominent Englishwomen, anatomizes political activity along gender lines, insisting that "to men belongs . . . the hard and exhausting labour implied in the administration of the national resources and powers . . . all the heavy, laborious, fundamental industries of state." Political activity, even in the physically unstrenuous form of voting, might cause women to "trespass upon the delicacy, the purity, the refinement, the elevation of her own nature, which are the present sources of its power" (Lewis 446).

If woman's body is imagined to be the source of her intellectual inadequacy, if it is precisely her physical state that ensures her exclusion from the world of politics, it makes sense that the right to vote would be figured, in pro–women's suffrage rhetoric, as something that could, quite literally, strengthen the female constitution. Women's suffrage propaganda frequently imagines the vote itself to be a kind of sustenance, a precious food historically stolen from women starved for political and social recognition. This connection between food and votes makes sense in light of the marketing of the women's suffrage movement: as we have seen, support for the politics of the suffrage movement could be demonstrated through an ethics of female consumerism in which women could purchase items related to food preparation—commodities that in turn offered political (if strangely domestic) messages for consumption and incorporation. But the Women's Social and Political Union also raised money by selling a variety of political posters and postcards that figured the battle for the vote as a struggle between men and women, or boys and girls, over the distribution of food. These posters are notable for their canny and humorous depictions of the sexual politics of hunger. One popular WSPU poster (fig. 4.3) depicts a young Johnnie Bull refusing to share a piece of his coveted "franchise cake" with his sister; he

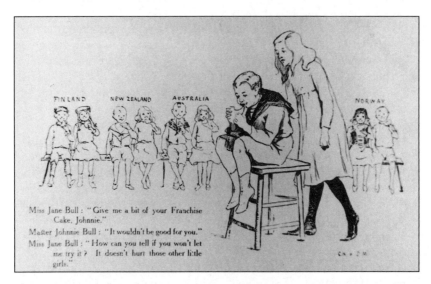

Fig. 4.3 Postcard. Suffragists would point out that women in other countries were allowed to vote, but anti-suffrage activists argued that this only demonstrated England's moral and political superiority. Courtesy of the Women's Library, London.

turns his back to her and crouches over his dessert possessively, telling her, "It wouldn't be good for you." She retorts, "How can you tell if you won't let me try it? It doesn't hurt those other little girls," referring to the girls in the background of the picture, from Finland, New Zealand, Australia, and Norway (countries that had already granted women the right to vote) who are sharing food with little boys. This postcard responds to the popular conception that political activity might damage or taint the innate delicacy of women, whose exclusion from the world of politics effectively protects them from that which would be bad for them. Similarly, a poster produced by the National Union of Woman's Suffrage Societies figures the suffragette as a harried mother serving her sons (whose bibs read "Trade Unions" and "Liberal Federation") from a pot marked "Political Help," while telling them, "Now you greedy boys, I shall not give you any more until I have helped myself"—the bowl from which she is eating reads "Votes for Women." A postcard entitled "Everything for Him— Nothing at all for Her" (fig. 4.4), published by the Artist's Suffrage League, demonstrates the ironic political stance of female antisuffragists. It depicts a mother feeding her son a pile of cookies; each cookie bears the word "Vote." As a group of seven girls looks on hungrily, the woman admonishes them, "Those who ask, shan't have; those who don't ask, don't want." These prosuffrage cartoons and post-

Fig. 4.4   Artist's Suffrage League postcard. The Mother Britannia figure represents the surprisingly large number of women who were against the vote. Courtesy of the Women's Library, London.

ers depict women not getting their fair share of political sustenance, and suggest that the answer can be found in the seemingly insatiable appetites of men. If political representation is coded in these images as a kind of food, it is a code made more easily comprehensible in the context of the debates surrounding the hunger strikes and forcible feedings.

Despite the fact that votes in prosuffrage propaganda, as we have seen, are figured as food, suffragettes, as represented in popular fiction of the early-twentieth century, never seem to eat. In Elizabeth Robins' *The Convert* (1907), largely based on the experiences of Christabel and Emmeline Pankhurst, a young suffragette suggests that between speeches and rallies, she can barely find time to sit down to a meal. The heroine (the convert of the novel's title) wistfully remarks that "in the house where I live, dinner is a sort of sacred rite. If you are two seconds late you are disgraced," suggesting that a blatant disregard for proper mealtimes indicates political responsibility and engagement (168). Gertrude Colmore's *Suffragette Sally* (1911) also comments on the seemingly necessary relationship between self-denial and political activism: refusing food allows the hunger-striking heroine to feel "weak, emaciated, sensitive in every part of her body, but proud in heart" (188). In these early-twentieth-century feminist novels, female self-denial is unabashedly valorized, with skipped meals serving as a reliable signifier for political dedication and militancy. Nowhere is this connection between denial and activism more clearly demonstrated, I want to suggest, than in Mrs. Humphry Ward's *Delia Blanchflower*. Indeed, despite her antiwomen's suffrage position, it is Ward's novel that most vividly demonstrates the complex and often contradictory messages generated by the hunger strikes.

By 1915, when *Delia Blanchflower* was published, Mrs. Humphry Ward was firmly established in the public's mind as an incisive literary critic, a formidable political activist, and one of England's most popular contemporary novelists. The phenomenal success of her second novel, *Robert Ellsmere,* made her a household name on both sides of the Atlantic: in the United States, the novel sold second only to *Uncle Tom's Cabin*. She was most frequently compared to Trollope, both for her prolific nature (she ultimately wrote twenty-five novels) and her sharp ability to dissect and chronicle contemporary political and social movements. Henry James, Ward's close friend and artistic mentor, suggested that her writing itself had the force and repercussions of a political act: "No agitation, on the platform or in the newspaper, no demand for a political revolution, ever achieved anything like the publicity or aroused anything like the emotion of the earnest attempt of this quiet English lady to tell an interesting story" (17). Ward's political influence was not limited to her novels alone, however. In July of 1908 she became the first president of the Women's National Anti-Suffrage League, and she was to be a vocal and committed "Anti," as they were known, for the rest of her life.

Though critics have largely dismissed *Delia Blanchflower* as "antifeminist" (presumably because of Ward's own regressive political stance), it can be read, I would suggest, as registering a more complicated ambivalence about the women's suffrage movement. Ward creates the familiar love triangle found in other "Woman Question" novels of the period (for example, James's *The Bostonians,* Gissing's *The Odd Women*) in which the intelligent, attractive, but confused heroine must choose between the allure of feminist politics and her attraction to the more conservative and traditional man who courts her. The suffragettes' hunger strikes, and women's appetites more generally, are central to the novel's discussion of female political and sexual agency. The novel actually opens with its hero, Mark Winnington, vacationing at a German hotel and commenting on what he sees as the general repulsiveness of women's hunger. Winnington, who functions as the novel's barometer of reasonable British behavior and judgment, seems strangely obsessed with the eating habits of his fellow female travelers. As he looks around the hotel, he first notices "a lady of enormous girth, whose achievements in eating and drinking at meals had seemed to him amazing"; he is further shocked by the seemingly insatiable appetite of the middle-aged German women, "who were almost all plump, plumper even than their husbands . . . the amount of Viennese beer they consumed at the forest restaurants . . . seemed to the Englishman portentous" (8). For Winnington, an excessive female appetite is inextricably linked to cultural otherness; it signifies a kind of barbaric behavior at the table that is apparently not typical of British women. Though Winnington reluctantly admits that the female guests are strangely attractive, and that it would be "difficult to find English women to rival the beauties at the German hotel," his attraction is tempered by disgust at their foreign, and decidedly unfeminine, eating habits (7). Observing one of the hotel's young beauties, he notices "with a revival of alarm, that she had a vigorous German appetite of her own. . . . [A]s he watched the rolls disappear he trembled for the slender figure and the fawn-like gait" (22). Winnington's "alarm" at the sight of the hungry German woman suggests that the vagaries of appetite are most destructive in their capacity to derail the normative trajectory of heterosexual attraction and desire: hunger ruins the female form, rendering even the most beautiful of women unappealing to men.

It is suggestive, then, that the suffragettes—the women the novel codes as most decidedly unfeminine—come to embody the ideal of female abstinence and reticence that Winnington initially deems sexually attractive. Gertrude, the novel's most dedicated suffragette and Winnington's main rival for Delia's political attentions and romantic affections, is described as being strangely disinterested in food and other seemingly normative pleasures of the body: "Food, clothing, sleep—no religious ascetic could have been more sparing than she, in her demands upon them. She took them as they came—well or ill-supplied; too pre-occupied to be either grateful or discontented" (200). Like other novels of the period, *Delia Blanchflower* repeatedly suggests that this religious commitment to the militant suffrage movement is necessarily linked to (and perhaps engendered by) a habitual disassociation from the body and its cravings. Delia, who finds herself inexplicably drawn to the heroics of the suffrage movement, is torn between the competing temptations of physical luxury and social idealism, but she soon gives up her love of domestic trifles for the more austere intellectual life of the suffragette. This capitulation is thematized through a discussion of Delia's sudden neglect of her physical needs: one breakfast scene, for instance, finds her surrounded "by letters and newspapers, to which she was giving an attention entirely denied to her meal" (198). Winnington, who deplores the fanatical methods of the suffragettes, becomes especially disturbed by the fact that Delia's beautiful apartment, once a recognizable space of traditional feminine domesticity, has been transformed into a site of militant political activity, a transformation that apparently poses a threat to Delia's physical welfare. He finds himself experiencing an unaccountable "irritation for Delia—who was to have no place apparently in her own flat for either rest or food" (317). Most horrible of all, to Winnington, is the inescapable fact that it is specifically the dining room, the center of domestic life and ritualized eating, that has been sacrificed to the cause: "The dining room . . . no less than the drawing room, had been transformed into an office and a store-room" (318). Here, the private, interiorized spheres of both the home (as a space of bourgeois respectability) and the female body (as a site of cultural and sexual reproduction) are seemingly emptied out, and forced to serve a political rather than a domestic function.

Female political and erotic power in *Delia Blanchflower* is thus predicated on an uncomfortable denial of the individual woman's body and its needs. Though Gertrude, like the other suffragettes in the novel, is characterized as thin and overworked, her body is strangely intimidating, even in its apparent weakness; Winnington realizes that Gertrude's "general effect was in some way formidable" (41). Indeed, it is paradoxically Gertrude's slenderness and delicacy that give weight to her political pronouncements; the narrator tells us that she has "a slender physique—trim, balanced, composed— suggesting a fastidious taste, nerves perfectly under control—a physique which had given special emphasis to her rare outbreaks of spoken violence. . . . [She possessed] refinement, seemliness, [and] 'ladylikeness' " (340). If it is Gertrude's "slender physique" that allows her to voice radical statements, it is striking that she grows even more intellectually threatening as she becomes weaker and thinner. It is her physical incapacity, especially after she has suffered in Holloway prison as a hunger striker, that makes her seem particularly intimidating to Winnington, that renders her an even more dangerous sexual and political rival. In this novel, female physical weakness signifies a kind of power that men, with their healthier constitutions, can never hope to attain: "How far more formidable to him in her weakness [was Gertrude] than in her strength! [Her] keen eyes were closed, the thin mouth relaxed and bloodless, the hands mere skin and bone. . . . Winnington realized her power through every vein!" (336). Gertrude's physical stature is therefore inversely proportional to her assumed political power; physical immobility, in this novel, translates into social and political mobility.

It is precisely Gertrude's starved form that captivates Delia, that draws her gaze, for in her physical weakness she is impossible to ignore. Even as Delia daydreams about Winnington, and begins to doubt the efficacy of the militant suffrage movement, the sight of Gertrude's body interrupts her thoughts: "She would not let herself think of Winnington.

One glance at the emaciated face and frame beside her was enough to recall her from what had otherwise been a heavenly wandering" (338). Gertrude's form, with her "emaciated face" and "skeleton hands," serves, for Delia, as a living text of the suffrage movement, one that bears the indelible scars of activism and suffering. The sight of the "willowy, intangible creature," at once compelling and aversive, redirects Delia's attention from the dictates of the heterosexual romance plot and posits self-negation (aligned here with a culture of homosociality) as a healthy form of political activism.

It is this tension between the public and the erotic, between political appetite and sexual desire, that is endlessly negotiated in discourses surrounding the women's suffrage movement. The ambivalent feelings registered in *Delia Blanchflower* regarding food and appetite have a clear analogue in broader turn-of-the-century discourses regarding that more problematic form of appetite, sexual behavior and desire. If late-nineteenth-century health reformers were frightened of and seemingly obsessed with controlling the vagaries of female appetite, the suffragettes, as many historians have argued, were similarly invested in subduing the apparently destructive and chaotic sexual appetites of men.[3] It was precisely men's baser, seemingly insatiable sexual needs and desires that were cited as the ultimate source of social inequality between the sexes, one that, for many early-century feminists, threatened to thwart the advancement of the race. As Lucy Bland has argued, turn-of-the-century feminist discourse often "subverted the dominant equation of Woman with Nature, Man with Culture and Humanity"; women were the bearers of decency and moral goodness who would help to purify the dangerous male ambitions and physical appetites that had a supposedly degenerative effect on both politics and the larger culture (81). The tendency to herald the advent of women's suffrage as a change that would usher in a new age of more civilized, less dangerous, behavior between the sexes is most clearly evidenced in Christabel Pankhurst's slogan "Votes for Women, Chastity for Men" (30). It should not surprise us, then, that the suffragettes, in their attempt to tame the wild appetites of men, might come to distrust appetite altogether, and reinforce an ideology of containment that sought to keep women free from passion and desire.

In a cultural context that posits habitual self-negation as constitutive of the feminine ideal, the suffragettes' disengagement from their bodily needs functions as an almost parodic commentary on the strictures of physical self-denial advocated by the writers of Victorian health manuals and etiquette books. Indeed, the decision to renounce the pleasures of food, while highly theatrical, was also, paradoxically enough, the most traditionally feminine of attention-getting strategies. The hunger strikes, despite their political efficacy, seem to employ the very structure of denial and renunciation that helped to shape the identity of the Victorian woman and heroine. This paradox was not lost on women's rights advocates of the period. In her critique of the militant suffrage movement, Teresa Billington-Greig (a former member of the Women's Social and Political Union) cited the "double shuffle between revolution and injured innocence" she saw as characteristic of suffrage rhetoric, blaming it on the "ages of self-suppression and the yielding up of self" that "have developed this capacity in women to such an extent as to make a vice out of a virtue" (138, 205). Indeed, it was precisely the suffragettes' tendency to commit acts of martyrdom and self-sacrifice (as opposed to their more violent, spectacular activities), that critics feared would make their campaign especially seductive to women. A letter to Herbert Gladstone from Edward VII in September of 1909 noted that "his majesty thinks that this short term of martyrdom is more likely to attract than deter women from joining the ranks of the militant Suffragettes" (Mackenzie 39).

The fear that hunger-striking might prove attractive to women, rather than repellant, points to the essential contradiction of an activity that is at once a sign of personal martyrdom and political militancy. The suffragettes' tendency to valorize martyrdom, even at the expense of health, is made explicit in the many illustrations that figure the hunger strikers as saints or angels, suggesting that even for the most politically radical of Edwardian woman, it was difficult to resist the seductions of martyrdom and self-abnegation (fig. 4.5). The hunger strikes, which called for a sacrifice of the most basic of physical needs, can be said to signify the extent to which the suffragettes were bound by Victorian scientific and cultural assumptions regarding women and their bodies. As we have seen, however, their refusal to eat was continually interpreted as a defiant act, as a refusal of precisely those cultural codes that taught women not to articulate or fulfill their physical and political desires. This reading is only possible, I would suggest, in the context of a culture that habitually posits self-sacrifice as a normative, appropriate model of female heroism. The fact that even during the struggle for women's equality self-abnegation could function as a kind of political resistance suggests that for women, there is more than a casual relationship between the vanishing of self and the making of history. It is these contradictory forces of deprivation and fulfillment, self-denial and self-assertion, that are powerfully articulated in the spectacle of the hunger-striking suffragette.

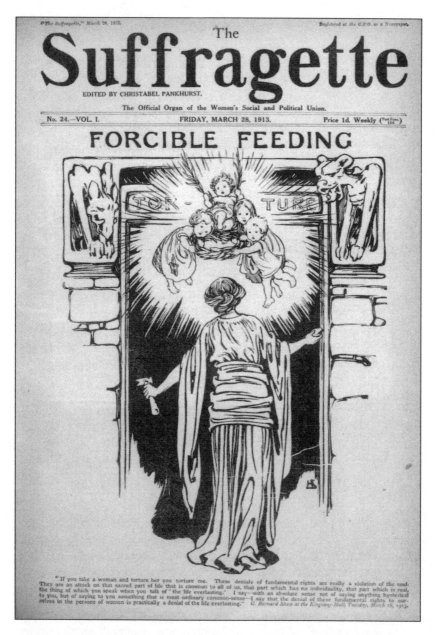

Fig. 4.5 Cover of the *Suffragette* March 28, 1913. A particularly striking illustration of the redemptive qualities of hunger striking. Courtesy of the Women's Library, London.

NOTES

1. On the marketing of the women's suffrage movement, see Diane Atkinson, *The Purple, White, and Green: Suffragettes in London, 1906–14.*

2. See Joan Jacobs Brumberg, *Fasting Girls: The Emergence of Anorexia Nervosa as a Modern Disease*, and Helena Michie, *The Flesh Made Word: Female Figures and Women's Bodies.*

3. See, for instance, Judith R. Walkowitz, *Prostitution and Victorian Society: Women, Class, and the State*, and Susan Kingsley Kent, *Sex and Suffrage in Britain, 1860–1914.*

WORKS CITED

Atkinson, Diane. *The Purple, White, and Green: Suffragettes in London, 1906–14.* London: Museum of London, 1992.

Beard, George Miller. *Eating and Drinking: A Popular Manual of Food and Diet in Health and Disease.* New York: 1871.

Billington-Greig, Teresa. "Emancipation in a Hurry." *The Non-Violent Militant: Selected Writings of Teresa Billington-Greig.* Ed. Carol McPhee and Ann Fitzgerald. London: Routledge & Kegan Paul, 1987.

Bland, Lucy. *Banishing the Beast: Sexuality and the Early Feminists.* New York: New Press, 1995.

Brumberg, Joan Jacobs. *Fasting Girls: The Emergence of Anorexia Nervosa as a Modern Disease.* Cambridge: Harvard UP, 1988.

Colmore, Gertrude. *Suffragette Sally.* London: Pandora Press, 1984 [1911].

Dodge, Grace H. *A Bundle of Letters to Busy Girls on Practical Matters.* London: 1890.

Dowson, Aubrey. *The Women's Suffrage Cookery Book.* London: Women's Printing Society, 1910.

Ellman, Maud. *The Hunger Artists: Starving, Writing, and Imprisonment.* Cambridge: Harvard UP, 1993.

Gissing, George. *The Odd Women.* London: 1890.

Gladstone, William E. "Female Suffrage: A Letter to Samuel Smith, MP." Rpt. in *Before the Vote was Won: Arguments for and Against Women's Suffrage.* Ed. Jane Lewis. London: Routledge, 1987.

Hardaker, M. A. "Science and the Woman Question." *Popular Science Monthly* 21 (1882).

Hardie, J. Keir. Letter to the Editor. *Daily News* 29 September 1909. Rpt. in Mackenzie 131.

Jacques, Daniel Harrison. *Hints Toward Physical Perfection.* New York: 1859.

James, Henry. "Mrs. Humphry Ward," *English Illustrated Magazine.* (February, 1892).

————. *The Bostonians.* London: 1886.

Kahane, Claire. "Hysteria, Feminism, and the Case of *The Bostonians.*" *Feminism and Psychoanalysis.* Ed. Richard Feldstein and Judith Roof. Ithaca, NY: Cornell UP, 1989.

Kent, Susan Kingsley. *Sex and Suffrage in Britain, 1860–1914.* Princeton, N.J.: Princeton UP, 1987.

Lytton, Constance and Jane Warton. *Prisons and Prisoners: Some Personal Experiences.* New York: George H. Doran, 1914.

Mackenzie, Midge. *Shoulder to Shoulder.* New York: Knopf, 1975.

Marcus, Jane. "Re-reading the Pankhursts and Women's Suffrage." *Suffrage and the Pankhursts.* Ed. Jane Marcus. London: Routledge, 1987.

Michie, Helena. *The Flesh Made Word: Female Figures and Women's Bodies.* New York: Oxford UP, 1987.

Moulilin, C. W. Mansell. "Artificial V. 'Forcible' Feeding." *The Suffragette* April 4, 1913.

Nicholson, Mervyn. "Magic Food, Compulsive Eating, and Power Poetics." *Disorderly Eaters: Texts in Self-Empowerment.* Ed. Lillian R. Furst and Peter W. Graham. University Park: Pennsylvania State UP, 1992.

O'Connor, Erin. "Pictures of Health: Medical Photography and the Emergence of Anorexia Nervosa." *Journal of the History of Sexuality*, 5.4 (April 1995): 535–72.

Pankhurst, Christabel. *The Great Scourge and How to End It.* London: E. Pankhurst, 1913.

Richardson, Benjamin Ward. *The Commonhealth: A Series of Essays on Health and Felicity for Every-Day Readers.* London: 1887.

Robins, Elizabeth. *The Convert.* London: The Women's Press, 1980 [1907].

Russett, Cynthia Eagle. *Sexual Science: The Victorian Construction of Womanhood.* Cambridge: Harvard UP, 1989.

Stowe, Harriet Beecher. *Uncle Tom's Cabin.* Boston: 1852.

Tickner, Lisa. *The Spectacle of Women: Images of the Suffrage Campaign, 1907–14.* London: Chatto, 1987.

Walkowitz, Judith R. *Prostitution and Victorian Society: Women, Class, and the State*. New York: Cambridge UP, 1982.

Ward, Humphry (Mrs.). *Delia Blanchflower*. London: Ward, Lock, 1915.

———. *Robert Elsmere*. London: 1888.

———. "An Appeal Against Female Suffrage." *Nineteenth Century* (June 1889).

Part 2

Grotesque, Ghostly, and Cannibalistic Hunger in Twentieth-Century Texts

5

"The Courage of Her Appetites": The Ambivalent Grotesque in Ellen Glasgow's *Romantic Comedians*

Debra Beilke

Judge Gamaliel Honeywell, the southern aristocratic protagonist of Ellen Glasgow's 1926 novel *The Romantic Comedians,* finds his twin sister Edmonia Bredalbane's excessive appetites the sign of a woefully "abandoned" attitude. He muses with distaste, "Her sinful past, for her many marriages had merely whitewashed it, had not saddened her, had not sobered her, had not even, he concluded, with his stern but just gaze on her broad and lumpy back, diminished her size. She had not only thrived, she had fattened on iniquity" (84).

As this quotation suggests, Glasgow is acutely aware of the cultural connection between women's unrestrained appetite for food and sexual misconduct. Her *Romantic Comedians* reveals the ways in which the southern lady's appetites are socially regulated in order to keep her in her place: lower in the southern hierarchy than white gentlemen but higher than Blacks. I argue in this essay, however, that this comedy of manners complicates the notion held by many cultural critics that the Bakhtinian grotesque is fundamentally transgressive. Glasgow does represent the comically grotesque female character of Edmonia Bredalbane in a potentially transgressive way, by giving her a witty, insightful voice and a life of unrepentant pleasure. However, Glasgow stops short of fully embracing her fictional creation; although readers are meant to laugh *with* Edmonia's words, we are nudged to laugh *at* her embodied presence. In other words, Edmonia produces two warring types of comedy: her own sense of humor, which is satiric and transgressive, and the grotesque humor of her body, the low comedy of the fallen woman. Glasgow's ambivalence towards her own creation may stem from her realization that, since her culture associates the excessive female body with the lower classes, especially African Americans, loosening the straightjacket of re-strained appetites would not so much liberate upper class white women, as lower their class status and the privileges that come with it.

The Romantic Comedians tells the story of sixty-five-year-old Gamaliel Honeywell's search for love after the death of his devoted wife Cordelia. A respected southern gentleman, Gamaliel has always done what was proper, including marrying a woman he did not love rather than com-promising her reputation. But, after a decent interval for mourning, Gamaliel experiences new stirrings of romantic interest—but only in girls young enough to be his granddaughter. Even though his long lost love Amanda Lightfoot has chastely waited for him for forty years, Gamaliel is no longer interested in her: at age fifty-eight, she is far too old for him. Instead, he pursues and marries a flighty young girl named Annabel who marries him for his money. Not surprisingly, Annabel leaves Gamaliel after a few months of marriage for a younger man. Gamaliel, of course, learns nothing from this misadventure and continues to hope for young love.

Despite its light-hearted tone, Glasgow's comedy of manners offers a serious critique of gender relations in southern culture of the 1920s.[1] While much of Glasgow's satire is overt, she also filters her concern with southern class and gender hierarchies through somatic symbols, demon-strating Carroll Smith-Rosenberg's point that "both through literal body language and through physical metaphor and image, the body provides a symbolic system through which individuals can discuss social realities too complex or conflicted to be spoken overtly" (268). I focus in this chapter on the way manners—especially manners concerning appetite—keep upper-class southern white women well regulated; well-bred ladies must control their mouths, and by extension their bodies, in order to achieve and maintain membership in the southern elite class.[2] The contrast between the strictly regulated manners of the proper late-Victorian southern lady of the 1880s and the looser manners of women in the textual present (the 1920s) forms the thematic core of this novel. (While Edmonia Bredalbane belongs chronologically to the Victorian cohort of the 1880s, her loose manners, which horrified her own generation but intrigue the youth of the 1920s, mark her as psychologically a member of the newer generation.)

Glasgow expresses these conflicting manners most dramatically by depicting two distinct body types: the slim yet curvaceous "queenly" body of the lady—Amanda Lightfoot—and the excessively fleshy body of the fallen woman—Edmonia Bredalbane. The text does not inscribe these two types haphazardly: they carry immense symbolic weight, so to speak, in articulating important social concerns about the regulation of female desire. Glasgow's fiction anticipates current feminist theorists such as Susan Bordo, who argues, "Viewed historically, the discipline and normalization of the female body . . . has to be acknowledged as an amazingly durable and flexible strategy of social control" (166). The disciplined body of Amanda Lightfoot represents the epitome of fine, upper-class manners, while the unruly, grotesque body of Edmonia, who had "indulged herself through life in that branch of conduct which was familiar to ancient moralists as nature in man and depravity in woman" (7), symbolizes the fallen standards for feminine conduct in the 1920s.

While the grotesque can take many forms, for the purposes of this chapter, I will focus on the grotesque as fat, protuberant, excessive body as theorized by Mikhail Bakhtin in his *Rabelais and His World*. Bakhtin argues that the medieval culture of folk humor is based on the concept of grotesque realism, in which images of the material bodily principle—particularly the lower body—play a large role. Carnivalesque laughter functions to "degrade and materialize": "To degrade also means to concern oneself with the lower stratum of the body, the life of the belly and the reproductive organs; it therefore relates to acts of defecation and copulation, conception, pregnancy, and birth" (21). Bakhtin insists than in the Medieval period, this exaggerated focus on the lower body rather than on abstract, spiritual principles had a "positive, assertive character. The leading themes of these images of bodily life are fertility, growth, and a brimming-over abundance" (19). More specifically, the bodily principle of grotesque realism is positive because it represents the collective body of the people rather than the atomized individual, and as such is disruptive of social hierarchies (19).

Recent feminist critics, informed by Bakhtin's theories, have argued that the category of the female grotesque is politically transgressive in that it undermines normative restrictions on female behavior and appearance. Mary Russo, for example, in her influential *The Female Grotesque*, asserts that the female grotesque can "be used affirmatively to destabilize the idealizations of female beauty, or to realign the mechanism of desire" (65). Russo is especially interested in the ways that "the grotesque, particularly as a bodily category, emerges as a deviation from the norm" (11), contending that "[t]he category of the female grotesque is crucial to identity-formation for both men and women as a space of risk and abjection" (12). Russo does, of course, recognize some of the drawbacks of Bakhtin's analysis for feminists, writing that "Bakhtin, like many other social theorists of the nineteenth and twentieth centuries, fails to acknowledge or incorporate the social relations of gender in his semiotic model of the body politic, and thus his notion of the Female Grotesque remains in all directions repressed and undeveloped" (63). Nevertheless, despite the drawbacks of this theory, Russo and other feminist critics interested in the grotesque tend to focus on its potentially transgressive elements. My own view is that while Bakhtin's analysis is powerful in its insistence upon "the relation between body-image, social context and collective identity" (Stallybrass and White 10), the cultural revulsion towards "low" comic figures often leads to hegemonic rather than transgressive implications. Because the grotesque is enmeshed within the deeply rooted cultural categories of high and low—with grotesque comedy being low and nonhumorous modes such as tragedy being high—deployments of the grotesque female body can reify rather than subvert hierarchical categories.

This description categorizes *The Romantic Comedians*. Using Edmonia Bredalbane as a mouthpiece for her own sharp wit and criticism of southern upper-class manners, Glasgow does on one level succeed in piercing through the veil of patriarchal constraints on women's lives. On a fairly overt narrative level, Glasgow's satire suggests that female appetites—for food, for sex, and for verbal expression—and the admired qualities of the southern lady are antithetical, indeed irreconcilable. The construct of the southern lady depends upon the severe bodily and psychic repression of women. After dismantling this unnatural construct, however, Glasgow finds she is not completely enamored with the results: the grotesque body and manners of Edmonia. On the one hand, the ravenous appetites and comic insights of Mrs. Bredalbane, echoing those of Rabelais, do resist the upper-class imperative that ladies contain their desires. But on the other hand, Glasgow undercuts the potentially transgressive qualities of this character because Edmonia's grotesque qualities mark her as dangerously close to the physicality stereotypically associated with the lower classes and especially African Americans in the South. Sincerely concerned with the debilitating effects of constrictive southern gender roles, Glasgow also belonged by birth to a privileged class and race, and these privileges were difficult for her to relinquish. *The Romantic Comedians*, then, encodes Glasgow's hesitation to embrace transgressive female characters because, for this author, a southern lady who laughs too loud and relishes her appetites falls from the high tragedy of the pedestal to the comic gutter of the appetites.

Ellen Glasgow, born in 1875, was not alone, of course, in classifying unrestrained female appetites as low in the American cultural hierarchy. Cultural historians document that by the end of the nineteenth century, American culture associated the fat female body with the lower classes. Joan Jacobs Brumberg, for example, asserts that "by the turn of the twentieth century, elite society already preferred its women thin and frail as a symbol of their social distance from the working classes" (185). She argues that female thinness and delicacy became a status symbol because it signified the "idle idyll of the leisured classes" (185). Unlike robust and "vulgar" working class women whose bodies signified manual labor, frail upper class women's unproductive and essentially decorative bodies advertised their elite social status. Susan Bordo convincingly argues that corpulence was no longer fashionable by the end of the century because "social power had come to be less dependent on the sheer accumulation of material wealth and more connected to the ability to control and manage the labor and resources of others. At the same time, excess body weight came to be seen as reflecting moral or personal inadequacy, or lack of will" (192). In a culture of overabundance, social status occurs through the ability to control one's appetites rather than to fulfill them.

The social stigma against female corpulence was even more acute in the American South of the late-nineteenth and early-twentieth century, however, because of the deeply rooted southern dichotomy between white lady as ethereal, sexless and refined spirit and African American woman as lustful, fleshy and "primitive" body. As numerous scholars of southern culture point out, the stereotype of the "high" self-sacrificing and pure white southern lady on her pedestal has historically been inextricably linked with its opposing definition of "low" and promiscuous African American womanhood.[3] These bodies are binary opposites in the southern symbolic matrix of this period in that white women's supposed sexual purity was integral to the system of racial hierarchy. As Catherine Clinton notes, "[p]ollution of the symbol of cultural purity—a white woman's body—threatened white supremacy" (58). In terms of male attitudes towards southern women, these divisions between pure and promiscuous bodies signify the difference between reverence and rape, providing the justification for white men's frequent, usually coercive, sexual liaisons with African American women.[4] One of the more famous articulations of the hierarchy of southern women's bodies is spoken by Mr. Compson of William Faulkner's *Absolom! Absolom!*:

> [T]he other sex is separated into three sharp divisions, separated (two of them) by a chasm which could be crossed but one time and in but one direction—ladies, women, females—the virgins whom gentlemen someday married, the courtesans to whom they went while on sabbaticals to the cities, the slave girls and women upon whom that first caste rested and to whom in certain cases it doubtless owed the very fact of its virginity. (109)

Given this cultural context, if a white woman is to remain high on her pedestal, she must remain vigilant about controlling her desires lest she cross that chasm from lady to woman and become contaminated with the unrestrained sexuality of African American females.

Diane Roberts usefully theorizes the southern distinction between white and African American female bodies in terms of Bakhtin's grotesque/classical opposition, with the white bodies as "classical," and the African American as "grotesque." Roberts argues compellingly that "if the female body tended toward the grotesque unless sternly regulated, the black body could never, in the mind of the slave South be *anything but* grotesque. Vigilance was required to keep white bodies from slipping toward blackness" (3). Thus, while Western culture traditionally associates men with mind and women with body, these binaries are complicated by class and race distinctions, complications that critics must address when theorizing the grotesque body.

Given this historical background in which the strict regulation of their appetites both oppresses (in terms of gender) and privileges (in terms of race and class) southern white ladies, it is little wonder that Ellen Glasgow's attitude towards unrestrained female desire, embodied in the excessive, grotesque body of fallen woman Edmonia Bredalbane, is deeply ambivalent.[5]

While *The Romantic Comedians* is fundamentally a novel of manners, Glasgow uses her characters' appetites metaphorically to differentiate between higher- and lower-class manners; bodies are significant mainly insofar as they symbolize the characters' control of their appetites. By manners, I mean socially recognized forms of behavior which serve to demarcate one group of people from another. In making this definition, I am drawing upon Lionel Trilling's famous dictum that manners are the "hum and buzz of implication . . . that part of a culture which is made up of half-uttered or unuttered or unutterable expressions of value . . . the things that for good or bad draw the people of a culture together and that separate them from the people of another culture" (201). Glasgow astutely realizes that manners not only bind people of a culture together, but also exert considerable social control over their bodies and minds. As one of her characters puts it, "If the world continued to grow away, not only from God, but from good breeding as well, what, she wondered despondently, could be trusted to keep wives contented and the working classes in order?" (194).

Restraint and reserve define aristocratic manners in this novel, as embodied by the appetites of Gamaliel Honeywell and the "true women" of his class and generation—Amanda and Cordelia. Gamaliel Honeywell, who represents the restrained, chivalric southern gentleman, is Edmonia Bredalbane's twin brother and one of her two foils (Amanda being the other). Judge Honeywell's desires, the narrator informs us, have long been subdued to his aristocratic "family inheritance of prudence, integrity, and reserve. Polygamous by instinct, like other men, he had confined his impetuous desires within the temperate zone of monogamy, where sober habit had preserved both his health and his appearance" (3). A moderate diet of bland food is, in his opinion, a sign of the "good taste which, like dyspepsia, was hereditary in the Honeywell family" (33). Gamaliel considers good taste or, in other words, self-regulated desire, as part of his aristocratic inheritance, a legacy which must be maintained by careful control of his dietary intake. That he considers good taste to be a hereditary trait suggests his view that class privilege is biologically justified. Therefore, characters such Edmonia who show obvious signs of bad taste despite their good blood profoundly upset his sense of natural entitlement.

Upper-class restraint, however, has its deleterious effects, which Glasgow humorously underscores through her dietary metaphor of dyspepsia; Judge Honeywell is burdened by "the taint of nervous dyspepsia that had been for generations the hereditary curse of his family" (6). His lifelong tendency towards indigestion can be read as a sign of his finding any ideas or behaviors extending beyond the strict confines of upper-class manners "hard to swallow." Reasoning that conventional standards are safest, he "was disposed to encourage liberty of thought as long as he was convinced that it would not lead to liberal views" (3). He was brought up under his father's belief that "if there is anything wrong with the Episcopal Church or the Democratic Party, I would rather die without knowing it" (9). In other words, a restrained appetite for sensuous pleasures also symbolizes restraint of thought, which Glasgow associates with orthodox southern values.

But while both men and women of the elite class must practice self-restraint, women must regulate their appetites even more strictly than do men. The repression of female appetites becomes a major figure in this novel for the patriarchal subordination of female desire. As Susan Bordo trenchantly observes, female appetite has been contained since the beginning of the industrial era by the "notion that women are most gratified by feeding and nourishing *others*, not themselves" (118). This cultural prescription certainly seems to be true in *The Romantic Comedians*, at least for good female characters. For example, Gamaliel's now-deceased first wife Cordelia (a character reminiscent of the self-sacrificing daughter of *King Lear*), whom he considers a perfect wife and mother, renounced her own appetites for the sake of his dyspepsia. She gave up "so much of the rich and highly flavored food to which her healthy appetite had inclined. For thirty-six years, she had sacrificed her appetite to his digestion" (175). Assuming that women are naturally self-sacrificing, Gamaliel took this self-denial for granted until confronted with the haphazard eating habits of his second wife, Annabel, and especially the voracious appetites of his twin sister Edmonia.

Glasgow comically contrasts Judge Honeywell's well-regulated appetites with Edmonia's intemperance to undercut patriarchal views of femininity as naturally self-sacrificing. Because of sexual misconduct, Mrs. Bredalbane, "an intrepid woman of liberal views and loose behavior" (7) fell from the pedestal as a young woman "not quietly, as was the custom in such matters, but with a loud explosion that had startled Queenborough" (7). In language echoing the stereotypical mammy figure of southern mythology, Edmonia is described as a "stout and disreputable dowager, [an] excessive . . . quadruple matron" (82). As opposed to the delicate frailty desired in upper-class white women, Edmonia's hearty physique suggests robust physical activity; she is "large, raw-boned, with strong, plain features, where an expression of genuine humour frolicked with an artificial complexion, and a mountainous bosom, from which a cascade of crystal beads splashed and glistened" (16). Edmonia's corpulence symbolizes her uncontained desire—her immoderate appetite for sensuous pleasures of all kinds, including food:

> But Edmonia, who had been born with the courage of her appetites, feared to be stout in age as little as she had feared to be scandalous in youth. A daring combination of American frankness and French epicurism, she was fond of succulent food and of wine, especially when it was red; and she had lived long enough abroad, he regretted, to acquire both the taste for gallantry and the horror of iced water. (16–17)

Edmonia's appetites suggest her hedonistic self-indulgence, a belief "in taking all the pleasure you can find" (21), with her body dramatically contradicting the dictum that women should cater to men's desires, not to their own. Because she indulges rather than restrains her appetite for sensuous pleasures, Edmonia transgresses not only the standards of upper-class reserve, but also the standards of white femininity. Although Edmonia is white skinned and of good family, her character paradoxically combines the good-humored obesity of the mammy figure with the promiscuous sensuality and tasteless love of finery stereotypically associated with the Jezebel figure.

Not surprisingly, combining such racial and class-based stereotypes into one character leads to comic—even grotesque—results. Honeywell, in fact, frequently uses the term *grotesque* to describe his sister. While eyeing her figure with distaste, he muses at one point, for example, "From her brown locks, which were piled high over a diamond bandeau, to her aching feet (they must be aching feet, he decided) in the most eccentric of French slippers, she was grotesque" (51). A far cry from her brother's self-regulation, Edmonia represents Mikhail Bakhtin's grotesque body as articulated in *Rabelais and His World*, which is associated with "food, drink, defecation, and sexual life . . . offered, moreover, in an extremely exaggerated form" (26) and which is "ugly, monstrous, hideous from the point of view of 'classic' aesthetics" (25). The grotesque body, according to Bakhtin, is identified with nonofficial low culture and with social transformation. As opposed to the classical body which represents the isolated bourgeois individual, the grotesque body represents the collective body of the people which is ever growing, abundant, and in the process of transformation. Although Bakhtin is making a historically specific argument, Glasgow's text demonstrates that the grotesque versus classical body dichotomy still has relevance in early-twentieth-century America. In its ideal form, the figure of the lady represents high culture by repressing all functions of the lower body—both social and physical. Edmonia's body, on the other hand, because of its associations with lower-class/Black womanhood, symbolizes the "return of the repressed" contents of the female body politic. As such, her figure represents social growth and change, particularly the social transformation in female manners during the 1920s.

One way in which Edmonia's grotesque body represents social transformation is by disrupting the notion of natural, inherent class status and the appetites that come with it. Gamaliel is particularly distressed by his sister's startling presence because, although they are twins and presumably have a very similar biological makeup, Edmonia did not inherit the Honeywell dyspepsia:

> Without delving into her character, there was, he felt, sufficient food for admonition in the recklessness with which she endangered her digestion. . . . That Edmonia, an exception to every rule, did remain well in spite of her greediness, was little less than an affront to his own abstemious diet. While he watched her, he longed to indulge in a veritable orgy of rebuke. (225)

Significantly, Gamaliel uses dietary metaphors to express his desire to control his sister. The phrases "food for admonition" and "indulge in a veritable orgy of rebuke" suggest that his own repressed hungers surface even while criticizing Edmonia's. Clearly, he resents Edmonia's satiety at least partially because of his own unfulfilled appetites.

Furthermore, Judge Honeywell also longs to rebuke Mrs. Bredalbane because the dyspepsia that she managed to bypass symbolizes his putatively hereditary good taste discussed above: "It was astonishing—it was positively amazing to him that Edmonia should have lived to her present age without acquiring the good taste which, like dyspepsia, was hereditary in the Honeywell family" (33). The context of this quotation makes clear that by "good taste" Gamaliel means keeping one's mouth shut, rather than talking, as Edmonia does, "incessantly of things that were unmentionable among delicate-minded persons" (52). Upper-class society defines good taste as keeping one's mouth shut—restraining both verbal output and caloric input. And since his twin sister, with her similar biological inheritance, seems congenitally incapable of good taste, Gamaliel feels threatened at some level by the suspicion that perhaps there is nothing natural after all about his privileged position in society.

Glasgow associates Edmonia with grotesque realism not only through her protuberant fleshiness, but also through her Rabelaisian or carnivalesque humor—laughter which discomfits the well-mannered in its embrace of all aspects of life, including food, drink, and sex. According to Bakhtin's *Dialogic Imagination*, Rabelaisian laughter is that which provides a "connection on the one hand with fundamental realities of life, and on the other with the most radical destruction of all false and verbal ideological shells that had distorted and kept separate these realities" (237). One distorted reality that Edmonia's laughter explodes is what Glasgow terms the "chivalric interpretation of biology" (40)—the self-serving patriarchal belief that men remain desirable until toppling into the grave while women lose their attractiveness with the first gray hair. With her "deep, thick laugh" that "gushes out" (85) uncontrollably, she laughs openly at Gamaliel's delusions. For example, because he does not want to accept the fact that he—at age sixty-five—is far too old to be marrying a woman of twenty-three, he tries to persuade Edmonia "that a man remains young longer than a woman of the same age" (27). While a well-mannered southern lady such as Amanda or Mrs. Upchurch would have murmured agreement to those words of wisdom, "Mrs. Bredalbane, who was settling herself in the softest chair in the room, laughed with the genial insolence which, it seemed to him, Nature had reserved for twin sisters. 'I wonder what lascivious old male first invented that theory?' she inquired, with amiable coarseness" (27).

Gamaliel, however, does not find Edmonia's presence and humor "amiable." She, in fact, repulses him, perhaps because on some level he recognizes her transgressive potential. He finds her propensity to say whatever is on her mind "vulgar," a word which underscores the fall in hierarchy that occurs when a woman lets herself go. But he also finds her corpulence distasteful, perhaps because, on some level, he senses that Edmonia's frank enjoyment of her fleshiness pollutes her (and by extension his) class and race identity. His disgust is important; as symbolic of upper-class attitudes more generally, it serves to differentiate Edmonia from her well-regulated peers. As Stallybrass and White have argued, "Differentiation, in other words, is dependent upon disgust. The division of the social into high and low, the polite and the vulgar, simultaneously maps out divisions between the civilized and the grotesque body" (191). Gamaliel's revulsion from the spectacle of Edmonia's appetites, insofar as it represents the standards of his class and generation, demotes Edmonia's status from high lady to low fallen woman.

It is not Edmonia's body size or even her sinful past per se that he finds grotesque, but her body's function as a symbol of her unrestrained appetites—more specifically, the pleasure she finds in them: "[I]t was not only Edmonia's past, it was her point of view that was disreputable" (16). Although Bella Upchurch, for example, is plump, Gamaliel heartily approves of her because she devotes her energy to flattering men rather than to pleasing herself:

> Physically, she embodied to perfection that indirect influence which had been formed by, and had formed in turn, the men of his time. Brisk, plump, pretty, with a way of her own, a short fringe, which was very becoming to her dove's eyes, and an expression of resigned but playful archness, she had gained by strategy everything she had ever wanted from life except a rich and indulgent husband. (17)

The difference between Bella and Edmonia—the difference between pleasingly plump and grotesquely fat—is less a distinction of size than of attitude. Edmonia directly appeases her own desires, rather than trying to get material or vicarious satisfaction out of men as Bella does.

Conversely, the appetites of Annabel, Gamaliel's new twenty-three-year-old bride, also become a source of his censure, even though her body is slender. As "light and graceful as a swallow in the air" (19), she has the slight figure so fashionable in the 1920s and symbolizes the amorality and disorder of the jazz age. Annabel's appetites are neither as heavy as those of Edmonia, nor as well regulated as those of Amanda. Instead, they are completely haphazard, disordered. Gamaliel discovers on their honeymoon, for example, that Annabel, very unlike his first wife, is utterly unconcerned with his need for regularity and wholesomeness in his diet. Instead, she orders meals only "irregularly" and indulges in her "perverted taste for eccentric dishes and dangerous French sauces" (175). Annabel, despite her lightness, is literally hard on Gamaliel's digestion: he comes down with a serious case of dyspepsia while on their honeymoon and needs to resort to the restorative powers of the waters at Vichy to recover. In summary, it is not fleshiness nor slimness per se that is important, but their function as signifiers for female appetite. Female appetites which are not directed towards serving male needs, whether they be disordered or excessive, merit disapprobation. Edmonia seems grotesque to her twin brother mainly because she indulges her appetites to please herself rather than restrain them to please someone else.

Although Judge Honeywell sternly disapproves of Edmonia's irreverent humor, Glasgow clearly appreciates her insight, at least to a certain extent. Edmonia, in fact, often sounds like a mouthpiece for Glasgow, especially when she pierces through the "evasive idealism" Glasgow found so destructive to southern women's lives.[6] Glasgow defined and defended the woman's movement as "a revolt from a pretense of being—it is at its best and worst a struggle for the liberation of personality" ("Feminism" 31–32). And as Marcelle Thiebaux demonstrates, Glasgow believed that women had denied their own humanity in responding to men's ideal of them: "The passivity of women, she felt, was not an innate quality but an acquired characteristic, one that would ultimately be cast off" (17). Mrs. Bredalbane's conduct, then, is certainly more in keeping with this author's concern for female emancipation than is Amanda's. Edmonia, the antithesis of passivity, speaks out consistently against hypocrisy and does everything in her power to liberate her personality from the rigid confines of polite manners. In short, Edmonia cannot be written off as someone who is only laughed *at*; she is certainly laughed *with* on some important level.

Nonetheless, a definite authorial ambivalence surrounds Edmonia, an ambivalence which is most evident in the descriptions of her body. The manner in which Glasgow represents Edmonia, especially in terms of her appearance, mitigates against the admiration readers might otherwise feel for her by turning her into a comic object as well as a comic subject. Not only does Glasgow describe her as "grotesque," but the author excessively dwells on Edmonia's physical unattractiveness. Because Glasgow always portrays Edmonia as sweating, huffing, eating, drinking, and wearing ill-fitting clothes on her lumpy, misshapen body, her effect becomes comic rather than compelling.

Thus, although Edmonia's courageous refusal to starve herself into social acceptability is laudable, it does not undermine the deep-rooted hierarchies of our culture in which women with voracious appetites and fat bodies occupy lower rungs in the social hierarchy; they are comically repulsive, and therefore less compelling. The scene during which Edmonia and Gamaliel have dinner together (chapter 8), illustrates this vexing problem in an especially vivid manner. During this dinner, Edmonia launches into an extended diatribe against the injustices of the social tradition which "hounded" her because she enjoyed herself too much, making comments such as "[Y]ou could have forgiven my committing a sin if you hadn't feared that I had committed a pleasure as well. . . . It wasn't my fall, it was my being able to get up again, that you couldn't forgive" (227). As she continues to poke holes in Virginia's venerable social traditions, Gamaliel starts to wonder if she may be right, asking if there might be "a leak, after all, in his inherited system of prudential morality" (229). However, although Edmonia's words are powerful, Gamaliel is finally unconvinced by her argument because of the repulsive spectacle of her voracious eating habits:

> It distressed Gamaliel to see Edmonia make the immoderate meal of an unbridled appetite. . . . Having been for so long the master of his appetite, if not of his fate, he could only regard Edmonia's indulgence as a melancholy spectacle, though naturally of a piece with the rest of her conduct. . . . [T]he charge that he had misjudged her had been unable to survive the sight of her hearty pleasure at the table. (231)

This scene is a good example of the power of somatic images: the repugnance Gamaliel feels before his sister's unbridled appetite finally outweighs the insight of her intellect. Granted, because Gamaliel's disgust colors much of the reader's view of Edmonia and because Gamaliel himself is an object of Glasgow's laughter, one could argue that the narrative undercuts this disgust. However, Glasgow does not portray Edmonia from any other character's point of view, even though she had the opportunity to do so, since many of the novel's scenes are written from the perspective of other female characters. We receive no contrasting perceptions of Edmonia from other characters; therefore, our impression of her cannot help but be tinged with Gamaliel's disgust.

While Edmonia's pleasure-loving irreverence certainly makes her an enjoyable character, her transgressive potential remains less assured. Paradoxically, the very qualities which mark her as transgressive—her insightful humor, her outspokenness, and her refusal to suppress her bodily desires in the name of southern ladyhood—are the same qualities which detract from her discursive power. The logic of the narrative, which continuously draws attention to the grotesque nature of Edmonia's presence, works to repulse and therefore discourage the reader from identifying with her. In other words, Glasgow portrays her as a comic figure: the reader is invited to laugh at her rather than try to emulate her.

The often unconscious power of somatic images to attract or repel becomes particularly apparent when Glasgow juxtaposes Edmonia's body with that of Amanda Lightfoot, the Victorian southern lady who remains high on her pedestal. A restrained, statuesque beauty in whom all emotions, desires, and lower bodily functions remain hidden, she represents the Bakhtinian classical body. In opposition to the grotesque body, which emphasizes transformation—growth and becoming—the classical body is a finished product in which all signs of connection between the interior body and the exterior world are hidden. Tall and curvaceous, with an imposing presence, Amanda is described consistently as "statuesque." Her emotions have been so constrained by propriety that even her eyes are like "blue enamel" (102), suggesting a hard surface glaze concealing any inner vitality. Victorian standards promote this remote, restrained beauty: "She had still what they used to call a perfect figure. Perfect! That was the reason, perhaps, that she had remained subdued to the queenly Victorian curves, though she was so slender that she might have worn one of those straight modern frocks like Annabel's without looking ridiculous" (56). The classical body is "isolated, alone, fenced off from all other bodies. All signs of its unfinished character, of its growth and proliferation were eliminated. . . . The ever unfinished nature of the body was hidden, kept secret; conception, pregnancy, childbirth, death throes, were almost never shown" (29). Virginal and impenetrable, Amanda's body and extreme self-discipline fence her off from all other bodies—she would die before letting anyone break through this fence.

Amanda's bodily perfection symbolizes her impeccable manners—impeccable, that is, by patriarchal Victorian standards. She never questions societal strictures because "she belonged to that fortunate generation of women who had no need to think, since everything was decided for them by the feelings of a lady and the Episcopal Church" (142). In her Victorian perfection, Amanda represents many of the characteristics Glasgow spent her life fighting against, especially the pretense and evasive idealism of southern culture. Living in a haze of sentimental delusion, Amanda remains unmarried, virginal and alone her entire life in tribute to her love for Gamaliel. After Cordelia's death, Amanda hopes, perhaps even assumes that the judge will marry her. She is, of course, wrong. As Mrs. Upchurch puts it, "The trouble is that Amanda has always lived in some world of sentimental invention. She has had absolutely no contact with reality" (311). And bringing southerners face-to-face with the cold hard light of reality is one of Glasgow's more important novelistic goals.

The reality of Amanda's exalted status is, as Glasgow makes clear, its prohibitive price: the complete denial of her appetites. Unlike Edmonia, who eats what she pleases, it requires "heaven knows what sacrifices" to keep Amanda's "late-Victorian figure" (60), and her figure symbolizes her strict self-discipline. The sacrifice necessary for her perfect manners, her exalted status, is the containment of all desire and emotion. Her inner life must remain completely inaccessible to the rest of the world because the "virtue of perfect behavior lies, not in its rightness, but in its impenetrability" (149). For example, she could have preempted Gamaliel and Annabel's marriage by admitting her feelings for the judge when Annabel asked her if she still cared. However, Amanda evades the question; she cannot admit her feelings for Gamaliel to anybody because "[n]ice women don't talk about their private affairs. . . . Nice women never, never ask each other such questions" (149). The effect of this containment on Amanda is, not surprisingly, loneliness and isolation. Although she has family and many social acquaintances, Amanda is cut off from intimate contact with anybody. Glasgow finds this intense loneliness of the traditional southern lady tragic. As she states in a nonfiction piece, "When I realize the lives of the women of the South, of the generation before me, I am fairly horror-stricken at the loneliness and depression they must have endured" ("No Valid Reason" 24).

Despite her suffering, however, Amanda's regal, classical body appeals strongly to the imagination. Her "statuesque beauty" (55) and "majestic height" (56) suggests a queenly presence which eschews the expression of lowly desires—either emotional or physical. Judge Honeywell admires this reserve because he finds the expression of female needs horrifying: "Nakedness of mind or body was abhorrent to him and mortifying episodes had taught him that when a woman begins to reveal her soul, she is seldom satisfied until she has stripped it bare" (87). This explains the powerful attraction women like Amanda have on his imagination:

> From Amanda herself, grave, stately, self-possessed, confirmed
> in queenliness, wrapped in her Victorian reserve as in a veil of

mystery, he knew that he should have nothing to fear. The
women of her generation had known how to suffer in silence.
What an inestimable blessing was this knowledge, especially
when it had passed into tradition! (55)

In summary, Amanda represents the "totally other-oriented emotional
economy" described by Susan Bordo, which she relates to unsatisfied
female hunger. In this emotional economy which, unfortunately, still
exists today, femininity requires that "women learn to feed others, not
the self, and to construe any desires for self-nurturance and self-feeding
as greedy and excessive" (Bordo 171). Female hunger—not only for
food but for independence, power, and sex—must be contained if a
woman is to be attractively feminine. Amanda is precisely such a contained figure, which explains why she is so admired by chivalrous gentlemen such as Honeywell: her figure is uncontaminated by the messiness
of the lower bodily desires or the unruliness of emotional needs.

But while Glasgow certainly mocks Honeywell in many ways, on
some level she shares his veneration for Amanda's type. Despite the
foolishness of Amanda's forty-year faithfulness to a married man, the
narrator's frequent descriptions of her presence as "queenly," "regal,"
"royal," and "majestic"—with no hint of irony—suggest that Amanda's
place is high in the hierarchy, an exalted figure closer to tragedy than to
comedy. While Amanda's behavior is often criticized by the narrator and
the other characters, Glasgow never disparages or mocks her imposing
presence. Her beauty and classic restraint, together with the intense
idealism she embodies, associate her with tragedy, a mode traditionally
considered much higher than comedy. This is partially because her classical body resonates with the restraint of classical tragedy as an art form.
Tragedy, as Norbert Elias observes, depends upon reserved behavior,
good form, and the repression of all that is vulgar:

> The importance of good form, the specific mark of every genu-
> ine "society"; the control of individual feelings by reason, a vital
> necessity for every courtier; the reserved behavior and elimina-
> tion of every plebeian expression, the specific mark of a particu-
> lar stage on the road to "civilization"—all this finds its purest
> expression in classical tragedy. What must be hidden in court
> life, all vulgar feelings and attitudes, everything of which "one"
> does not speak, does not appear in tragedy either. People of low
> rank, which for this class also means of base character, have no
> place in it. Its form is clear, transparent, precisely regulated, like
> etiquette and court life in general. (16)

Like French tragedy, the fine manners of the Victorian South require that
individual feelings be tightly corseted and hidden from the public. Glasgow
seems to be aware that the effects of this repression are tragic, not only

in the sense of wasted human potential, but also in the sense of an exalted, higher form of art and life. Mrs. Upchurch, for example, finds Amanda's faithfulness "magnificent, of course, but it was not human" (131). The magnificent classical body stands on a higher level than average humans with their messy desires: "Beside her majestic height the thin slips of girls revolving around her appeared as trivial as painted dolls" (56). In other words, the compelling effect of her queenly body mitigates against Amanda's silliness, suggesting the (often subconscious) power of somatic images. Tragic figures, after all, tend to capture the imagination more compellingly than do comic figures, however much we may enjoy laughing.

Furthermore, not only is tragedy generally considered a higher mode of art in Western culture, but it is also more specifically associated with southern identity. The eminent southern historian C. Vann Woodward argues that southerners have a distinctly regional identity at odds with the national emphasis on optimism, success, and progress: "The experience of evil and the experience of tragedy are parts of the southern heritage that are as difficult to reconcile with the American legend of innocence and social felicity as the experience of poverty and defeat are to reconcile with the legends of abundance and success" (21). Having lost the Civil War and many revered antebellum traditions, while at the same time recognizing at some level their guilt in upholding slavery, white southerners, according to Woodward, tend to view life through a darker lens than that of northerners, and indeed, the tragic but exalted figure of the defeated cavalier and the virtuous but much-abused southern lady are popular, compelling figures in southern literature. On some level, then, Amanda represents this icon of tragically maligned southern identity.

In summary, this novel presents an interesting paradox: Glasgow somatically portrays Amanda as the higher figure, even though in most areas, Glasgow is closer to Edmonia in her beliefs. Even though the text depicts Amanda's romantic delusion and wasted life as faintly ridiculous, her somatic representation as Bahktin's classical body suggests the opposite. While Glasgow underscores Amanda's romantic idealism as a mere illusion, still, by consistently describing her as "queenly" and "tragic," the author suggests that a majestic, regal dimension adheres to this evasive idealism, just as something low tinctures the liberated woman. This social differentiation between the tragic high figure of the repressed southern lady and the comic low figure of the fallen woman is expressed most succinctly by Bella Upchurch. Observing that being a fallen woman is no longer the tragedy it once was, she asks herself with consternation, "What . . . could be more deplorable than the swiftness with which the high tragedy of one generation declines into the low comedy of the next?" (288). The fact that Glasgow chooses (consciously or unconsciously) to emphasize the comically unappealing side of Edmonia while she represents the vapid Amanda as such a strikingly tragic figure suggests her own ambivalence about unrestrained female desire, a metaphor for female emancipation.

Why, since Glasgow spent her life revolting against the evasive idealism and sexual subordination of women in her culture, would she portray Amanda as so compelling and Edmonia as so comically grotesque? Glasgow critics have generally attributed her ambivalence towards southern manners to her historical position in between Victorianism and modernism. I would add, however, that her ambivalence is also aesthetic—her revulsion towards the excessive appetites of low comedy, a revulsion stemming from her class and race privileges. As I suggested earlier, Glasgow's social position as an upper-class southern lady leaves her with contradictory urges. While she does want upper-class white women to gain equality with upper-class white men, she realizes that resisting the imperative to control female appetites is not an entirely satisfactory option for achieving this goal. Representing the fallen woman as a grotesque body does indeed degrade the category of the lady on her pedestal. However, this degradation does not collapse the categories, a collapse which would be necessary for true social change. Instead, the degradation only moves around its players. The fact that Edmonia falls from the pedestal does not change the definition of a true lady; it only moves her to a lower rung in the hierarchy—a rung contaminated with the physicality of lower-class and African American bodies.

NOTES

1. *The Romantic Comedians* is the first novel of Ellen Glasgow's "Queenborough trilogy," with Queenborough generally considered a pseudonym for Richmond, Virginia. Glasgow referred to the trilogy of *The Romantic Comedians* (1926), *They Stooped to Folly* (1929) and *The Sheltered Life* (1932) as her "Tragicomedy of Manners," explaining, "[T]hese [novels] depict the place and tragicomedy of the individual in an established society. They illustrate the struggle of personality against tradition and the social background" (*Rouse* 206). While some critics view all three novels as tragicomic, I would not include *The Sheltered Life* under that rubric, seeing it as almost completely tragic.

2. According to diet historian Hillel Schwartz, the ideal of the "regulated body" was a pervasive discourse circulating during the years 1880–1920, the years in which Glasgow came of age. He documents that in this period new slimming techniques emerged that "were nicely compatible with the new kinaesthetic ideal of a dynamically balanced body. . . . All four techniques dealt with abundance as if it were a threat to the system, a moral as well as a physical danger" (113). One of the butts of Glasgow's satire in this novel is this view of abundant intake as a danger to the system—both the physical and social systems.

3. Although the southern lady on her pedestal is similar to Victorian true womanhood of the North, historians agree the image of southern lady differs

from the northern by being much more extreme, more long-lasting and, most important, symbolically central to southern identity. As Anne Goodwyn Jones has argued, "[T]he southern lady is at the core of a region's self-definition; the identity of the South is contingent in part upon the persistence of its tradition of the lady" (4). For full-length treatments of the white southern lady, see historian Anne Firor Scott's *The Southern Lady* and literary critic Anne Goodwyn Jones's *Tomorrow Is Another Day*.

4. The critical and historical literature on the complicated tangle of race, sex, and gender in the South—what Lillian Smith termed the "race-sex-sin spiral"—is vast. See, for example, Angela Davis, bell hooks, Nell Irvin Painter's "Social Equality Miscegenation, Labor and Power," Elizabeth Fox-Genovese, Hortense Spillers, Rennie Simson, Barbara Omolade, Joel Williamson, Lillian Smith, Patricia Hill Collins, and John D'Emilio and Estelle Freedman.

5. Previous critics have overlooked the ambivalence of Glasgow's humor in this novel. For a useful overview of Glasgow's comic technique and themes in her Queenborough trilogy, see C. Hugh Holman's "The Comedies of Manners," Kathryn Lee Seidel's "The Comic Male: Satire in Ellen Glasgow's Queenborough Trilogy," and Caroline King Barnard Hall's "'Telling the Truth about Themselves': Women, Form and Idea in *The Romantic Comedians*." Holman, who focuses on the formal elements of her work, believes *The Romantic Comedians* to be "unsurpassed as an American comedy of manners" (127), a judgment with which Glasgow herself heartily agreed. Seidel concentrates on the satiric portrayals of the male characters in the trilogy, arguing that Glasgow varies from Juvenalian to Horatian satire in ridiculing and condemning "the limitations that society imposes on men who therefore both define themselves in comically limited ways and are thus predetermined to impose related limitations upon women" (16). Hall, finally, combines a feminist perspective with a formal analysis and concludes that the novel is about the truth of the female perspective of southern life as contrasted with the "paucity of inherited wisdom and the failure of prewar, male-dominated structures" (194). My analysis differs from the above critics in its attention to the relationship between representations of the body and the comic mode.

6. See, for example, "'Evasive Idealism' in Literature: An Interview with Joyce Kilner" in *Ellen Glasgow's Reasonable Doubts*, edited by Julius Rowan Raper, in which she lambasts the popular "literary pabulum" which revels in evasive idealism: "And furthermore, I think that this evasive idealism, this preference for a pretty sham instead of truth, is evident not only in literature, but in every phrase of American life" (124).

WORKS CITED

Bakhtin, Mikhail. *The Dialogic Imagination*. Ed. Michael Holquist. Trans. Caryl Emerson and Michael Holquist. Austin: U of Texas, 1981.

———. *Rabelais and His World*. Trans. Helene Iswosky. Bloomington: Indiana UP, 1984.

Bordo, Susan. *Unbearable Weight: Feminism, Western Culture, and the Body.* Berkeley: U of California P, 1993.

Brumberg, Joan Jacobs. *Fasting Girls: The History of Anorexia Nervosa.* Markham, Ont.: New American Library, 1989.

Clinton, Catherine. "Southern Dishonor." *In Joy and In Sorrow: Women, Family, and Marriage in the Victorian South.* Ed. Carol Bleser. Oxford: Oxford UP, 1991.

Collins, Patricia Hill. *Black Feminist Thought: Knowledge, Consciousness, and the Politics of Empowerment.* New York: Routledge, 1991.

Davis, Angela. "Rape, Racism and the Myth of the Black Racist." *Women, Race and Class.* New York: Random House, 1981.

D'Emilio, John, and Estelle Freedman. *Intimate Matters: A History of Sexuality in America.* New York: Harper, 1988.

Elias, Norbert. *The History of Manners.* Trans. Edmund Jephcott. New York: Pantheon, 1982.

Faulkner, William. *Absalom, Absalom!* New York: Modern Library, 1964.

Fox-Genovese, Elizabeth. *Within the Plantation Household: Black and White Women of the Old South.* Chapel Hill: U of North Carolina P, 1988.

Glasgow, Ellen. "'Evasive Idealism' in Literature: An Interview with Joyce Kilner." Rpt. in Raper 122–129.

———. "Feminism." Rpt. in Raper 26–36.

———. "No Valid Reason Against Giving Votes to Women: An Interview." Rpt. in Raper 19–26.

———. *The Romantic Comedians.* Garden City, N.Y.: Doubleday, 1926.

———. *The Sheltered Life.* Garden City, N.Y.: Doubleday, 1932.

———. *They Stooped to Folly: A Comedy of Morals.* Garden City, N.Y.: Country Life, 1929.

Hall, Caroline King Barnard. "'Telling the Truth about Themselves': Women, Form and Idea in *The Romantic Comedians.*" *Ellen Glasgow: New Perspectives.* Ed. Dorothy M. Scura. Knoxville: U of Tennessee P, 1995. 183–195.

Holman, C. Hugh. "The Comedies of Manners." *Ellen Glasgow: Centennial Essays.* Ed. M. Thomas Inge. Charlottesville: UP of Virginia, 1976. 108–128. Rpt. of "April in Queenborough: Ellen Glasgow's Comedies of Manners." *Sewanee Review* 82 (1974).

hooks, bell. *Talking Back: thinking Feminist, thinking black.* Boston: South End Press, 1989.

Jones, Anne Goodwyn. *Tomorrow Is Another Day: The Woman Writer in the South, 1859–1936.* Baton Rouge: Louisiana State UP, 1980.

Omolade, Barbara. "Hearts of Darkness." Snitow, Stansell, and Thompson 350–367.

Painter, Nell Irvin. "'Social Equality,' Miscegenation, Labor and Power." *The Evolution of Southern Culture*. Ed. Numan V. Bartley. Athens: U of Georgia P, 1988.

Raper, Julius Rowan, ed. *Ellen Glasgow's Reasonable Doubts: A Collection of Her Writings*. Baton Rouge: Louisiana State UP, 1988.

Roberts, Diane. *The Myth of Aunt Jemima: Representations of Race and Region*. London: Routledge, 1994.

Rouse, Blair. ed. *The Letters of Ellen Glasgow*. New York: Harcourt, 1958.

Russo, Mary. *The Female Grotesque: Risk, Excess and Modernity*. New York: Routledge, 1994.

Schwartz, Hillel. *Never Satisfied: A Cultural History of Diets, Fantasies and Fat*. New York: Macmillan, 1986.

Scott, Anne Firor. *The Southern Lady: From Pedestal to Politics, 1830–1930*. Chicago: U of Chicago P, 1970.

Seidel, Kathryn Lee. "The Comic Male: Satire in Ellen Glasgow's Queenborough Trilogy." *Southern Quarterly* 23.4 (1985) 15–26.

Simson, Rennie. "The Afro-American Female: The Historical Context of the Construction of Sexual Identity." Snitow, Stansell, and Thompson 229–235.

Smith, Lillian. *Killers of the Dream*. 1949. New York: Norton, 1994.

Smith-Rosenberg, Carroll. "The New Woman as Androgyne: Social Disorder and Gender Crisis, 1870–1936." *Disorderly Conduct: Visions of Gender in Victorian America*. New York: Oxford UP, 1985 245–296.

Snitow, Ann, Christine Stansell, and Sharon Thompson, eds. *Powers of Desire: The Politics of Sexuality*. New York: Monthly Review Press, 1983.

Spillers, Hortense. "Interstices: A Small Drama of Words." *Pleasure and Danger: Exploring Female Sexuality*. Ed. Carole S. Vance. Boston: Routledge, 1984. 73–100.

Stallybrass, Peter, and Allon, White. *The Politics and Poetics of Transgression*. Ithaca: Cornell UP, 1986.

Thiebaux, Marcelle. *Ellen Glasgow*. New York: Frederick Ungar, 1982.

Trilling, Lionel. "Manners, Morals, and the Novel." *The Liberal Imagination*. Garden City, N.Y.: Doubleday, 1954.

Williamson, Joel. *The Crucible of Race: Black-White Relations in the American South Since Emancipation*. New York: Oxford UP, 1984.

Woodward, C. Vann. "The Search for Southern Identity." 1958. *The Burden of Southern History*. 3rd ed. Baton Rouge: Louisiana State UP, 1993.

6

"Death Is a Skipped Meal Compared to This": Food and Hunger in Toni Morrison's *Beloved*

Ann Folwell Stanford

"How do we get to that promised motherland?"

—Marilyn Nelson Waniek,
"X Ennead I. Vi," *Magnificat*

we will wear
new bones again.
we will leave
these rainy days,
break out through the mouth
into sun and honey time.

—Lucille Clifton ("new bones," *Good Woman:*
Poems and a Memoir 1969–1980)

Among a dazzling array of other things, Toni Morrison's *Beloved* connects historical rage, resistance, and the process of "rememory" for African American slaves and their descendants with hunger, starvation, feeding, and chronic overeating. Morrison's use of food and hunger imagery in this complex story calls into question the relation of the dysfunctional body to racial oppression and historical memory. Significantly, the social pathology undergirding the institution of slavery (and slavery's aftermath) is inextricably linked to the physical, emotional, and spiritual pathologies of bodies that deny themselves food (as Sethe does in her obsession with feeding her apparently returned from the dead daughter, Beloved), or chronically overeat (as Beloved does in her desire to become real), or that simply live with an abiding and nameless hunger (as does Sethe's surviving daughter, Denver). Marked in and on the bodies of slaves and their descendants, the institution of slavery itself is figured as an infecting agent of illness, much as abolitionist writing saw "slavery as a poison or disease that affects both the body and politic of the nation and the body natural of each citizen" (Titus 200). In *Beloved*, one of the manifestations of that illness is the relatively quotidian, quiet starving and excessive eating that today sends scores of women to treatment centers, therapy, and self-help groups, and is typically looked upon as a problem of middle-class white women.[1] In Morrison's hands, however, the issue is not control of food in order to create superior bodies, but the survival of bodies rendered inhuman and useful only for work and reproduction under the economy of slavery.

Having fled Sweet Home plantation nine months pregnant with a network of raw and still bleeding whip wounds on her back, Sethe gives birth to a baby girl in the woods and manages to make it to freedom, meeting up with her other children and her freed and gifted mother-in-law, Baby Suggs, where she lives until the slave master hunts her down. Refusing to be recaptured or submit her children to a life of slavery, Sethe cuts the baby's throat and attempts to kill the others before she is stopped. The slave master decides she is not worth keeping and she is soon freed from jail, living with her mother-in-law (until her death) and other children in a rural area close to Cincinnati, Ohio. The murdered baby haunts the house for years, driving away Sethe's two sons, Howard and Buglar when they are old enough to flee. After Sethe's friend Paul D (and himself a former Sweet Home slave) comes to live at 124 Bluestone, the ghost leaves but returns in embodied form, as the girl, Beloved.

What does it mean that a novel set in the slave era employs representations of overeating, starvation, and complicated notions of embodiment? Unlike many contemporary theories of women and eating disorders that tend to focus on low self-esteem, childhood abuse, and other family dysfunction as etiological factors, and even those that contextualize eating disorders within a social context, *Beloved* adds the dimension of historical memory and institutionalized, as well as internalized, racism. I am not suggesting that Morrison is particularly interested in revising current notions of women and eating disorders in *Beloved*, but that her use of the imagery raises important questions about the nature of such issues and their connection not just to the individual body (or the familial body) but the body politic as well.[2] Becky W. Thompson, in her book on women of color and eating disorders, argues that "portraying [eating problems] as individual 'disorders' rather than responses to physical and psychological distress is part of a historical tendency to mislabel the results of social injustices as individual pathologies" (6). Morrison creates both: a pathologized body and the reality of gross social injustice, refusing to separate the two.

In the 1980s, a body of work by women began looking at food, eating (or dieting) and the function of slenderness along with its relation to gender and social control.[3] In *Beloved*, however, Morrison appropriates overeating and starvation as tropes for marking historical memory on the bodies, minds, and souls of African Americans. The returned ghost child, Beloved, fantasizes her mother, Sethe, "chew[ing] and swallow[ing]" her, but, conversely, "Beloved ate up [Sethe's] life, took it, swelled up with it, grew taller on it" (250). As boundaries erode by way of food transactions, Morrison interrogates the limits of human interdependence and its extremes of symbiosis. Food in *Beloved* provides an analytic frame for the destructive mechanism of internalized racism. Sethe's body becomes the site of racism's agency, turning against itself as she slowly starves, carrying out the brutal work of dehumanization rooted in slavery, but in this instance, unaided by slave owners or cruel foremen. Instead, racism is maintained by, and finds fulfillment in, Sethe's body itself as she comes to be literally consumed—and enslaved—by Beloved's hunger. For Denver, the starvation is less literal, but the loss of boundaries, a sense of self, as well as her tremendous hunger for Beloved to recognize and bestow identity upon her is no less significant.

Surrounding the women's individual hungers are the sounds of "voices that ringed 124 like a noose" (183). These voices come from "[t]he people of the broken necks, of fire-cooked blood and black girls who had lost their ribbons. . . . What a roaring" (181). The sounds of the "Sixty million and more" play like a drone throughout the novel, never letting readers forget that the individual pain and disturbance represented in *Beloved* cannot possibly be comprehended without their historical and social context. While James Berger argues that the historical trauma is also "introduced into the narrative primarily through the figure of the returning and embodied ghost" (415), it is also mapped on Sethe's body in the shape of the tree that was left on her back after the whip lashes healed and in her slowly starving body after Beloved returns and begins to consume her. The voices that ring the house—the potentially liberating memory of historical outrage—become paradoxically the noose that makes possible the perpetration of more injustice and suffering and is replicated inside the house as the two women become so tied to Beloved and her rage that they are nearly destroyed.

Within slavery's logic, Sethe—and all slaves—must be considered as non- or subhuman for the system to maintain itself. To justify commodification, slaves must be seen as bodies only. Susan Bordo observes that slavery deepens the already powerful dehumanization of racism, commenting that "the legacy of slavery has added an additional element to effacements of black women's humanity. For in slavery her body is not only treated as animal body but is property, to be taken and used at will. Such a body is denied even the dignity accorded a wild animal; its status approaches that of mere matter, thing-hood" (11). Thompson describes "the existential nightmare of slavery," where "no self was legally recognized and therefore the body could not exist for the self either" (17). In *Beloved*, Sethe and Denver repeat the existential nightmare as they become enslaved to Beloved's demands and they cease to exist for/as/to themselves. To complicate things, the slave body, maintained solely to work for a white master, carried within it the potential of becoming an anti-body under racism's yoke, one that could lose its ability to resist the infection of slavery and its dehumanizing commodification, and ultimately turn against itself. Even though the female slave body was accorded value only as a commodity that added to the owner's capital, Sethe resisted while she was a slave, choosing instead (rather than being arbitrarily marked as a breeder) the man with whom she would have children, and fleeing with those children when their survival was at stake. As a slave, she had known powerful resistance to "thing-hood," so much so that she fled Sweet Home, her back ripped open by the whip, and in her final month of pregnancy. This rage to survive, however, later turns against her when that resistance leads her to extraordinary violence and she is haunted by the guilt of her actions. Killing her "already crawling" baby and attempting to murder her other children to save them from slavery, Sethe becomes crushed by it, ironically, paradoxically, fulfilling racism's function, much as an antibody would in an immune system—a system of resistance—when that system breaks down, leaving it open to serious, often fatal illness.

Baby Suggs knows that the slave body is ultimately disposable once its utility is gone. Moreover, a slave body that loves itself is subversive, dangerous to a society that relies on slave capital. It is for this reason that Baby Suggs leads the community in a body-loving, body-affirming worship each week, telling her people that, "the only grace they could have was the grace they could imagine" (89) and that imagination and self-love was an act of powerful resistance because it flew in the face of racist (and slaveholding) beliefs and practices:

> And O my people they do not love your hands. Those they
> only use, tie, bind, chop off and leave empty. Love your hands!
> Love them. Raise them up and kiss them. Touch others with
> them, pat them together, stroke them on your face 'cause they
> don't love that either. *You* got to love it, *you*! And no, they
> ain't in love with your mouth. Yonder, out there, they will see
> it broken and break it again. What you say out of it they will
> not heed. What you scream from it they do not hear. What
> you put into it to nourish your body they will snatch away and
> give you leavins instead. No, they don't love your mouth. *You*
> got to love it. (88)

"They," the white world, will deny nourishment to the African American
body, much as Beloved finally does to Sethe. In this powerful homily,
Baby Suggs at once critiques slavery and racism, situating them in human
evil, and invokes the slave body as human—created to be powerful,
nourished, and beloved.

For Sethe, however, who has attempted to shut down the memories
of slavery at Sweet Home and the killing, the beloved one is not her
body, but an "other," the insatiable ghost who comes to haunt and
destroy her. Beloved becomes the "they" who "do not love your flesh,"
but "despise it," as Baby Suggs says. Resistance in Baby Suggs's terms—
self-love—is broken down as Sethe becomes more and more isolated
from the community and fights to keep the memories submerged, leaving her vulnerable to destructive power. Instead of self-love and a nurturing community, Sethe embraces Beloved as a cure for the pain of
slavery and for the lacerating memories of the murder. It is not the
heroism of her past that haunts Sethe ("collected every bit of life she had
made all the parts of her that were precious and fine and beautiful, and
carried, pushed, dragged them through the veil, out, away, over there
where no one could hurt them" [163]), but the guilt of murder. This
guilt is reinforced by the community's complicity in Sethe's isolation and
by Paul D's condemnation when he later learns what had happened.
Sethe's need to be relieved of her guilt allows Beloved to become a
totalizing force in her life and thus to fulfill racism's agenda of annihi-
lation of the strong African American woman-self Sethe had been in the
past. Indeed, Sethe's attempt to satisfy Beloved becomes a form of self-
consumption, as her own body begins to break down from lack of food
(that Beloved eats instead).

Beloved's monstrousness is, in many ways, a projection of Sethe's
own perception of herself as the monstrous mother/other as it is
constructed in nineteenth-century racist discourse. The nineteenth-
century ideal of domesticity and the effacing, nurturing (white, middle-
class) mother throws into bold relief Sethe's actions, making them

seem even more horrible. Sethe yearns and fights for her children's freedom, but under slavery, is forced to see herself as murderous. Henderson says, however, that at the heart of Sethe's struggle is a desire for counternarrative: "Sethe must compete with the dominant metaphors of the master('s) narrative—wildness, cannibalism, animality, destructiveness. In radical opposition to these constructions is Sethe's reconceptualized metaphor of self based on motherhood, motherliness, and motherlove" (79). As she works toward another way of seeing herself, Sethe struggles with the dismembered bits of her past in the metaphors of the internalized narrative and thus they are intolerably painful to her. The master narrative only allows her to see herself as that mother who murders and drives away her children. Thus, her heroism is eclipsed by her notion of herself as devouring mother—ironically reversed as the devoured child returns to devour her.

SETHE AND THE COST OF FORGETTING

When Paul D comes back into Sethe's life years after they had been slaves at Sweet Home plantation, he observes her eyes "like two wells into which he had trouble gazing," and remarks to himself that they "needed to be covered, lidded, marked with some sign to warn folks of what that emptiness held" (9). Sethe seeks to fill her emptiness after Beloved returns in embodied form, with obsessively feeding the once-dead child. She does this to satisfy her own need to obviate the trauma, to erase the memory of her slave past and to have, not only the memory of Beloved's murder dissolved, but also the very act itself, and to find a way to that sense of herself as a (fiercely) loving mother. As long as Beloved remains embodied, Sethe is "excited to giddiness by the things she no longer [has] to remember" (183), since Beloved "understands it all. I can forget how Baby Suggs' heart collapsed; how we agreed it was consumption without a sign of it in the world. Her eyes when she brought my food [in prison], I can forget that, and how she told me that Howard and Buglar were all right but wouldn't let go each other's hands" (183–184).

Not only is Sethe haunted by her notion of herself as a monstrous mother and trapped by the burden of slavery's history, but, she later realizes, she is also haunted by her past as a daughter. Much as a trauma survivor would do, Sethe suddenly remembers, while talking with Beloved, "something she had forgotten she knew." This was "something privately shameful that had seeped into a slit in her mind" (61), the time Nan, the woman who cared for her after her mother was hung, told her that her mother had thrown away all of her children but Sethe: "The one from the crew she threw away on the island. The others from more whites she also threw away. Without names, she threw them. You she gave the name of the black man. She put her arms around him. The others she did not put her arms around. Never. Never. I am telling you, small girl Sethe" (62).

For Sethe, this moment of memory is much like the Auschwitz survivor for whom her testimony, her remembering marks a moment of profound change. Unlike the Auschwitz survivor, however, for whom remembering is a "breaking out of Auschwitz even by her very talking" (Laub 62), for Sethe there is no breaking away. Sethe's newfound knowledge is "not simply a factual given that is reproduced and replicated by the testifier, but a genuine advent, an event in its own right" (Laub 62), but leaves her still trapped in the frightening knowledge that her mother, too, murdered her children. The lone survivor of her brothers and sisters, Sethe struggles under the weight of that and other memories (significantly figured as food), which she futilely fights.

> She shook her head from side to side, resigned to her rebellious brain. Why was there nothing it refused? No misery, no regret, no hateful picture too rotten to accept? Like a greedy child it snatched up everything. Just once, could it say, No thank you? I just ate and I can't hold another bite? . . . But my greedy brain says, Oh thanks, I'd love more—so I add more. And no sooner than I do, there is no stopping. (70)

Beloved's advent is so powerful precisely because she has the power—or so Sethe thinks—to change the past, and thus, to change Sethe's sense of self. Reversing the process of her hungry, greedy brain eating the terrible memories, Sethe compulsively feeds Beloved instead, eventually at the expense of her own body. With Beloved's presence, Sethe becomes fixed, not with resisting or rewriting the master narrative, but appeasing it—as manifested in her frantic attempts to please Beloved. Within the discourse of oppression, Sethe's memories cannot come together in a healing counternarrative, but continue to haunt her with the unspoken (and unspeakable) possibility that she has always been the monstrous mother, and is the daughter of a monstrous mother as well.

Sethe's driving hunger to feed Beloved is also linked to the violent and traumatic interdiction of maternal desire she experienced at Sweet Home, what Lynda Koolish calls a "rupture of maternal love" (425), when Schoolteacher's nephews held her down and "took [her] milk." One obvious and powerful way of resisting thing-hood, under the terms of slavery, is to give nurture to one's own chosen child. Koolish argues that this rupture is

> signified not only in the murder of Beloved but also in Sethe's frantic, failed attempt to provide sufficient breast milk to her nursing babies. The extraordinary unquenchable thirst and

> hunger of Beloved is the mirror of Sethe's obsession with
> getting milk to her daughter, enough milk, milk she alone
> could provide. . . . Even before the theft of her breast
> milk. . . . Sethe's breasts did not—could not contain milk
> enough to feed all who hungered. (425)[4]

The need to feed one's child is so elemental that Sethe's desire becomes
another way she is rendered vulnerable to Beloved's power to overtake
her. The theft of her milk and Sethe's response to it signals the profoundly complicated relationship of maternal desire to the commodified
female slave body. Paul D's incomprehension at the punishment Sethe
received for telling on the boys is eclipsed by Sethe's outrage at the
original act itself:

> After I left you, those boys came in there and took my milk.
> That's what they came in there for. Held me down and took
> it. I told Mrs. Garner on em. . . . Them boys found out.
> . . . Schoolteacher made one open up my back, and when it
> closed it made a tree. It grows there still. . . . "They used
> cowhide on you?" "And they took my milk." "They beat you
> and you was pregnant?" "And they took my milk!" (17)

The boys' act underscores Sethe's function as a slave: to produce food
for whites as they consume her. The maternal slave body becomes yet
another function in the economy of slavery—providing a valuable re-
source to whites—motherhood stripped of agency, a motherhood of
absence. Thus, in the terms of the master narrative, Sethe becomes the
terrible mother doubly, not only because she kills her child, but also
because she subverts the slave economy by doing so. This act of resistance complicates and intensifies Sethe's guilt in the eyes of the law: she
is not only a monster of a mother, but she is also an enemy of the state.
    It is no accident that Beloved "laps devotion like cream" (243)
and that for Sethe, Beloved represents the opportunity to try to reclaim her desired role as nourisher and undo not only the murder, but
the always present theft of her milk. It is by way of the desire to
nourish and nurture her children that racism's power overtakes Sethe
through Beloved. As a slave woman, Sethe simply cannot win. As the
mother who denies herself, she begins to approximate the prescribed
role for nineteenth-century women, but it nearly kills her. Thus the
novel exposes the catch-22 for Sethe. As long as she attempts to negotiate her identity as mother to Beloved within the crucible of nineteenth-
century (white) domesticity and the institution of slavery, her sense of
self is eroded more and more.
    Arriving from under a bridge, literally just born from the water,
Beloved is exhausted and violently thirsty. Immediately upon seeing

Beloved in the yard, Sethe's bladder fills "to capacity" and bursts forth, much as it would if her water had broken from the womb. Significantly, Sethe's first observation is that Beloved is "[p]oorly fed" (51). Indeed, Beloved's craving for the sweets ("sugar could always be counted on to please her" [55]) and other foods with which Denver and Sethe ply her suggests that those foods are only appetizers: what she truly wants is Sethe herself, as her eyes "lick," "taste," and "eat" Sethe (55). Beloved explains to the lovestruck Denver that Sethe is "the one. She is the one I need. You can go but she is the one I have to have" (76). As she attempts to feed Beloved (and thus quell the pain of memory) Sethe slowly starves. The first thrill of realizing that Beloved had "come back to her," and, ironically, her belief that she would never have to be haunted by the memories again, turns to anguish as Beloved becomes both accusing and increasingly demanding: "Beloved . . . said 'do it,' and Sethe complied. . . . Beloved accused her of leaving her behind. Of not being nice to her, not smiling at her." The present becomes conflated with the past as Sethe tries to explain her actions to Beloved, who only throws the history of slavery and hunger in her face:

> And Sethe cried, saying she never did, or meant to—that she had to get them out, away, and that she had the milk all the time and had the money too for the [grave]stone but not enough. That her plan was always that they would all be to- gether on the other side, forever. Beloved wasn't interested. She said when she cried there was no one. That dead men lay on top of her. That she had nothing to eat. (241)

Storytelling becomes another way to feed Beloved, and so Sethe becomes locked to her not only through food, but by constantly keeping Beloved entertained. Sethe's connection to the ghost child becomes symbiotic as her need for forgetting and mercy grows in proportion to Beloved's rage to be re-membered, embodied, and, always, fed. But while Sethe is desperate to "beat back the past," she also is "[l]oaded with [it] and hungry for more" (70). The burden of the past haunts Sethe as much as the disembodied baby ghost, and later becomes the embodied ghost. As hungry as she is to mother Beloved, she is also desperate to make sense of the past, to "re-memory" it, and in so doing, to loosen its hold on her. Beloved's demands on Sethe, however, become more and more intense, "and when Sethe ran out of things to give her, Beloved invented desire" (240). She wants Sethe's company, she dresses in Sethe's clothes, imitates her, and even carries herself "the same way down to the walk, the way Sethe moved her hands, sighed through her nose, held her head" and sometimes, for Denver, "it was difficult . . . to tell who was who" (241). But Beloved grows in size, becoming obese, and Sethe shrinks. Sethe cannot sleep and loses all interest in taking care of her physical body, sitting in a chair, "licking her lips like a chastised child while Beloved [eats] up her life, [takes] it, [swells] up with it, [grows] taller on it" (250). And so Sethe diminishes with the force of her own hunger. Rather than consuming food, Sethe becomes food for the embodied ghost.

Although her children are able to care for themselves (Howard and Buglar have long since run away from the frightening house), Sethe has lived constantly with the pain of not being able to nourish her babies. That, along with the need to fight off, to obviate, the past, shifts with Beloved's presence, which becomes the embodiment of all the horrors Sethe has tried to escape. Instead of facing them, however, she mistakenly believes Beloved's presence will erase them, and relieve her of any guilt or blame. In Sethe's mind, Beloved has to remain with her. They are locked in an exhausting symbiosis. When Sethe coughs up something that isn't food, but is a part of her own body, Denver finally realizes that she is literally dying of starvation.

DENVER AND THE EROTIC GAZE

When Beloved comes to live at 124 Bluestone, Denver becomes a ghost to herself. Having known loneliness for most of her life, Denver is starved for community. The house had become an island of isolation after the baby's murder, "no visitors of any sort and certainly no friends" for twelve years (9). Baby Suggs's withdrawal and eventual death severed Denver's connection with life-affirming energy. Her loneliness is figured in the text also as hunger. Her secret hideaway is an "emerald closet," made up of the space within "five boxwood bushes ringed round . . . closed off from the hurt of the hurt world, [where] Denver's imagination produced its own hunger and its own food, which she badly needed because loneliness wore her out. *Wore her out*" (29). Denver describes her extreme loneliness and the undercurrent of fear that she lived with always, and how she had only had the disembodied ghost for company all her growing up years (for Beloved had haunted 124 Bluestone for years before her embodiment), confessing,

> I love my mother but I know she killed one of her own daughters, and tender as she is with me, I'm scared of her because of it. . . . [A]nd there sure is something in her that makes it all right to kill her own. All the time, I'm afraid the thing that happened that made it all right for my mother to kill my sister could happen again. I don't know what it is, I don't know who it is, but maybe there is something else terrible enough to make her do it again. I need to know what

> that thing might be, but I don't want to. Whatever it is, it
> comes from outside this house, outside the yard, and it can
> come right on in the yard if it wants to. So I never leave this
> house and I watch over the yard, so it can't happen again and
> my mother won't have to kill me too. (205)

But "whatever it is" does come back and, through the mechanism of her
desire and fear, is nurtured, held, and maintained in Denver's life. Beloved is she whom both Denver and Sethe assume they want when in fact
she brings slavery's institutional energy—racism. Beloved's appearance
sharpens Denver's sense of loneliness and she becomes possessively attentive to the girl who arrives with a fever, "breathing like a steam engine"
(53). In addition, Beloved defuses Denver's fear; for if Beloved was killed
and has returned, then Denver can maintain the illusion that she is
(relatively) safe from the thing that made Sethe kill once before. Accordingly, Denver's attentiveness becomes an obsession with Beloved as she
nurses her back to health, forgetting to eat or even to visit her former
hideaway, the emerald closet.

Intensely erotic, Denver's gaze at Beloved becomes "food enough to
last. But to be looked at in turn was beyond appetite; it was breaking
through her own skin to a place where hunger hadn't been discovered"
(118). Denver also "nurs[es] Beloved's interest like a lover whose pleasure was to overfeed the loved" (78). In such passionate moments, Denver
loses all sense of herself; her "skin dissolve[s] under that gaze" and she
"float[s] near but outside her own body" (118). And yet, while she
imagines herself disembodied, she also has the sense of being seen, being
made visible by Beloved ("You are my face. You are me" [216]). Denver's
enslavement to Beloved is manifested in the lengths she would go to
preserve the loss of self/reconstruction of self that Beloved catalyzes:

> The present alone interested Denver, but she was careful to
> appear uninquisitive about the things she was dying to ask
> Beloved, for if she pressed too hard, she might lose the penny
> that the held-out palm wanted, and lose, therefore, the place
> beyond appetite. It was better to feast, to have permission to
> be the looker, because the old hunger—the before-Beloved
> hunger that drove her into the boxwood and cologne for just
> a taste of a life, to feel it bumpy and not flat—was out of the
> question. Looking kept it at bay. (119–120)

For Denver, "anything is better than the original hunger" that grew out
of the ordeal of witnessing her own and her brothers' near-extinction at
their mother's hands and Sethe slitting Beloved's throat. Loneliness and
the isolation that came when Sethe refused the community's sympathy
("trying to do it all alone with her nose in the air" [254]) motivated

Denver's retreat with her mother into the world of 124 Bluestone. Denver's panic at the thought of losing Beloved, whom she imagines to be her only tie to a textured life is ironically rooted in her own loss of self:

> If she stumbles, she is not aware of it because she does not know where her body stops, which part of her is an arm, a foot or a knee. . . ."Don't," she is saying between tough swallows. "Don't. Don't go back." . . . Now she is crying because she has no self. Death is a skipped meal compared to this. She can feel her thickness thinning, dissolving into nothing. She grabs the hair at her temples to get enough to uproot and halt the melting for a while. (123)

It is, however, Beloved's ephemeral body that cannot exist without the bodies of Denver and Sethe. And yet, both Denver and Sethe believe that without Beloved they will in one way or another cease to exist. All three characters struggle to be real, articulated human beings, but they look for that realness to come from the other. Beloved's realness is contingent upon Sethe's and Denver's isolation and unfed hungers—always connected to the institution (slavery) and events (atrocities at Sweet Home) that led up to her murder in the shed. For Sethe, realness depends upon Beloved exonerating her for the murder, something she is incapable of doing, since she embodies not only her own rage, but the rage of millions of dead slaves. In attempting to find freedom in Beloved, Sethe entraps herself in a life-draining enterprise, for it is from a cipher that she attempts to feed her hunger for forgiveness. And for Denver, the realness she seeks exists in relationship, only the relationship is with a ghost who drains the sense of identity necessary to maintaining human relationships. She pleads with Beloved, "You are my face; I am you. Why did you leave me who am you?" (216).

COMMUNITY AND RESISTANCE

By mapping all three characters' hungers, it is possible also to see the lineaments of resistance and healing. Sethe and Denver, while marked by the history of slavery, are also survivors. But institutional barbarity moves in and through bodies, its symptoms manifesting in various ways. In *Beloved*, the trope of hunger and overeating foregrounds how the body simultaneously adapts to oppression and resists it. As Sethe and Beloved grow more tightly entwined and their boundaries increasingly dissolve, hunger (both Beloved's and Sethe's) and food render Sethe virtually invisible to herself. Sethe seeks to ease her guilt and grief, to become the mother/self she could not be under slavery by giving over her volition to Beloved. Similarly, as Denver feeds Beloved, she loses all sense of herself except as she is reflected in Beloved.

Sethe's insistence on feeding her own children, on guarding her "milk," has isolated her more and more from the community. This isolation is compounded by the community's own judgment of the murder and isolation of Sethe for what they perceive as her prideful ways, creating the chasm in which Beloved thrives.[5] Because of Sethe and Denver's hungers, it is not surprising that food becomes a means to community and healing, and inverts the existing structure of isolation at 124 Bluestone. While feeding Beloved only makes her more monstrous, when Denver and Sethe accept the gift of food from women in the community, they necessarily open their hands, a gesture signifying the end of the totalizing hold Beloved has required to stay embodied. For once they let go of her, Beloved floats away. They cannot do this alone, and it is only when Denver observes Sethe and comes to realize the seriousness of the situation that things begin to change:

> [T]he flesh on her mother's forefinger and thumb was thin as china silk and there wasn't a piece of clothing that didn't sag on her. Beloved held her head up with the palms of her hands, slept wherever she happened to be, and whined for sweets although she was getting bigger, plumper by the day. Everything was gone except two laying hens. (239)

Driven by the greater fear that they would all starve to death, Denver, "step[s] off the edge of [this] world" (239), into another that awaits her, drawing upon the affirming spirit (a different kind of ghost presence) of her grandmother, Baby Suggs, who has come to help her make the crossing from isolation into community. Denver is terrified:

> "But you said there was no defense."
> "There ain't."
> "Then what do I do?"
> "Know it, and go on out the yard. Go on." (248)

There is no defense against racism and death and Baby Suggs knows this well, but she also knows the absolute necessity of being for and with each other, feeding and being fed, being a healing community in the face of evil.

After Denver walks out of the house, she goes to her former teacher. When Lady Jones provides rice, eggs, and tea, she becomes the first to break the community's silence. For one as hungry and isolated as Denver has been, the act of receiving food from another woman represents the beginning of a radically disruptive, new way of thinking: "having a self to look out for and preserve" (252). In this moment, Denver begins to create a new discourse for herself—one that resists the master narrative within which the body could not exist for the self. As food begins to appear in the yard regularly, Denver leaves home to return the empty baskets to each woman, being welcomed back into the community with every visit. Each woman leaves a sign of her identity on her gift of food so that Denver will not only return thanks and the empty bowl or pan, but she will have direct contact, thereby reestablishing her links to the world outside 124 Bluestone. The names inscribed on the baskets and bowls of food proclaim identity, selfhood, and bodies who want to keep themselves, along with Denver and Sethe, alive. Denver is not the only one who breaks through to another narrative, however. In the process, the women begin to remember life with Baby Suggs (who was the community's preacher), "the days when 124 was a way station, the place they assembled to catch news, taste oxtail soup, leave their children, cut out a skirt" (249), and they soften in their condemnation of the pride that filled Sethe's house. They learn from Janey Wagon (with whom Denver has begun working as a domestic) just why Sethe is in such straits: "Sethe's dead daughter, the one whose throat she cut, had come back to fix her" (255). In addition, by drawing on their own memories of violation and trauma, the women build solidarity with Sethe and find within themselves empathy for her suffering that creates a bridge over and out of the endlessly circulating guilt and self-destructive power that Beloved's presence maintains.

Through her fear for her mother, Denver slowly lets go of her obsession with the destructive, eating ghost, and allows herself to be nourished by others. Denver's compulsion to hold on to Beloved's presence is every bit as painful and difficult to let go as an addiction. The point is that she cannot and does not have to come to this in a vacuum. First Baby Suggs's ghost and then strong African American women intervene to empower Denver. It is in the act of moving out of the loop of isolation at home and allowing herself to be nurtured, nourished, by other women, that Denver's healing begins and that the chain binding Sethe and Denver to Beloved is weakened.

Beloved complicates the notion of community, however. One could argue that Denver, Beloved, and Sethe form their own community. Obviously, just because it is a community does not make it liberating. Theirs is closed, tightly constructed, and ultimately destructive. The text bids readers to ask, what are the terms of a healthy community? In the closed community, boundaries blur and are transgressed as identities break down. As Denver leaves this community for another, she goes where she is fed, moving from starvation to being nurtured by hands other than her own. But Denver has taken the first step. She draws on the life-affirming spirit of Baby Suggs and moves out into the dangerous but potentially healing world. In addition, the women have done their own shifting, seeing Sethe's plight differently than before. Without them,

Sethe is not empowered to move beyond Beloved's hold. When she hears the women's rage (all thirty of them), which connects them to the rage of the sixty million dead slaves, she listens, comes to the door. This same power expressed by the women is that which led Sethe to kill (and therefore save from slavery) her daughter, but unfocused and isolated, it turned against her, leading her to forget that which the women's voices awaken:

> They grouped, murmuring and whispering, but did not step foot in the yard. Denver waved. A few waved back but came no closer. Denver sat back down wondering what was going on. A woman dropped to her knees. Half of the others did likewise. . . . [A]mong those not on their knees, who stood holding 124 in a fixed glare, was Ella, trying to see through the wall, behind the door, to what was really in there. . . . Ella had been beaten every way but down. She remembered the bottom teeth she had lost to the brake and the scars from the bell were thick as rope around her waist. She had delivered, but would not nurse, a hairy white thing, fathered by the "lowest yet." It lived five days never making a sound. The idea of that pup coming back to whip her too set her jaw working and then Ella hollered. (258–259)

Ella's yell ruptures the shell of silence around 124, and while Denver is the link between the community and Sethe, Ella first connects directly with Sethe through the hell of her own experience, and the other twenty-nine women quickly join her. Although she had previously shunned Sethe, Ella taps into her own knowledge of suffering and leads the rest of the women into a powerfully articulated anger: "Instantly the kneelers and the standers joined her. They stopped praying and took a step back to the beginning. In the beginning there were no words. In the beginning was the sound, and they all knew what that sound sounded like" (259).

The healing fury of the community is set against the evil of racism, not the bodies on and in which racism has done its evil. As Ella remembers—with power—her rape and the birth of the "hairy white thing" and her resistance to becoming a victim, she focuses that same rage and resistance against the rapaciousness of Beloved. She also connects her own acts of infanticide with Sethe's and sees them both as profoundly painful acts of resistance to dehumanization and the master narrative that structures such dehumanization. This fury is not leveled against the dead child, but against the monster that racism has created and that Sethe's desire has permitted, the monster that seeks to devour her and Denver.

Collectively, the women drive Beloved from 124, thus ending the murderous nooselike isolation that has choked Sethe and Denver. An agent in her own healing, Sethe finally walks out of the house and into the group of women; they do not drag or even bring her out. She allows herself to be re-membered into the community, but not dissolved into it. This process is figured as a reverse of Beloved's coming, when Sethe lost her water and became lost in Beloved. Here, the sound of the women's voices "[breaks] over Sethe and she tremble[s] like the baptized in its wash" (261). Her figural rebirth back into a community of strong women protects Sethe when she mistakes Mr. Bodwin (the man who "had kept [her] from the gallows in the first place"), for the slave catcher. As she runs towards him with an ice pick, reenacting what had happened years before, the women "make a hill. A hill of black people, falling" and obstruct her (262).

And so Sethe's obsessive, isolated feeding of Beloved ceases with the embodied ghost's departure. She has eaten food made and offered by women from the community, has allowed herself to be fed, and has been strengthened enough to receive the gift of their intervention when the women come into her yard to "save her from a futile cohabitation with loss" (Handley 699). In this way, Sethe has opened her hands to receive food and to let Beloved go when the women come to drive her away. The erased self is reinscribed by food and the women's presence. Food allows Sethe not only to survive physically, but becomes the means for her to rejoin a powerful community—rich in historical memory and knowledge. As Sethe and Denver leave their isolation, they also experience what Beloved had taken from them: a sense of identity as well as personal boundaries. They both have the opportunity to discover and relearn interdependence within this community as Denver's first acceptance of food begins to weaken the circulation of slavery and racism's power binding the three women.

Sethe's grief at losing Beloved is intense, but Paul D tells her it isn't Beloved, but Sethe herself who is her own "best thing." This is not a concept to be internalized easily, and yet Sethe begins to reclaim her identity and her memories, and the annihilating work of racism is interdicted through hers and the community's powers of resistance. Beloved's memory remains, but it is a rememory, one that has the potential to cure rather than destroy. For Beloved's power as embodied suffering—of the sixty million and more—cannot, should not, be forgotten. Once Sethe no longer needs to run from the memories, however, she can use them as she creates a life-affirming resistance to racism, based on presence rather than loss. It is in human bodies that the evil of racism plays itself out and it is through the process of becoming re-membered (into oneself and into a healing community) and allowing the self to be nurtured—fed—that the body encounters the power to resist destruction. In *Beloved*, food and feeding have the potential to both destroy and heal. Morrison's text becomes a space in which history's horrible record of racism and slavery is played out within female bodies and through hunger. Beloved the child will never be forgotten, should never be forgotten, just as the "sixty million and more" should not be forgotten. But neither should their memory continue slavery's bitter legacy. The women have brought food. The noose is loosened. Sethe the starved becomes Sethe the fed, and is on her way, quite possibly, to becoming Sethe, her own best thing.[6]

NOTES

I am, as always, grateful to my colleague, Marisa Alicea, for her thoughtful comments on earlier drafts of this essay, and to Tamar Heller for her helpful suggestions.

1. Edwidge Danticat's novel *Breath, Eyes, Memory* is a notable departure from the usual connection of eating disorders with white middle-class women. In it, the protagonist, a Haitian-American, struggles with bulimia and the struggle to come to terms with her sexuality, her family heritage, and her identity.

2. This is not the first time Morrison has employed the trope of food and eating to construct a narrative of trauma focusing on the destructive effects of racism. In *The Bluest Eye* Morrison uses food—specifically Mary Jane candies— to signal Pecola's desire to annihilate her (Black) self and become a blue-eyed (white) self:

> Each pale yellow wrapper has a picture on it. A picture of little Mary Jane, for whom the candy is named. Smiling white face. Blond hair in gentle disarray, blue eyes looking at her out of a world of clean comfort. The eyes are petulant, mischievous. To Pecola they are simply pretty. She eats the candy, and its sweetness is good. To eat the candy is somehow to eat the eyes, eat Mary Jane. Love Mary Jane. Be Mary Jane. (43)

3. See, for example, Susie Orbach, *Fat is A Feminist Issue: The Anti-Diet Guide to Permanent Weight Loss*; Orbach, *Hunger Strike: The Anorectic's Struggle as a Metaphor for Our Age*; Kim Chernin, *The Obsession: Reflections on the Tyranny of Slenderness*; Chernin, *The Hungry Self: Women, Eating and Identity*; Joan Jacobs Brumberg, *Fasting Girls: The Emergence of Anorexia Nervosa as a Modern Disease*; Michelle Mary Lelwica, *Starving for Salvation: The Spiritual Dimensions of Eating Problems Among American Girls*; and Lilian Furst and Peter W. Graham, eds. *Disorderly Eaters: Texts in Self-Empowerment*.

4. Koolish also points out that the "extravagant feast" given by Sethe and Baby Suggs after Sethe's escape is "Sethe's failed attempt to provide a community stay against spiritual and physical hunger, metaphorically, to feed "Sixty million and more," to feed a hunger that spanned continents and time frames, to quench a thirst that the subsequently arriving Beloved will bring from another time, another place" (425).

5. I think Koolish has it right when she asserts that the community is protecting themselves from the terrible knowledge of "what Sethe's act implicity reveals"—that the consequences of slavery were many times worse than Beloved's murder—and it is for this reason that they reject Sethe (426).

WORKS CITED

Berger, James. "Ghosts of Liberalsim: Morrison's *Beloved* and the Moynihan Report." *PMLA* 3.3 (May 1996): 408–420.

Bordo, Susan. *Unbearable Weight: Feminism, Western Culture, and the Body.* Berkely: U of California P, 1993.

Bromberg, Joan Jacobs. *Fasting Girls: The Emergence of Anorexia Nervosa as a Modern Disease.* Cambridge: Harvard UP, 1988.

Chernin, Kim. *The Hungry Self: Women, Eating, and Identity.* New York: Times Books, 1985.

———. *The Obsession: Reflections on the Tyranny of Slenderness.* New York: Harper, 1981.

Clifton, Lucille. *Good Woman: Poems and a Memoir 1969–1980.* Brockport, NY: BOA, 1987.

Danticat, Edwidge. *Breath, Eyes, Memory.* New York: Vintage, 1995.

Furst, Lilian, and Peter W. Graham, eds. *Disorderly Eaters: Texts in Self-Empowerment.* University Park: Pennsylvania State U, 1992.

Handley, William R. "The House a Ghost Built: Nommo, Allegory, and the Ethics of Reading in Toni Morrison's *Beloved.*" *Contemporary Literature* 85.4 (1995): 676–701.

Henderson, Mae G. "Toni Morrison's *Beloved*: Re-Membering the Body as Historical Text." *Comparative American Identities: Race, Sex, and Nationality in the Modern Text.* Ed. Hortense J. Spillers. New York: Routledge, 1991.

Koolish, Lynda. "Fictive Strategies and Cinematic Representations in Toni Morrison's *Beloved. African American Review* 29.3 (1995): 421–438.

Laub, Dori. "Bearing Witness or the Vicissitudes of Listening." *Testimony: Crises of Witnessing in Literature, Psychoanalysis, and History.* Ed. Shoshana Felman and Dori Laub. New York: Routledge, 1992.

Lelwica, Michelle Mary. *Starving for Salvation: The Spiritual Dimensions of Eating Problems Among American Girls.* New York: Oxford UP, 1999.

Morrison, Toni. *Beloved.* New York: Knopf, 1987.

———. *The Bluest Eye.* New York: Simon & Schuster/Washington Square, 1970.

Orbach, Susie. *Fat is a Feminist Issue: The Anti-Diet Guide to Permanent Weight Loss*. New York: Berkley Books, 1978.

———. *Hunger Strike: The Anorectic's Struggle as a Metaphor for Our Age*. London: Faber, 1986.

Thompson, Becky W. *A Hunger So Wide and So Deep: A Multiracial View of Women's Eating Problems*. Minneapolis: U of Minnesota P, 1994.

Titus, Mary. " 'This Poisonous System': Social Ills, Bodily Ills, and *Incidents in the Life of a Slave Girl*." *Harriet Jacobs and Incidents in the Life of a Slave Girl: New Critical Essays*. Ed. Deborah M. Garfield and Rafia Zafar. New York: Cambridge UP, 1996.

Waniek, Marilyn Nelson. *Magnificat: Poems*. Louisiana State UP Baton Rouge, LA, 1994.

7

"There Is No God Who Can Keep Us from Tasting": Good Cannibalism in Hélène Cixous's *The Book of Promethea*

Chris Foss

In Hélène Cixous's *The Book of Promethea* images of hunger and appetite abound as metaphors for both sexuality and creativity. The most striking element in this figurative vocabulary is the trope of cannibalism that, in many ways, is central to the text's re-visioning of the self-other relation. In her recourse to this controversial trope of cannibalism (usually reserved by feminists for masculinist appropriation of the feminine Other), Cixous effects a consciously ironic, at times playful, but ultimately revolutionary rescription of a masculine economy that traditionally has disempowered women. She bases this rescription on an ethic of generosity that grows out of the text's revolutionary re-visioning of the self-other relation. Ultimately it is this ethic of generosity (with its emphasis on "taking in" rather than "taking over") that enables *Promethea* successfully to transform the traditional masculine economy of love/ desire, along with the phallogocentric myths and tropes that undergird it, into an empowering feminine alternative and an expression of a truly liberating love.[1]

Promethea's narrator explicitly relates her own cannibalism to that primal linking of sex and eating in the Garden of Eden: "And cannibalism? Once one begins to smell it, putting the apple in one's mouth

149

doesn't take long" (57). She explains, "Of course, when it is a woman the movement is very slow but eventually there is no god who can keep us from tasting" (57). Such cannibalism, she suggests, is "good cannibalism" (59), a cannibalism that is not ghastly or ghostly or grotesque, but rather generous and loving and fulfilling. One usefully may see such good cannibalism as a textual embodiment of Cixous's alternative feminine economy—and, thus, an examination of the dynamics of this trope offers substantial insight into the dynamics (and, ultimately, the outcomes) of this feminine economy.

In "The Author in Truth," Cixous claims that "the genesis of 'femininity' goes by way of the mouth, through a certain oral pleasure, and through the nonfear of the inside" (151).[2] This brief statement highlights a central concern of Cixous's throughout her distinguished career, namely, the relationship between orality and feminine writing (*l'écriture féminine*). At the same time, it also subtly suggests an emphasis on re-visioning what for Cixous is the founding myth of Western culture, the Book of Genesis and its scene of the apple. "The Author in Truth" is Cixous's almost worshipful meditation on Clarice Lispector's *The Hour of the Star* and, more specifically, on the "libidinal education" it offers its readers. According to Cixous, texts of libidinal education such as Lispector's are "always on the trail of the first story of all human stories, the story of *Eve and the Apple*" (149). "In these stories," she states, "the fate of the *so-called feminine economy* is at stake" (149).

Cixous's feminine economy presents itself as an alternative to the appropriating logic of phallogocentrism. Her frustration with the phallogocentric use of language as a cultural system that imposes oppressive binary values is readily apparent in her willingness to grant that *feminine* is itself a problematic descriptor for an economy which "is not the endowment solely of women" (149). For Cixous, because one always finds oneself "preceded by words," it is important both to acknowledge the role of words in reducing unformed and fluid thought expressions to particular meanings and to challenge the limits of words by opening up their forms and making them more fluid: "[W]e could replace them with synonyms, which would become as closed, as immobile, and petrifying, as the words 'masculine' and 'feminine,' and they would lay down the law for us. And so? There is nothing to be done, except to shake them all the time, like apple trees" (150). For Cixous, writing is a daring, if not transgressive, activity that restages the scene of the apple, a scene in which one (re)negotiates one's relationship to desire and to prohibition, to pleasure and to the Law, and ultimately to the thought process itself and to language.

Cixous, then, while acknowledging its limitations, utilizes the term *feminine* to qualify one's "relationship to pleasure" (150). For her this feminine relationship to pleasure is positive, is open, and is distinctly oral. In her re-visioning of the scene of the apple—the struggle between "the word of the Law (or the discourse of God) and the Apple" (150)—she observes that "knowledge could begin with the mouth, the discovery of the taste of something" (151). The apple, she says, "is visible, is promise, is appeal—'Bring me to your lips'; it is full, it has an inside" ("Author" 151). Indeed, in this particular scene of the apple Eve (standing in for all participants in the feminine economy) discovers "the inside of the apple, and this inside is good" (151). Eve's "relationship to the interior, . . . to the touching of the inside, is positive" (152). In this one grasps why "the genesis of 'femininity' goes by way of the mouth, through a certain oral pleasure, and through the nonfear of the inside"—Cixous's feminine scene foregoes the forbidden to focus on the fruit. Thus, "Every entrance to life finds itself *before the Apple*" (150).

Susan Rubin Suleiman has noted that Cixous's mode of writing gradually developed away from the anger of the "ironic feminist polemic" in "The Laugh of the Medusa" and toward "a mode of feminine lyrical celebration" (xvi) whose themes revolve around "the relations between writing, giving, nourishment, love, and life" (viii). She associates this development with the influence of Lispector (among other influences), and thus "The Author in Truth" represents a crucial text in this shift.[3] At the same time, that essay is first and foremost about Lispector, and as such should not be expected to provide extended insight into Cixous's own feminine writing (however similar their projects may be). Cixous's *Promethea*, a novel from roughly the same period that has been largely ignored in America, offers precisely such an opportunity for in-depth study.[4]

Promethea, the story of the love relationship between a goddess-like embodiment of feminine writing (Promethea) and her partner (the narrator), is an expression of love as much as it is a book about love. Cixous always has stressed that writing is intimately connected to love's open, outgoing gesture toward the other. In "Coming to Writing" she claims, "I write for, I write from, I start writing from: Love. I write out of love. Writing, loving: inseparable. Writing is a gesture of love" (42). In "The Laugh of the Medusa" she suggests she owes her own opportunity to write to earlier poets who were "capable of loving love and hence capable of loving others" (283). Such poets thus express the "other love" that generates *l'écriture féminine*, the "new love" that "dares for the other, wants the other, makes dizzying, precipitous flights between knowledge and invention" ("Laugh" 297). Cixous concludes the essay by explicitly positing writing and love as inextricably interrelated: "When I write, it's everything that we don't know we can be that is written out of me, without exclusions, without stipulation, and everything we will be calls us to the unflagging, intoxicating, unappeasable search for love" (297). For her "the text is always written under the sweet pressure of love" ("Coming" 43), the same love which creates "the space and the desire for endlessness" ("Coming" 44). *Promethea* (as a novel) allows Cixous to explore/exploit the "desire for endlessness" she sees as characteristic of both love and writing through extended metaphors of hunger and appetite, and in the process offers more detailed insight into the orality of this "other" sort of love.

Promethea is Cixous's most extended, in-depth portrayal of the sort of self-other relation made possible through the desire for endlessness embodied in the act of love/writing.[5] Near the end of "The Author in Truth" Cixous posits that one of the most important themes in *The Hour of the Star* is "recognition of the difference of the other . . . accompanied continually, for the subject, by the possibility of being the other" (177). This is one of the most important themes in *Promethea* as well, where Cixous brings her project of rescripting phallogocentric myth to bear on how love/writing leads to a new self-other relation based upon a feminine libidinal economy. *Promethea* simultaneously re-visions the Genesis and the Prometheus myths, restaging both the scene of the apple and the scene of the eagle by means of a figurative vocabulary of orality in which images of hunger and appetite serve as metaphors for how love/writing "dares for the other, wants the other."

Prometheus, of course, brought the gift of fire to humanity and consequently was punished by Zeus, who nailed him to a mountain peak where an eagle fed upon his liver daily. Aeschylus credits Prometheus with providing humanity with many of the arts of civilization and, in his revision of Aeschylus, Percy Bysshe Shelley specifically links his fire bringer to the powers of poetry in *Prometheus Unbound*.[6] In her own re-visioning of the Prometheus myth, Cixous's imagery revolves around the main Promethean motifs of the eagle and of fire. Significantly, in both cases her utilization of these motifs is informed by the dynamics of hunger and appetite. This recourse to imagery of orality links her own scene of the eagle with the scene of the apple as a scene of love/writing.[7]

In other words, Cixous's recourse to images of hunger and appetite effects a continual restaging of the scene of the apple. Her narrator at one point offers Eden as her stomach's geographical equivalent when, in explaining why she does not "rest easy on this earth," she echoes *Paradise Lost:* "I have a small uterus that contracts too often, east of my stomach" (31). Later she claims to have made her book "in the hollow of the Tree of Knowledge" (198). It is her trope of good cannibalism that allows her to couple her rescripted scene of the eagle and scene of the apple in such a way that the former is revealed as itself simply another version of the latter. Before turning to Cixous's rescripting of phallogocentric violence and punishment, however, one must first delineate the radical re-visioning of the self-other relation that underlies such figurative strategies.

Promethea follows the development of its couple's relationship as Promethea leads the narrator to abandon the more traditional self-other relation for one characterized by a fluxional process of continuous transformation and "self"-dissolution in which the very boundaries between self and other are intentionally blurred. At first, the narrator can only dream of the freedom Promethea seems to embody. Cixous establishes an explicit contrast between a Promethea who is so "naked" and "innocent" and a narrator who is "girded in suspicions, [is] feathered in forebodings, arguments, word constructions" (10). Part of the narrator's armor is her split persona, a division between her living self (which she refers to as *H*) and her writing self (the narrative voice of the text). This division represents a crack already present in the wall of the narrator's ego boundaries, yet for the most part the split is more regressive than revolutionary. Although divided, both of these selves are fairly clearly demarcated from the outset, which not only prevents them from collapsing into one another but more importantly preserves both personas as indisputably self, never potentially othering. Promethea, one learns, has reproached the narrator for this "little maneuver" (12). Through her relationship with Promethea, however, the narrator will move increasingly closer to the possibility of being "the same woman who lives and writes" (11). Promethea, as "the person who has not cut the cord binding words to her body" (154), embodies the love inspiring the narrator's exploration of their relationship through writing: "I write to come close to Promethea" (14). Fittingly, the narrator represents their love as a writing on one another's hearts (92–93).

In *Promethea* love/writing enchants "without respecting the famous invisible and shimmering line between different sorts of things" (6). Both partners see the boundaries of their "self"-constructions become increasingly more fluid, to the point that the pair seem—like writing and love—inseparable. Such blurring becomes more and more apparent as the book moves along. Early on the narrator confesses that distancing herself from Promethea is like distancing herself from her own heart (27). Cixous intensifies such fusion in her use of ambiguous pronominal antecedents: the reader is unsure whether such pronouns refer to Promethea or to the narrator. At one point the narrator confesses, "I no longer know if 'she' is Promethea or me, in these notes" (139). The narrator actually only compounds the confusion by signaling that these distinctions are simply not always that important. A number of times she is merely content to write that "one of us" (meaning either her or Promethea, or even H) said this or did that, implying not only that it is something not clearly attributable to one or the other, but also perhaps that either way it was rather both of them anyway—or perhaps even that ultimately it is simply not important who it was, or if it was one or both.

Promethea continually shifts between an endless number of roles and analogues, from Shelley's Prometheus to Christ, Acteon, Genie, Amazon, and (perhaps most frequently) Pegasus. These shifts are not limited to specific analogues, however; she is also an arrow, a city, a doe, a lioness, a mountain, the rain, the sea, a ship, and a vampire, among countless others. She assumes these roles and analogues almost simultaneously: "Promethea is a woman? Yes. Is a mare? Yes. Is also a Yes? Yes to all I want" (150), claims the narrator. Her wild ride on Promethea's back through myriad positionings encourages her own transpositional process, and that begins to break down the traditional self-other relation. The narrator flows through her own diverse stream of roles (including an army, a bird, a fish, and a shadow) and analogues (including Moses, Jonah, Diana, and Prometheus). Yet in the relation between these two lovers—both of whom move through such roles and analogues not simply in isolation but often in connection with the other's figural shifts—Cixous redraws the traditional boundaries between self and other. In fact, the two flip-flop between positions in a number of paired roles, including hunter/prey, queen/slave, and (most noticeably) mother/child.[8]

This fluid commingling of roles and analogues serves to problematize standard conceptions of those roles and analogues. For example, in the intentional conflation of the roles of mother and child, Cixous forces the reader toward a parodic new logic that breaks down the traditionally defined boundaries of those roles, illogically accepting the new relations that somehow allow for such fluid crossovers.[9] On the same page, for instance, the narrator tells Promethea both "Already I am in your belly" and "I brought you into the world. I nursed you" (114). The blurring is even more explicit when at one point the narrator offers a sentence in which she is mother to Promethea ("Give me your thirsts so I can give you my breast") and then in the very next sentence reverses the roles ("Give me your thirsts so I can drink them, suckle me with the milk of your fears") (117). What one means by *mother* or *child* is no longer clearly definable; these terms are complicated rather than clarified by their relation to one another. Here, in this fluid representation of breastfeeding (with its emphasis on taking in, not just taking), flows the generosity of Cixous's feminine economy. Such feminine fluidity leads to the dissolution of self-other boundaries in the relationship, a relationship in which it is less a matter of one person appropriating the other to herself than it is a matter of discovering the impossibility of knowing where one person's boundaries begin or where the other's end.

Promethea may be "always in transfiguration" (152), but at the same time she still is first and foremost a woman (151). Cixous's narrator, against the ever-present "danger of gynocide," also insists from the beginning on her experience as a woman's experience: "I owe it to all the veiled women in the world to believe that I must still stubbornly utter the magical, unveiling credential words 'I am a woman'" (9). Significantly, despite her wariness of the words *masculine* and *feminine*, Cixous does not dispense with biology. *L'écriture féminine* does not "cut the cord binding words" to the body; it writes the body, and the particular body Cixous writes (as a woman) is the female body.

This emphasis on the body in fact leads Cixous to a view of writing as a bodily function. Writing seizes her "from some bodily region" ("Coming" 9), she claims, "from an inconceivable region deep down inside [her] but unknown" (10). Not surprisingly, then, she employs a figurative vocabulary drawing from bodily processes in order to express the sort of dynamic produced by an openness to love/writing. Thus, *Promethea*'s narrator frequently figures writing along the lines of the nourishment of the mother's milk, the ultimate gesture of love. Indeed, in "Coming to Writing" Cixous explicitly links these two bodily processes: "[W]riting, too, is milk. I nourish. And like those who nourish I am nourished" (49). If writing is nourishment, so too is love. *Promethea*'s narrator insists "there is no barrier" between the mouth/the palate/the throat and the breast/the heart (113). If, as I have argued, throughout *Promethea* Cixous shows how the act of love/writing leads to a blurring of boundaries between self and other (between the one who writes and the one who is written, between the one who loves and the one who is loved), then it is this act's fundamental connection to bodily processes such as nourishment that invites Cixous to represent the process of re-visioning which it embodies by means of metaphoric evocations of hunger and appetite.

Early on Cixous's narrator describes her transformative experience of loving/writing Promethea as a process both terrifying ("I am scared to death") and mouth watering ("It is delicious") (12). In fact, the word *delicious* reappears throughout the book as an apt descriptor of love/writing. The narrator characterizes her experience of a lovemaking in which there seems to be "only one body" as "Delicious closeness" (54).[10] She later describes her "art" of writing as an attempt "to capture the moment" with words: "I want to toss [a beautiful moment] handfuls of delicious words so gluttony will keep it there" (112). Still later she refers to her writing as an "odd sort of gluttony" that "regurgitate[s] and taste[s] all over again the figurative Promethea" while the real one is away (158).[11] Love too is figured as hunger, both "delicate hunger and raging hunger" (65–66). All of this leads the narrator to speak of her "sublime appetite" where Promethea is concerned (53).

Promethea, like her male mythological counterpart, is a fire giver. Cixous's narrator reports, "Promethea has rekindled dreams of fire in me," and, "Promethea brings the fire of all dreams up into reality" (24). As one might expect, however, the characteristic Cixousian blurring allows for the narrator to be cast as the fire giver as well: "[A]nd what if Promethea does not like my plateful of fire? . . . I want you to taste it; eat my fire, Promethea" (36). Fire in *Promethea* represents writing/love/desire/sex all at once, though sometimes figured more explicitly as one or the other in a particular passage. The narrator speaks of writing her book about Promethea as a fiery experience. She speaks of crawling to a "dish of coals" at which she will "suck real fire," wondering if one can eat and sing at the same time (24–25).[12] She wants to "translate fire into songs": "I want to understand its tongue, I want to grasp its words, I want to put them in my mouth, suck on them. . . ." (40–41). This Promethean fire connotes more than her writing, however; it is specifically linked to her love for Promethea as well. When the narrator's vision turns "more fiery more burning," she claims, "I am describing you to me, I am describing desire" (67). Later, shortly after confessing that love "eats" her up, she asks Promethea, "[T]ake me into your fire and consume me" (144).

In that same passage she describes her "suffering" in the fire of love: "[A]lready I am dying, silently, entangled gazes moaning" (144). The age-old double entendre in *dying* as sexual orgasm is clearly in play here, and one might extend this back into an ironic wordplay in God's punishment of death for tasting the apple (especially given the intimate connection between the Tree of Knowledge and sexual knowledge). Indeed, sexual puns and connotations dominate much of the fire imagery. The sexual implications are at times extremely explicit: "Sometimes this is a burning bush. Crouching before the fire I contemplate it and adore it until it gives in and calls me. Then I move up, I slide between its burning breasts, I suckle the flames. I cry "Softer! Harder!" I blow on my own pyre. . . . I say: "Don't burn me too fast! I want to taste every spark" (62–63). Even here appetite and eating inform Cixous's figurative vocabulary. Just as good cannibalism is both "torment and feast," so the fires of love/writing are all the more pleasurable for their pain. The experience of fire and its appetites is both consuming and transforming, both violent and ecstatic. Given Cixous's view of writing as bodily function and her view of it as an act of love, the double entendre others have read into the title of her "seminal" essay "Coming to Writing" seems almost too obvious. Certainly this sense of *coming* is in play when *Promethea*'s narrator explains "why [fire's] coming feels so violent" (41).

Such metaphorical linking of violence with sex/love/writing pervades *Promethea*, particularly in Cixous's restaging of the scene of the eagle. At different places in the text the narrator is the eagle to Promethea's tortured Titan only to suffer a reciprocal torture in which Promethea is her eagle. Thus in one passage the narrator writes, "[A]nd her, spread out, it was as if Promethea was waiting for her eagle . . . feeling so hungry, so hungry for that pain" (140); in another, "'Be the eagle!' I ask Promethea. And she does. 'Dig in!' I say. And she does" (42–43). The function of these passages as metaphoric descriptions of lovemaking rescripts some of the connotations of violence and domination at the heart of patriarchal appropriation. These figurative representations of love/writing[13] employ a vocabulary of hunger and appetite to rescript oppressive constructions reinforcing the Law of the Father into sexually and creatively liberating options re-visioning traditional cultural meanings.

One effect is simply to drain such violence of its figural power by utilizing it ironically and playfully. Cixous also drains its figural power by blurring the very distinction between such violence and feminine lovemaking, by going so far as to incorporate it into and subsume it within such lovemaking. At the same time, attributing selfish, possessive, even violent urges (though only metaphorical) to her female lovers deftly deconstructs "self"-less femininity. Indeed, taking this even one step further, Cixous also encourages us to see such urges as actual tendencies within both Promethea and the narrator. Acknowledging that such feminine-oriented individuals are not immune to the more regressive tendencies of human nature makes them and their love more real, more human (instead of representing some naïve, idealized perfection).

The most powerful, if not the most controversial, of Cixous's figural rescriptions remains her trope of cannibalism. This trope does not simply repeat the process of rescripting phallogocentric violence set in motion by the more general hunger imagery and by the more specific fire and eagle imagery, but rather actually underlies virtually all of the figurative reconceptions of love/writing delineated above. Invitations to consume, to devour, to dig in certainly in their own way reflect cannibalistic urges. That one may see the trope of cannibalism as underwriting all of these evocations of hunger/appetite returns one to the scene of the apple, to the "genesis of 'femininity' " through the "certain oral pleasure" that is love/writing as good cannibalism. Seen in this light, as scenes of love/writing in which one's relationship to pleasure is transformed ("[E]ventually there is no god who can keep us from tasting"), *Promethea*'s scenes of the eagle and all of its hunger imagery in general are revealed to be—on a fundamental level—part of a continuous restaging of the scene of the apple. Above and beyond these, however, there are enough passages in which Cixous's imagery unmistakably refers to the appetite for and eating of one another's flesh to establish this trope as perhaps the major motif in *Promethea*. Given Cixous's yoking of her good cannibalism with the scene of the apple, one justifiably may expect that attention to this motif will bear much fruit, providing a fuller understanding of her conception of love/writing.

Predictably, Cixous's cannibalistic imagery refers to both love and writing. "The story of love," according to *Promethea*'s narrator, is "that one starts loving the things one will end up devouring" (58). Her own book, she says, is sometimes called "Promethea delivered" because "it delivers a pound of Promethea" (63). Promethea's reaction to this is to tell the narrator, "[Y]ou can cut me up in bits and eat me," to which the narrator replies, "I've already done it some. I just wrote that" (63). The allusion to the famous "pound of flesh" from William Shakespeare's *Merchant of Venice* implies it is Promethea's heart that is delivered up as the price of love/writing. This cannibalistic love/writing is a delivery not only in the sense of "to hand over" but also "to produce" (along with this meaning's association with "to give birth"). The childbirth metaphor clearly in play here is especially significant in that its association of the delivery of the narrator's book (love/writing) with the delivery of a baby serves to deconstruct the phallogocentric binary of male creativity versus female procreativity. This maneuver shows love/writing to be a truly liberating activity for the narrator, and in so doing opens up yet another level of meaning to *delivery*, "to rescue" or "to set free." The narrator in fact prepares the reader for such an association a few pages earlier when she fantasizes about being food in the marketplace, "waiting there for Promethea to come and choose me, deliver me, taste me, swallow me, absorb me the way I want to eat her" (59).

In typical Cixousian fashion, the dynamics of hunger and eating are multi-dimensional and multi-directional. The narrator tells Promethea both, "My flesh is what I have to serve you," and, "I need your body to feed my daily being" (122). The imagery at times is quite graphic: "I shall tear you apart. I shall make your blood spurt out. . . ." (64). Yet this violence seems to be what makes her cannibalism's restaging of the scene of the apple possible, delivering Cixous's characters from the stain of original sin. At one point the narrator reads Promethea's cry of "I want you to split open my breast, I want you to set my heart free" as an invitation ("eat my heart") that is actually a request ("I want to be the apple between your teeth, take my life" [154]). Later, H's desire to eat Promethea, to "bite her, cut her throat, consume her, yes, die from the need," is represented as a punishment for Promethea's innocence in order to "make her feel the terrible delights of primal suffering" (179).

The narrator occasionally presents this restaged and cannibalistic scene of the apple as defying all logic. Just as Promethea's desire to have her heart eaten, "to be the apple," is "[i]nexplicable" (154), so the narrator's own desire ("the need to enter [Promethea's] flesh, the need to sink my whole self into her belly") is "[i]ncomprehensible" (118). It is indeed incomprehensible, she continues, "the way we cannot avoid becoming primitive, ruthless gods" (118). Yet the narrator's elaboration on what she means by "becoming primitive, ruthless gods" (namely, "The need to bring her to her knees, to get down on my knees" [118]) does in fact offer some sort of insight into the parodic "illogic" behind Cixous's cannibalistic yoking of violence to love/writing. Her recourse to cannibalism—with all its talk of licking, sucking, tasting, and eating—obviously on one level is a playful depiction of lovemaking between two women (as is, here, being down on one's knees). But certainly it is also more than that, as it is more than merely an ironic appropriation of tropes (holy communion, prayer) traditionally associated with "the word of the Law (or the discourse of God)."[14]

The key to the illogic behind Cixous's cannibalism lies in its continually breaking down/through the traditional boundaries insisted upon by rational logic. The blurring of self-other boundaries accomplishes part of this assault: at any given moment one of the lovers is burning, devouring, eating, on her knees; at the next, the other is; at the next, they both are. Cixous's ironic rescripting of love as violence (and violence as love) also contributes to her undermining of phallogocentrism. As I argued above in relation to her scene of the eagle, this too is a revolutionary blurring of sorts. *Promethea*'s narrator refuses to accept, to be locked into, a comfortable mindset of preestablished rules and definitions. In forcing us to consider love/writing and violence together, she prevents the concrete of their conventionally antithetical construction from setting, from hardening. Just as she speaks of a good cannibalism, so she speaks of a "pure violence" (39), of "the vital violence of life" (19). Inhaling this "vital violence" allows one to voice the simultaneous "admiration" and "terror" of life "without false modesty" (19). It allows one to discover "the ordinary marvelous banal human violence of her emotions," that one is a "devourable devouring human being" (131). The working out of Cixous's aesthetic of *l'écriture féminine* in the trope of cannibalism, in other words, forces one to confront the interimplication of love/writing and violence.

As a result, this cannibalistic aesthetic expresses rather than represses aggressive/regressive urges—but in the ever-shifting ground of the relationship there is no room for such urges to take root. They are immediately followed by another (perhaps completely contradictory) urge and yet another, without allowing any single urge to define the relationship. Cixous's narrator admits, "[I]n love not all is love"—there is also "injustice, anger" (65). It is both "innocent hungers and cruel hungers" (66). In coming to terms with how "in love not all is love," she remembers to note "with drops of blood, sweat, and urine, before everything *dries*," that in love/writing one has "to forget, to not forget, to distance savagery" (64). Here one finds an embrace of the duality (or, rather, multiplicity) to human experience and one recalls the lesson of Robert Louis Stevenson's *Jekyll and Hyde*, that it is not healthy to develop the sort of split personality fostered by the rigid logic of binary thinking. She will continue the process of loving and learning generosity while admitting she still feels (violent) urges for control.

Cixous's approach to love/writing is thus perhaps a more honest, less idealized one in that her narrator acknowledges the range of human desire and emotion in a way that refuses the fairy tale vision of an untainted love destined to dispose of the forces of evil in an airbrushed happily ever after ending. Acknowledging that no love is perfect, or perfectly selfless, is the first step in preparing oneself (and one's relationship) for the inevitable moments of tension and conflict. It is to refuse to deny human selfishness and violence, and thereby to attempt to be able to defuse their ability to surprise and overcome one's love (or, perhaps more appropriately, one's "other love").

In this way Cixous powerfully rescripts the dynamics of phallogocentric thought into a liberating alternative, beating the Master's tools/spears of violence into plowshares in hopes of a more fertile future for her "other love." *Promethea*'s narrator claims, of the dynamics of love/writing, "it is a matter of possession" (71)—only to insist that the lesson in this is that one "had to begin learning dispossession" (85). Thus, she later comments, "Rereading this book I notice that it has a unity: a book on relinquishment, dispossession and possession" (136). Verena Andermatt Conley has argued that "the most difficult part is to keep the love in movement, to remove it from a dialectic of *avoir, non-avoir*, linked to possession" (128). As Cixous herself puts it in "Clarice Lispector," "[T]he trick is "not to absorb the thing, the other, but to let the thing present itself" (63). Accordingly, as Betsy Wing has astutely observed, "[M]uch of Cixous' work has been concerned with love and how it may be lived without one member of the couple (or both—though in our culture, most frequently the woman) being destroyed through a passive incorporation into the other" (v).

What is truly ironic about Cixous's project in *Promethea* is that she presents this "other love" (which does not possess, incorporate, destroy) through images of hunger and appetite, and of violent cannibalism. The narrator claims that her "cannibalistic tendencies" are feelings of which in the past she would "almost have been ashamed," but that now they make her "almost proud. Or at least at peace" (56), that "if there is such a thing as good cannibalism then ours is it" (59). What makes this cannibalism good is "the secret of good taking": instead of taking over, "if you take something, take it in, learn" (159). This "good taking"

(taking in rather than taking over) is at the heart of the ethic of generosity informing Cixous's conception of love/writing. According to the narrator, "I used to call what I now call generosity, dependency, and I thought it was bad" (55). Through Promethea she learns that, while "it is easy to love and sing one's love," "true greatness" consists in "letting oneself be loved, entering the magic and dreadful circle of generosity, receiving gifts" (20). Unlike the one who loves, who remains focused on oneself (one sings about oneself in declaring "I am in love" or "I love her"), the one who is loved must be willing to abandon this self-centered positioning in order to admit one's need for the love of another (one's dependence upon the other) and, perhaps more importantly, to acknowledge another's love for oneself. In this way one considers the other as subject rather than object ("s/he loves me") so that one can begin to take in and learn rather than to take over and appropriate.

One may usefully compare this ethic to the "hymn-to-want," to the "economy of positive lack," which Cixous delineates in her discussion of Lispector's *Passion According to G. H.* in "The Author in Truth" (164). In such an *"economy of recognition,"* one understands how "hunger is faith" (164). One understands that to need is a "strength": "Needing is a spiritual offering of one's hand to the other, and offering one's hand is not a demand; it is a greeting to the world, a giving place" (166). For *Promethea*'s narrator, then, it is better to receive than to give: "Giving requires no courage, but to receive love so much strength, so much patience, and so much generosity must be extended. Only then can love descend upon us the way it wants" (105). Such an ethic represents a revolutionary re-visioning of an existing ethic of generosity—the Christian "It is better to give than to receive."[15] "Receiving" here is in a sense to acknowledge one's need for the other in a way that accepts that other as a legitimate self in its own right (a self worthy of learning from). But it is also more than that. It is "entering the magic and dreadful circle of generosity" in which one is both self and other, other and self. One both gives and receives (takes in)—one both loves and is loved, writes and is written, eats and is eaten. One enters into a literal give-and-take in which the boundaries between the two selves are no longer quite so clear cut.

Ultimately, of course, good cannibalism is only a metaphor, and this fact is in itself only fitting given the deconstructive embracing of process-oriented "illogic" it embodies in the text. As the narrator confesses of her desire to possess Promethea, "I only dream of doing all this . . . I just want to starve you a little—all the better to feed you immediately" (106). Continuing on, she writes, "I want only to imagine how I could achieve your transmutation, but how terrible if I tried, if I succeeded, if I lost you!" (106). However extreme, Cixous's cannibalistic imagery speaks bodily desire in a way that does not repress such desire but that also does not allow its violence to become actualized beyond its expression as desire. Its temporary positioning therefore cannot be established as a defining trope over and against the imagery of generosity. Immediately after the preceding passage, the narrator adds, "As far as war is concerned I am truly a woman: I do not want to win" (106). Here Cixous explicitly links her good cannibalism to an economy of love which rescripts phallogocentric taking over as feminine taking in. She explains, "I do not really want to eat Promethea the way Penthesilea was determined to eat Achilles" (59). Or, one might add, the way Achilles (who fights and kills her only to realize he has fallen in love with her in the process) was determined to eat Penthesilea. No, the narrator explains, "As for our cannibalism, it remains unfulfilled in reality"; "I will never have to eat Promethea" (59).

Still, this good cannibalism is a powerful and empowering metaphor: "If I imagine a piece of Promethea in my mouth . . . I don't let go of my pen . . . and I love it, because I love [her]" (60). It is powerful because even if "unfulfilled in reality," it still "makes itself felt, very real indeed, in the stomach, in the esophagus, in the palate, because in terms of passion, that's where we are: at that untenable distance that threatens always to disappear" (59). "Keeping it," the narrator continues, "is a matter of delicate balance" (59). It is empowering because it figures forth the feelings of hunger and appetite which, as expressions of bodily desire, reinforce the notion of process one must embrace if one is to preserve this delicate balance between love/writing and violence. For this reason "one must never stop giving [love] limits to devour" (120).

Cixous's narrator tells us, "[W]hen we sleep on the brink of the abyss we dream of hell and of paradise. I would like to emphasize that it is there, on the edge of the world, that paradise begins" (60). "Love's real hell," she says, is that "beyond the edge of the world everything must be created," requiring "superhuman" effort (60). Yet, she confesses, "the truth is that the process of arriving in paradise is pure paradise" (59). This process is, she says, like gardening, both "a joy and backbreaking labor," for "if one wants to stay everyday one must accomplish the impossible again" (60). Here again one finds oneself in a garden in paradise, at the scene of the apple. A bit later on the narrator claims, "We are creatures for recreating and recreating. Our constant recreation is what is at stake" (87). One may read *recreation* both as "creating again"/"creating anew" and as "play"/"leisure"/"diversion," and in this one sees how Cixous's paradise is both "a joy and backbreaking labor." It is both, not one or the other, simultaneously the recreation growing out of its feminine orientation to pleasure and the re-creation growing out of its rescripting of phallogocentric myth/thought. This process of continually living/loving/writing the delicate balance that is good cannibalism can be, like much hard work, truly invigorating—and one certainly works up an appetite! Thus, in Cixous's cannibalistic re-staging of the scene of the apple, "We are not of the first paradise—the one that could only be lost. Here it is all to be won" (60). And even if, as the narrator remarks, there are "no free apples these days," surely apples so dearly purchased are "even more delicious, even more astounding, for being won" (60).

NOTES

1. I use *feminine* (as opposed to *lesbian* or *female*) here, and throughout the chapter, in an attempt to avoid being construed as making an essentialist argument, since Cixous herself insists that *feminine* is not a gender-specific term. Granted that, because the love relationship she portrays in *Promethea* is shared by two women, one therefore might claim that Cixous's re-visioned economy is a specifically lesbian one. Certainly her own knowledge of "the feminine" is necessarily informed by her experience as a woman in a way that, say, Jean Genet (whom Cixous cites numerous times as a feminine writer) would not have experienced it as a man. Yet, while types of difference such as sexual preference and biological sex do provide distinct (and therefore important) inflections of such economies, and while Cixous's feminine economy perhaps is more likely to be most pronounced in lesbian relationships, Cixous would insist that gay, heterosexual, and other love relationships also might be based upon the same ethic of generosity (even if, especially in the case of heterosexuality, such a possibility might be less likely).

2. Cixous writes, "It is not anatomical sex or essence that determines us in anything; it is, on the contrary, the fable from which we never escape, individual and collective history, the cultural schema, and the way the individual negotiates with these structures, with these data, adapts to them and reproduces them, or else gets around them, overcomes them, goes beyond them, gets through them—there are a thousand formulas—and connects with or never connects with a universe 'without fear and without reproach' " ("Author" 155).

3. Of course, as Suleiman acknowledges, this is not to say the early texts (including "The Laugh of the Medusa") lack their own moments of feminine celebration. She cites "Coming to Writing" (1977) as "a text in point, astonishingly varied in tone and mode" (vxi).

4. Cixous originally presented an early version of "The Author in Truth" as a lecture in 1984. The revised version is collected in *"Coming to Writing" and Other Essays* (1991). *Promethea* originally appeared in French in 1983 (not long before the aforementioned lecture) and was published in English in 1991 (fittingly, the same year as "The Author in Truth").

5. Because for Cixous these two actually are "inseparable," I have chosen to represent them as one act (*love/writing*) that always in a sense entails both even when seemingly applied specifically to one or the other. *Love* here encompasses feelings of desire and acts of lovemaking (sexuality) in addition to its broader sense of strong, heart-felt affection. *Writing* refers primarily to the feminine writing Cixous dubs *l'écriture féminine*, but it also invokes creativity in general.

6. Shelley, like Cixous, saw writing as a gesture of love. In *A Defence of Poetry*, he suggests that both Love and Poetry involve "a going out of [one's] own nature" (487) whereby one "put[s] [one]self in the place of another and of many others" (488). Jerrold E. Hogle, in his landmark Shelley book, argues that Shelley's poetics reveal an aesthetic of what he calls *radical transference*. This aesthetic, "a centerless displacement of figural counterparts by one another" (10), employs a strategy of disruptive mythography as one of its means of re-visioning the Prometheus myth. I find a remarkably similar disruptive mythography at work in *Promethea*.

7. Given Cixous's recourse to images of hunger and appetite, it is interesting to note that, according to Hesiod, Prometheus already had angered Zeus by saving choice meat from the sacrifices to the gods to help feed humankind.

8. One may see the first two of these paired roles as participating in the same rescripting of phallogocentric violence and punishment that Cixous effects in her cannibalistic scenes.

9. I derive my emphasis on continually shifting definitions and categories evolving out of an aesthetic based on relationship from Hogle's virtuoso delineation of the "illogic" (197) of parody in Shelley's poetics. Hogle builds on Dorothy van Ghent's teasing out of "parody's most literal signification, its placing of one 'song [*ode*] next to [*par*]' another" (196). In this version of parody a "set of words" such as mother/child becomes "a 'beside song' where a construct is positioned alongside (or at a slight distance from) the source of its own, now reworked, materials" (Hogle 196). This "newer formation presents those ingredients as radically disrupted and reorganized by a totally different gravitation between elements," offering in place of the traditional definitions a "relational order" in which the "juxtaposition of similar groups of figures blatantly definable only by different lexicons or modes of interrelation is exactly what forces [the] reader into working out how the new logic could operate" (Hogle 196). Ultimately, then, the reader "must construct the new option, not just by proposing the redefinitions" of particular sets of terms like mother/child, but even more so "by accepting . . . the incessant transformation of all the reworked terms" (Hogle 197)—here of not only all the roles and analogues associated with either the narrator and/or Promethea, but also all the various rescripted scenes (and, in particular, the scene of the apple).

10. Interestingly, even here one finds that characteristic Cixousian blurring in that it is not clear whether one of the partners has been subsumed into the other or whether they truly have become one. In a passage representative of many others, the narrator reports, "I claim mine was the body taken, Promethea swears she was invaded" (54).

11. Cixous utilizes multiple linkings of cooking and writing throughout the text. See, for example, 28–29 and 184–86.

12. This section calls to mind the famous passage from Shelley's *Defence* in which he figures "the mind in creation" as a "fading coal" (503–04).

13. The violent imagery in Cixous's scenes of the eagle refers to the experience of writing Promethea as well as loving her. For instance, in the sentence immediately preceding the sentence in which the narrator asks Promethea to be the eagle and dig in she confesses, "The pages closest to my heart are the ones that hurt me most to write" (42).

14. One is reminded of Christina Rossetti's sexually charged appropriation of eucharistic imagery/vocabulary in the famous line 471 of *"Goblin Market"* ("Eat me, drink me, love me"), an appropriation all the more charged for having followed Lizzie's request of Laura in the preceding lines 466–68: "Come and kiss me. / Never mind my bruises, / Hug me, kiss me, suck my juices."

15. The Christian ethic is obviously a revolutionary ethic in its own right, though weakened by ages of lip service. The good cannibalism of the narrator and Promethea offers a very different sort of lip service indeed.

WORKS CITED

Cixous, Hélène. "The Author in Truth." Trans. Deborah Jenson, Ann Liddle, and Susan Sellers. Cixous, *"Coming to Writing" and Other Essays.* 136–81.

———. *The Book of Promethea.* Trans. Betsy Wing. Lincoln: U of Nebraska P, 1991.

———. "Clarice Lispector: The Approach." Trans. Sarah Cornell, Susan Sellers, and Deborah Jenson. Cixous, *Coming to Writing" and Other Essays.* 59–77.

———. *"Coming to Writing" and Other Essays.* Ed. Deborah Jenson. Cambridge: Harvard UP, 1991.

———. "The Laugh of the Medusa." Trans. Keith Cohen and Paula Cohen. *The Signs Reader: Women, Gender, and Society.* Ed. Elizabeth Abel and Emily K. Abel. Chicago: U of Chicago P, 1983. 279–97.

Conley, Verena Andermatt. *Hélène Cixous: Writing the Feminine.* Lincoln: U of Nebraska P, 1984.

Hogle, Jerrold E. *Shelley's Process: Radical Transference and the Development of His Major Works.* New York: Oxford UP, 1988.

Rossetti, Christina Georgina. "Goblin Market." *The Pre-Raphaelites and Their Circle.* Ed. Cecil Y. Lang. Chicago: U of Chicago P, 1975. 130–143.

Shelley, Percy Bysshe. *Shelley's Poetry and Prose.* Ed. Donald H. Reiman and Sharon B. Powers. New York: Norton, 1977.

Suleiman, Susan Rubin. "Writing Past the Wall or the Passion According to H. C." Cixous, *"Coming to Writing" and Other Essays.* vii–xxii.

Wing, Betsy. "A Translator's Imaginary Choices." Cixous, *The Book of Promethea.* v–xiv.

8

"I Cannot Eat My Words but I Do": Food, Body, and Word in the Novels of Jeanette Winterson

Suzanne Keen

Among the works of contemporary British novelists, Jeanette Winterson's fiction is uniquely pervaded by food: real and symbolic food; food as metaphor and plot device; food as shorthand for characterization and social class; and food as magical link between more and less fantastical worlds. As the titles of her first and second-to-last novels suggest, from *Oranges are Not the Only Fruit* (1985) to *Gut Symmetries* (1997),[1] Winterson's fiction invests tasting, digesting, and discriminating among foods with more than ordinary significance. Food, body, and word come together in a set of practices strongly confirming the aims of Hélène Cixous's version of *l'écriture feminine*, combining sexual, spiritual, physical, and conceptual ecstasy, or *jouissance*.[2] A decade before Winterson's first novel appeared, Cixous challenged women writers to write through their bodies in order to avoid operating within male discourse: "It is time for [the woman writer] to dislocate this 'within,' to explode it, turn it around and seize it; to make it hers, containing it, taking it in her own mouth, biting that tongue with her very own teeth to invent for herself a language to get inside of" (257). Winterson's representations of masticated and savory foods, bodies, and words enact her enthusiastic writerly self-creation as a prolific and devouring poetic genius who consumes and transmutes her materials. Through repeated appearances in her novels, oranges, kippers, porridge, bananas, chicken, trotters, cake, leeks, toast, stewed rabbit, spaghetti, and frozen prawns acquire talismanic status, as individual foods evoke disgust and sympathy, alienation and recognition. Their consumption contributes to a sacramental theory of authorship organized around metaphors of incorporation, communion, and sexual ecstasy.

Few readers encounter Winterson's fiction without knowing of the writer's open lesbianism. As Bonnie Zimmerman notes, some lesbian writers "have succeeded in creating, or recreating, a symbolic system for sex through writing about food," in which food conveys "the intimacy, nurturance, warmth, and sensuality that women claim to find in lesbian sexuality" (104). In the following discussion, I show that some aspects of Winterson's representations of food, gender, and sexuality confirm this insight. However, I also argue in this chapter that a fuller understanding of Winterson's complex uses of food depends upon specifically religious contexts adopted and subverted as Winterson writes the woman writer's body, consuming her lovers, her reading, her meals, and her rejected Christianity to produce a new Logos of sublime self-creation.

The story of that self-fashioning and the perils of taking Winterson's words literally begins with her debut novel, *Oranges are Not the Only Fruit*. Those readers who discovered Winterson with *Oranges* are likely to forget neither its coming-out story, nor the disavowed Pentacostal evangelicalism of Winterson's upbringing, memorably embroidered, honored, and lampooned in the most comical of her novels. The transformed and fantastical medium of *Oranges* does not obscure its autobiographical elements, but Winterson insists from the start that her creations be read as fictions, as the "Deuteronomy" chapter of *Oranges* makes plain: "People like to separate storytelling which is not fact from history which is fact. They do this so that they know what to believe and what not to believe. This is very curious. How is it that no one will believe that the whale swallowed Jonah, when every day Jonah is swallowing the whale?" (93). In her 1995 book of essays, *Art Objects*, Winterson also cautions her readers not to assume that her lesbianism inflects her writing in any obvious way, arguing that one writer's "chosen sexual difference" does not "bind her in semiotic sisterhood with any other writer" just because that writer is "also lesbian" (103). She bluntly asserts, "I am a writer who happens to love women. I am not a lesbian who happens to write" (104).

Respecting Winterson's wish not to be labeled a lesbian writer can be a challenge, for in interviews with journalists strategically timed to create publicity for her books, she often refers to her sexual adventures. Around the time of the publication of *Gut Symmetries*, Winterson informed Ginny Dougary that when she was younger, she swapped sex with "lonely married women" for Le Creuset cookware, which these women from the Home Counties could more easily acquire than cold cash.[3] Not unjustifiably suspicious that Winterson was pulling her leg, Dougary presents the revelation as one of a series of Winterson's shifting statements of self-fashioning, but also relates the comment of Winterson's publisher at Granta Books that "for someone who is not known for her cooking, Winterson does have a remarkably large collection of Le Creuset" (9).[4] Those real or imaginary Le Creuset pots, changing hands in a barter version of lesbian prostitution, weigh down any attempt to raise a discussion of food in Winterson above the level of *fabliaux*. Indeed, the carnivalesque spirit of much of Winterson's work comes in part from her Rabelaisian admixture of food and sex. In *Sexing the Cherry* (1989), a hapless male perks up at the thought of the fellatio he thinks he is being offered, but Winterson's ecofeminist character wants to swallow her in-adequate lover whole, "every single bit, straight down the throat like an oyster, [his] feet last, [his] feet waving in [her] mouth like a diver's flippers. Jonah and the Whale" (145). Gluttony, sexual vengeance, mon-strosity, and a revisionist typology of the Bible are gleefully claimed as key components of what Marilyn Farwell aptly describes as "the gro-tesque and exaggerated female body that conditions postmodernism's metaphoric construction of the lesbian body" (185).

The gulping down of a man oyster-fashion evokes the consumption of the aphrodisiac in an unusual context, after unsatisfying sex. Winterson characteristically disorders the elements in familiar symbolic trajectories and relationships, rewriting love triangles, apprenticeships, quests, and traditional recipes for stirring up desire. "Is food sexy?" the ambiguously gendered first person narrator of *Written on the Body* (1992) inquires. The answer that follows first debunks the traditional associations of food with eroticism as hypermasculine and infantile: "*Playboy* regularly fea-tures stories about asparagus and bananas and leeks and courgettes or being smeared with honey or chocolate chip ice-cream." Worse, "Au-thentic Pina Colada flavour" body oil only makes the tongue of the lover "come out in a rash" (36). Yet lunch with Louise, the beloved of *Written on the Body*, inspires this erotic wish:

> When she lifted the soup spoon to her lips how I longed to be that innocent piece of stainless steel. I would gladly have traded the blood in my body for half a pint of vegetable stock. Let me be diced carrot, vermicelli, just so you will take me in your mouth. I envied the French stick. I watched her break and butter each piece, soak it slowly in her bowl, let it float, grow heavy and fat, sink under the deep red weight and then be resurrected to the glorious pleasure of her teeth. (36)

The foods invoked in this passage (bread, vegetable stock, diced carrot, vermicelli) add new entries to the lexicon of erotic eatables: they are humble, healthful, soft, and wet. Even the French stick gains libidinal power as it is broken, buttered, and sunk in broth. As Bonnie Zimmerman has observed, "some of the most sensual language in lesbian literature" can be found when sex, food, and cooking are "deliciously intertwined" (104). Beyond the bread, certain key words (*innocent, blood,* and *resurrected*) subtly conjure up the sacramental in this scene of desire. Winterson's flirtation with blasphemy is deliberate: rearranging the counters in the drama of communion, the narrator instructs her lover with words that echo Christ's command regarding the Eucharist: "Eat of me and let me be sweet" (*Written* 20).

A concordance of references to food and eating in Winterson's fiction would reveal not only that every one of her works includes copious allusions to food, but also that a significant cluster characteristically associates food with sexuality, spirituality, and artistry. The web of references to food in Winterson's fiction always includes strands spun out of religious themes: consolation, communion, and Winterson's sacramental theory of authorship. The placement of Winterson as a lesbian writer sometimes obscures this religious context. Marilyn Farwell's comprehensive *Heterosexual Plots and Lesbian Narratives* asserts that "the topic of much lesbian postmodern writing is language and the body" (170). We need not disagree with this sensible assessment to recall, as Caroline Walker Bynum so memorably demonstrates, that language and body also come together in the metaphors and practices of women's spirituality.[5] Bynum's work on medieval women provides a salutary caution to readers who would separate an understanding of religion and spirituality from gender, sexuality, and the body, or vice versa. Of course, Winterson is not a medieval woman, but her deep familiarity with the Bible and theology inform her feminism, her narrative art, and her theory of authorship. With the lyricism of the Song of Solomon, the fertility of blasphemy, and the irreverent humor of habitual taboo breaking, Winterson anchors her most far-flung metaphors and imaginings in a fundamental metonymy of food and body derived from Christian theology, by way of William Blake's contrary Proverbs of Hell.

Following a reference to oranges in the imaginary concordance of Winterson's food words, for instance, would lead to this instructive passage from the "Joshua" chapter of *Oranges are Not the Only Fruit,* Winterson's quasi-autobiographical debut novel:

> On the banks of the Euphrates find a secret garden cunningly walled. There is an entrance, but the entrance is guarded. There is no way in for you. Inside you will find every plant that grows growing circular-wise like a target. Close to the heart is a sundial and at the heart is an orange tree. This fruit had [*sic*] tripped up athletes while others have healed their

wounds. All true quests end in this garden, where the split fruit pours forth blood and the halved fruit is a full bowl for travellers and pilgrims. To eat of the fruit means to leave the garden because the fruit speaks of other things, other longings. So at dusk you say goodbye to the place you love, not knowing if you can ever return, knowing you can never return by the same way as this. It may be, some other day, that you will open a gate by chance, and find yourself again on the other side of the wall. (123)

On one level, the passage presents a *mise-en-abyme* of the surrounding *Bildungsroman* plot: Jeanette and her fantastic alter ego Winnet will have to find a way in the world by other means. The girl must face the risk that she may never return to her home, a place strongly associated with her adoptive mother. A glance at the imaginary concordance shows that Jeanette's mother is symbolically linked to oranges. She offers them to Jeanette as tokens of (or substitutes for) love and comfort; she insists for most of the novel that they are "the only fruit" (29). Jeanette's mother is horrified by the sexuality of "Next Door" (53), by "unnatural passions" (7) and the "Breeding Ground" (16) of the world outside the home and church. She raises her adoptive daughter to be a missionary, going so far as to rewrite the end of *Jane Eyre* to provide a positive role model—Jane married to St. John Rivers (74). The oranges she proffers only temporarily bind a relationship that will be impossible to sustain after Jeanette matures: "So at dusk you say goodbye to the place you love" (123). Oranges make a poor substitute for true mother love.

The obvious connection between the female anatomy, inside "a secret garden cunningly walled," and the orange that heals, bleeds, endangers, and (like the fruit of the tree of knowledge) exiles those filled with "other longings," makes female sexuality the *locus amoenus* of "all true quests" (123). Laura Doan describes Winterson's oranges as emblems of a reversible inward/outward dichotomy: "[T]he orange (with a rough, thick, seemingly impenetrable exterior that contains a soft, delicately segmented inner fruit, at once sweet and tart) operates most simply as a metaphor for the self/world or self/other dichotomy . . . representing the separation between inner and outer" (147). As an illustration of how tightly the inner and the outer fit, Jeanette's degree of discomfort with herself, her lover Melanie, and her mother, can be gauged by how difficult she finds peeling the fruit. During a health crisis, she attempts to build an igloo out of orange peels, symbolically converting the debris of her mother's gift into an emblem of shelter and escape.

Though clearly gendered female, the nature of the sexual identity associated with oranges remains ambiguous: do oranges form a "scum," as the novel's first epigraph from Mrs. Beeton's recipe for marmalade announces? Do they signify the limitations of a conventional existence, as the second epigraph, Nell Gwynn's remark, "Oranges are not the only fruit," suggests? Jeanette's lesbianism often seems to be set against the ubiquitous conventional oranges, but her aura and her personal demon are both orange-colored; from the orange demon she receives a clitoris-like talisman, the "rough brown pebble" (114) that protects her alter ego Winnet in the interpolated fairy tales. (These fragments of a quest romance, omitted from the television version of *Oranges*, form a significant psychological subplot to the realistic story of breaking away from a repressive community.[6]) If the sexual metaphors embodied by the split orange and halved orange evoke menses, mother's milk, and oral sex, these mythic fruits do not reveal all the secrets of oranges. Leaving home, Jeanette vows to support herself with any kind of work: "The only thing that worried me was the thought of having to work on a fruit stall. Spanish Navels, Juicy Jaffas, Ripe Sevilles" (137). This might seem to express Jeanette's resolution not to sell herself, or to avoid backsliding into her mother's world. Though the passage calls up a version of the perils of Christina Rossetti's *Goblin Market* (1862), it suggests self-denial rather than self-protection.[7] Nor do the allusions to Eden provide a simple key. The passage virtually mandates the consumption of the fruit, in a communion that reverses the forbidden apple, but it also mirrors the expulsion from Paradise, which can be read in personal terms as a fortunate fall. Winterson's self-instructing allegory can be evasive, undercutting and revising itself with the ambiguous accessibility of religious parable. If the meaning of oranges and other foods in this one novel becomes slipperier the more instances we consider, the picture becomes even more complicated in later novels.[8]

Just as her female artist Picasso performs an apprenticeship painting in mustard before she acquires a palette representing a broader spectrum, Winterson's earlier novels, *Oranges are Not the Only Fruit* and *Boating for Beginners* (1985), use food in a relatively schematic way to figure and explore variations in human sexuality.[9] Her mature novels, including *The Passion*, *Sexing the Cherry* (1989), *Written on the Body*, *Art and Lies: A Piece for Three Voices and a Bawd* (1994), and *Gut Symmetries* make of food an ever-more complex mixture of associations with eroticism, gender, adventure, memory, deception, the fear of confinement, aggression, predation, grotesquerie, political tyranny, and national character.

The critics who have commented on the nexus of food and body in Winterson's work have identified it with the writer's lesbianism. Laura Doan, for example, argues that "Winterson's use of the fruit metaphor is more . . . than an icon; it is her first tentative mechanism for imagining the fruition of a postmodern lesbian existence" (148).[10] Yet as Doan concedes in a 1991 interview with Helen Barr, Winterson answers the question, "Why fruit?" with more traditional words emphasizing the relationship between bodily experience and representation: "'The things we can see, touch, smell, taste and hear delight me. . . . This is the awe and wonder of the natural world, which, largely now, we just close our eyes to" (qtd. in Doan 148). Rather than characterizing this answer as "somewhat evasive" as Doan does (148), I see instead Winterson's extension of ecstatic religious language to the "awe and wonder" of the natural world. The representation of fruit as part of a mystical communion is reinvented in Winterson's imagination. Though the metonymy of food and body does in places refer to the experiences of lesbian sexuality, Winterson's maxim—autobiography is nothing but art and lies—reminds us of the centrality of words, and not only those words denoting the lived experience of the author, in interpreting the images and fictions of the edible in her novels. In Winterson's works, words become the central ingredient of an alternative faith which invests the writer with uncanny power, for through the writer the substitute for grace flows: "The more we ask of language, the more we shall receive" (*Great Moments* 76).

Detractors and admirers alike notice the immodesty of Winterson's manifestoes for the word. The blurb from her companion Margaret Reynolds' book, *Erotica: Women's Writing from Sappho to Margaret Atwood*, describes Winterson as employing "a vocabulary at once simple and large, combined with an arrogant assumption of privileged vision," which "allows her narrative a precise and relentless erotic power" (358). An eroticism made out of words requires the key ingredient of authorial attitude. Though insisting on the value of alternative perspectives in telling and interpreting events, Winterson's fictions share the flavor of this "mustard of her own" (*Oranges* 95): a recognizable narrative voice, intermittently droll, deadpan, allusive, down-to-earth, satirical, and pompously high-flown. The copresence of food, body, and word in all the novels points repeatedly to a literary experience of reading as incorporation: the writer takes in (for example) the works of Virginia Woolf; the reader subsequently takes in not only Winterson, but those whom Winterson has digested: "Eating words and listening to them rumbling in the gut is how a writer learns the acid and alkali of language. It is a process at the same time physical and intellectual. . . . The writer finds that words are visceral, and when she can eat them, wear them, and enter them like tunnels she discovers that the alleged separation between word and meaning between writer and word is theoretical" (*Art Objects* 172–3). The metaphors employed to describe the writer's reading, her art, and her relationship to her reader invoke Eucharist and transubstantiation, placing the writer first in the position of communicant, then (mystically) in the role of the host. As we will see, the implicit cannibalism of this kind of intimacy reappears as a shocking plot device in Winterson's recent novel, *Gut Symmetries*.

Before approaching (in *Gut Symmetries*) the surreal scene that represents the culmination, thus far, of Winterson's thinking about the way lovers and readers consume the beloved, some groundwork on the disagreeable meatiness of males must first be laid. Winterson's celebration of the corporeality and appetite of disorderly female eaters such as *Sexing the Cherry*'s gigantic Dog Woman (the character who devours her hapless lover's penis) repeatedly brings together femininity and vegetarianism. The Dog Woman's mistake about male members derives from her gardening (as well from inexperience): she imagines that the snapped-off penis will grow back, like a plant. To distinguish the sympathetically depicted fruit-and-vegetable-consuming female characters from their male foils, Winterson evokes disgust at masculinity with a set of allusions to red meat. In Winterson's Noah story, *Boating for Beginners*, the entrepreneurial Ham hires Mrs. Munde to produce Hallelujah Hamburgers (31), for "you are what you eat," and her daughter Gloria (Munde) worries that, having consumed the phallic sausages from the chain store butchershop "Meaty Big and Bouncy," she cannot truthfully claim "on her wedding night that she'd never had a man inside her" (46). Winterson conflates meat eating and sex with men in a straightforward image of contamination. In Winterson's third novel, *The Passion*, Villanelle considers the marriage proposal of a lover who earns his living selling meat and horses to the occupying French army, but falters, for she would "be marrying a meat man" (64). The ultimate meat man in this work is Napoleon, who indulges his excessive appetite for chicken despite the fact that everyone else is starving. This historical injustice desecrates even the communion wafer: "I took the wafer on my tongue and it burned my tongue. The wine tasted of dead men, 2,000 dead men" (42). In Winterson's 1994 fiction, *Art and Lies*, the protagonist Sophia (who names herself Picasso) suffers in the home of her dysfunctional family: the house itself smells of "hung meat" (159) and the bed of her brother and rapist smells "of meat and drains" (157). If men are pigs, (*Oranges* 71), women ought to at least try to avoid contamination by watching what they eat and whom they marry. But like the victims in fairy tales, women cannot always avoid being eaten up themselves, and sometimes survival requires eating or suffering things that profane the body.

When males in power cannot be dodged, the perspective of meat men degrades women's bodies. In *Art and Lies*, a surgeon contemplates the breasts he has removed: "[S]o often he had looked at them; a jelly of tissue and fat, the puckering dead skin and the useless nipple on the tin plate. What could he do with those breasts, sliced like kiwi fruit, soft variegated off-coloured flesh? He scraped them into the bin. Binsful of breasts, although a country colleague of his used to take them home to feed the pigs, why not?" (188). Food metaphors defamiliarize the body as Winterson's characters exchange salvoes from entrenched positions in an exaggerated gender war. The chilling conversion of women's breasts into pig slops contrasts strikingly with the Rabelaisian treatment of the Dog Woman's castration of her sex partners in *Sexing the Cherry*. Informed that "men like to be consumed in the mouth," and encouraged by the swooning of her first victim, a flasher with a "thing" that grows from pea-pod to cucumber dimension, Dog Woman does as the man suggests, putting it in her mouth, "swallowing it up entirely and biting it off with a snap" (40). Disgusted, she spits out the "leathery thing" and feeds it to one of her dogs. Later she learns that men's members do not grow back: "This seems a great mistake on the part of nature," she opines, "since men are so careless with their members and will put them anywhere without thinking" (120). Though Winterson's female characters could scarcely avoid the charge of promiscuity, male sexual adventuring appears more predatory and gross. As Jove, the male physicist in *Gut Symmetries* confesses, "[L]ike any other young man, I used to visit the meat-houses around Times Square" (193).

Jove's understanding of the cannibalism he commits underlines not only the equation of wife and meat, but the power of the word to make two people one flesh: "I did it so that it would not have disgusted either of us. She was my wife. I was her husband. We were one flesh. With my body I thee worship. In sickness and in health. For better or for worse. Till death do us part. . . . I parted the flesh from the bone and I ate it" (200). When Alice (Alluvia, lover to both Jove and Stella) finds the butcher and his victim, she vomits when she sees that Stella's buttock and hip have been "chopped away" (213). Taken thus far, the ritualistic perversion of marriage and communion seems to underscore Winterson's disgust with meaty men and their rites. Yet the victim Stella first introduces the idea of cannibalism when she declares that she will seduce her husband's lover, Alice: "Give me a pot and let me turn cannibal. I will feast on her with greater delight than he. If she is his titbit then I will gourmet her. Come here and discover what it is to be spiced, racked and savoured. I will eat her slowly to make her last longer. Whatever he has done I will do. Did he eat her? Then so will I. And spit her out" (29).

Though it sounds grisly, this declaration in fact leads to the most passionate and enduring liaison of the novel, as Alice (Alluvia) proves to be Stella's true Astrophil. In a coy allusion to Philip Sidney's and Adonis's wound, Stella's mutilated thigh exposes the diamond she has always insisted lies embedded in her bone. (Her mother, craving diamonds during pregnancy, compulsively eats a number of jewels, one of which cannot be retrieved, for it has nourished the fetus [89–91].) Extracted from her body, cleaned off and laid on Stella's tongue, the diamond ("articulate with light" [213]) miraculously revives Stella, who will live to walk with a limp after plastic surgery. Thus the mother's legacy ("you are what you eat") protects the child in a revivifying communion. Carbon in its most beautiful form signifies the substances that make us part of one another, consumed and consuming: "The medievals thought that the damned lived in Satan's belly, hot pouch of indigestion, but damned or saved, what we were continues in the lungs of each other. Nitrogen, oxygen, tell-tale carbon" (216). Though Winterson denies an afterlife, in the incarnation of inspired word, the writer creates a substitute "intimacy of thin air" (217), recycling the matter of life, which "constantly escap[es] from the forms it inhabits" (216).

Winterson's combination of physics, philosophy, and Jewish mysticism in *Gut Symmetries* has been criticized by Robert Alter as implausible (36–38), but from this imperfect novel the diamond that connects the oranges, pebbles, and olive pits of earlier works can be retrieved. After the diamond has done its miraculous work on Stella's tongue, the novel leads the reader to conclusive images of safe harbors. At the end of the novel, a kiss is accompanied by a corny technicolor transcendence: "They were letting off fireworks down at the waterfront, the sky exploding in grenades of colour. Whatever it is that pulls the pin, that hurls you past the boundaries of your own life into a brief and total beauty, even for a moment, it is enough" (223). Winterson's clitoral symbols offer not only sexual fulfillment, but also renewal, healing, and paradise. The purely personal desire to give and receive sexual satisfaction leads to utopian visions of plenty and nurture. Though the seventeenth-century Dog Woman of *Sexing the Cherry* possesses an orange-sized clitoris too huge to be stimulated, her twentieth-century incarnation gets political satisfaction by strong-arming world leaders to share their food surpluses: "We change the world, and on the seventh day we have a party at the wine lake and make pancakes with the butter mountain and the peoples of the earth keep coming in waves and being fed and being clean and being well" (139). As Bonnie Zimmerman observes, "Nurturance begins with feeding, and women, whether lesbian or straight, are the feeders of the world" (104). The narrator of *Written on the Body* celebrates her beloved in terms reminiscent of the Song of Songs, leading from food to eroticism to an earthly paradise:

> My lover is an olive tree whose roots grow by the sea. Her fruit is pungent and green. It is my joy to get at the stone of her. The little stone of her hard by the tongue. Her thick-fleshed salt-veined swaddle stone.
>
> Who eats an olive without first puncturing the swaddle? The waited moment when the teeth shoot a strong burst of clear juice that has in it the weight of the land, the vicissitudes of the weather, even the first name of the olive keeper.
>
> The sun is in your mouth. The burst of an olive is breaking of a bright sky. The hot days when the rains come. Eat the

day where the sand burned the soles of your feet before the
thunderstorm brought up your skin in bubbles of rain.
    Our private grove is heavy with fruit. I shall worm you to
the stone, the rough swaddle stone. (137)

Here in the private grove, the lyrical narrator seems to have found a way
back into the "secret garden cunningly walled" of *Oranges are Not the
Only Fruit* (123). Further, the reader is joyfully invited to share the feast.

In Winterson's revision of the Paschal mystery, her own words possess the transforming power of the Eucharist and provide the way to
paradise. She reverses, in *Art and Lies,* those most famous lines of W. H.
Auden's "In Memory of W. B. Yeats": "The words of a dead man / Are
modified in the guts of the living" (ll. 22–23). In Winterson's sacramental theory of authorship, the writer acts on the reader who consumes her
words: "Read me. Read me now. Words in your mouth that will modify
your gut. Words that will become you. Recite me until you know me off
by heart. Lift up a flap of skin and the word sings. On the operating table
the word sings. In the grave the words push up the earth. Ashes to ashes,
dust to dust, the living word" (*Art and Lies* 55). If the gut of the reader
is modified by incorporating Winterson's undying words, the author
herself participates in a circular consumption of her own creation: "I
cannot eat my words but I do. I eat the substance, bread, and I take it
into me, word and substance, substance and word, daily communion,
blessed" (55). The nexus of eroticism, utopian vision, and a writer's
passionate invocation of her own words come together in Winterson's
ecstatic religion of herself.

NOTES

1. This piece was completed before the publication of Winterson's *Power
Book* (2000).

2. See Hélène Cixous's essay, "The Laugh of the Medusa," for a sample of
her poetic, punning, and challenging aphorisms on writing the body, feminine
writing, and on the need to dislocate the rules, categories, and controlling features of phallogocentric writing. Ursula K. Heise speculates that some of
Winterson's work responds to the theories of Cixous and the other French
feminists (547).

3. See Marilyn R. Farwell's account of the difficulties in identifying Winterson,
and Winterson's unruly fictions, as "lesbian," in *Heterosexual Plots and Lesbian
Narratives* (178–79).

4. See also Joanna Bale, 3.

5. From among the works of Caroline Walker Bynum, see especially *Holy
Feast and Holy Fast,* and "Introduction: The Complexity of Symbols" (1–20).

6. See the filmscript for *Oranges* in Winterson, *Great Moments*. On the influence of Malory's Morte D'Arthur on Winterson's revised grail quest, see Cosslett (15–28).

7. Jeanette's elderly friend Elsie cheers her up by reading Christina Rossetti's *Goblin Market* (*Oranges* 30); this internal allusion, though unexplicated when it appears, suggests the traditional link between fruit and eroticism. See Christina Rossetti, *Complete Poems* (11–26). See also "Consumption," in Reynolds, *Erotica* (249–50).

8. For instance, repulsive funeral baked meats and potted beef justify the purifying vegetarianism of the later stages of Jeanette/Winnet's quest.

9. Winterson's repudiated second novel *Boating for Beginners* was published very soon after her first and it does not measure up either to the standard set by *Oranges* or to the achievements of her subsequent work. Its somewhat crude use of food motifs throws into relief the more complicated patterns in later novels. For an unusual defense of the novel's humor, see Heise 546–7.

10. In an article that came out while this chapter was under review, Christy L. Burns comments briefly on the ingestion of words, transubstantiation, and the eroticism of reading. (371).

WORKS CITED

Alter, Robert. "Sexing the Jewry." *New Republic* (April 7, 1997): 36–8.

Auden, W. H. "In Memory of W. B. Yeats." 1940. *Collected Shorter Poems: 1927– 1957.* New York: Random House, 1960: 141–3.

Bale, Joanna. "Lesbian Novelist Tells of Sex for Le Creuset Saucepans." *Times* [London] January 4, 1997: 3.

Blake, William. *The Marriage of Heaven and Hell.* 1790–93. *William Blake's Writings.* Vol. 1. *Engraved and Etched Writings.* Ed. G. E. Bentley, Jr. Oxford: Clarendon P, 1978. 74–99.

Burns, Christy L. "Powerful Differences: Critique and Eros in Jeanette Winterson and Virginia Woolf." *Modern Fiction Studies* 44. 2 (1998): 364–92.

Bynum, Caroline Walker. *Holy Feast and Holy Fast: The Religious Significance of Food to Medieval Women.* Berkeley: U of California P, 1987.

———. "Introduction: The Complexity of Symbols." *Gender and Religion: On the Complexity of Symbols.* Ed. Caroline Walker Bynum, Stevan Harrell, and Paula Richman. Boston: Beacon, 1986: 1–20.

Cixous, Hélène. "The Laugh of the Medusa." *New French Feminisms: An Anthology.* Ed. Elaine Marks and Isabelle de Courtivron. New York: Schocken, 1981: 245–64.

Cosslett, Tess. "Intertextuality in *Oranges Are Not the Only Fruit:* The Bible, Malory, and *Jane Eyre.*" *'I'm telling you stories': Jeanette Winterson and the Politics of Reading.* Ed. Helena Grice and Tim Woods. Postmodern Studies 25. Amsterdam: Rodopi, 1998: 15–28.

Doan, Laura. "Jeanette Winterson's Sexing the Postmodern." *The Lesbian Postmodern.* Ed. Laura Doan. New York: Columbia UP, 1994: 137–55.

Dougary, Ginny. "Truth or Dare." *Times Magazine* [London] January 4, 1997: 9–11.

Farwell, Marilyn R. *Heterosexual Plots and Lesbian Narratives.* New York: New York UP, 1996.

Heise, Ursula K. "Jeanette Winterson." *British Writers.* Supplement 5. Ed. George Stade and Sarah Hannah Goldstein. New York: Scribners, 1999: 541–59.

Kester, Gunilla Theander. "The Forbidden Fruit and Female Disorderly Eating: Three Versions of Eve." *Disorderly Eaters: Texts in Self-Empowerment.* Ed. Lilian R. Furst and Peter W. Graham. University Park: Pennsylvania State UP, 1992: 231–40.

Reynolds, Margaret, ed. *Erotica: Women's Writing from Sappho to Margaret Atwood.* London: Pandora, 1990.

Rossetti, Christina. *Goblin Market.* 1862. *The Complete Poems of Christina Rossetti.* Ed. R. W. Crump. Vol. 1. Baton Rouge: Louisiana State UP, 1979: 11–26.

Winterson, Jeanette. *Art and Lies: A Piece for Three Voices and a Bawd.* London: Cape, 1994. New York: Knopf, 1995.

———. *Art Objects: Essays on Ecstasy and Effrontery.* London: Cape, 1995. New York: Knopf, 1996.

———. *Boating for Beginners.* London: Methuen, 1985.

———. *Great Moments in Aviation and Oranges are Not the Only Fruit. Two Filmscripts.* London: Vintage, 1994.

———. *Gut Symmetries.* London: Granta Books, 1997. New York: Knopf, 1997.

———. *Oranges are Not the Only Fruit.* London: Pandora Press, 1985. New York: Atlantic Monthly Press, 1987.

———. *The Passion.* London: Bloomsbury, 1987. New York: Vintage, 1989.

———. *The Power Book.* London: Cape, 2000.

———. *Sexing the Cherry.* London: Bloomsbury, 1989; New York: Vintage, 1991.

———. *The World and Other Places.* London: Cape, 1998.

———. *Written on the Body.* London: Cape, 1992; New York: Alfred A. Knopf, 1993.

Zimmerman, Bonnie. *The Safe Sea of Women: Lesbian Fiction 1969–1989.* Boston: Beacon, 1990.

Part 3

Food and Cooking: Patriarchal, Colonial, Familial Structures

9

Rewriting the Hysteric as Anorexic in Tsitsi Dangarembga's *Nervous Conditions*

Sue Thomas

In *Nervous Conditions* (1988) the anorexic Nyasha Sigauke is examined after a breakdown by two white psychiatrists, the first of whom tells her family that she "could not be ill, that Africans did not suffer in the way" that they reported she did, and suggests to them that firm control is all that she requires (201). As Becky W. Thompson observes, "[T]he stereotype that eating problems are 'white girl' phenomena has led many highly trained professionals to either misdiagnose or ignore women of color" (12). Jacqueline Rose's comments on the racial and gender assumptions embedded in the practice of colonial psychiatry in Africa are also apposite. African women were thought, she writes, to lack "'interiority'—twice over, as African and as woman. According to the dominant mythology, African identity was collective not individual (read more dependent, immature), but African man had gained the rudiments of individual personhood from his contact with the European, a contact which African women lacked" (103). An evolutionary paradigm was invoked: African women, Megan Vaughan notes in *Curing their Ills: Colonial Power and African Illness*, " 'were said not to have reached the level of self-awareness' " necessary to develop psychological problems (qtd. in Rose 103). *Nervous Conditions* is a "sociodiagnostic" examination[1] of the somatic manifestations of the psychological and epistemic violence inherent in the cultural production and reproduction of black colonial identity and Shona gender norms in late 1960s Rhodesia. The characteristically perspicacious Nyasha terms the nervous dis/ease "hysteria" (84). In her portrait of Nyasha's anorexia, Tsitsi Dangarembga, who studied psychology at the University of Zimbabwe during the 1980s, contests or supplements historically available psychoanalytic theorizations of colonial nervous dis/ease and anorexia nervosa, such as the view of the first psychiatrist who examines Nyasha, T. Buchan and L. D. Gregory's "Anorexia Nervosa in a Black Zimbabwean," and Frantz Fanon's *Black Skin, White Masks* and *The Wretched of the Earth*. Noting the "absence of non-white victims" in the medical literature on the condition, Buchan and Gregory claim that their case history of a twenty-four-year-old woman is the "first record of unequivocal anorexia nervosa occurring in a black Zimbabwean whose presenting symptoms meet the diagnostic criteria laid down by Feighner" (326). The woman's history to early adolescence accords in many ways with biographical information about Dangarembga herself as well as aspects of her representations of both Nyasha and her cousin Tambudzai (Tambu), the first-person narrator.[2] Like Frantz Fanon, Dangarembga is attentive to the "intersections of racial subjectivity and social power" (Bergner 76), yet implicitly critiques his assumptions about gender.

In rewriting the hysteric, Dangarembga uses tropologies of food, eating, digestion, and hunger to represent the stakes of ingesting both local patriarchal and colonial English cultural assumptions, especially those about traditional Shona femininity and race. In this sense *Nervous Conditions* endorses the view of Mainini, Tambu's mother, that stomaching, or adopting, Englishness (203) alienates the Shona of the black colonial elite from their ancestors, racial heritage, and sustaining ties with the mother, especially the tie of shared language; it kills psychically and spiritually, if not physically. Tambu likes to think of her move from rural poverty into the ranks of a mission-educated colonial elite as her "reincarnation" (92). Her word is appropriate: the assimilative imperative to internalize a white middle-class religious poetics of taste, cleanliness, and decency disrupts and cognitively remaps her sense of her own embodiment as a Shona woman.[3] In *Nervous Conditions* ingestion and food are highly charged signifiers of cultural and maternal affiliations, and the ambiguities and contradictions attendant on the internalizing of both English texts and the values inscribed in them, as well as the performative scripts of Shona femininity and masculinity.

The novel is set in the early period of the guerilla warfare (Chimurenga Two) launched by the Zimbabwe African National Union on April 28, 1966, the settlement of which in 1980 brought about Zimbabwe's legal independence from Britain and black majority rule. Dangarembga's epigraph—" 'The condition of native is a nervous condition' "—is from

Jean-Paul Sartre's preface to Frantz Fanon's *Wretched of the Earth*. In the preface Sartre discusses the repressed sources of the horizontal violence which precedes wars of independence from colonizing powers:

> [A]t first it is not *their* [the natives'] violence, it is ours [the colonizing power's] which turns back on itself and rends them; and the first action of these oppressed creatures is to bury deep down that hidden anger which their and our moralities condemn and which is however only the last refuge of their humanity. Read Fanon: you will learn how, in the period of their helplessness, their mad impulse to murder is the expression of the natives' collective unconscious.
>
> If this suppressed fury fails to find an outlet, it turns in a vacuum and devastates the oppressed creatures themselves. (16)

Western culture, Sartre claims, bewitches the "carefully selected unfortunates" of Fanon's black colonial elites: "Our enemy betrays his brothers and becomes our accomplice; his brothers do the same thing. The status of 'native' is a nervous condition introduced and maintained by the settler among colonized people *with their consent*" (16–17). The hysteric in *Nervous Conditions* is a product of precariously repressed rage at patriarchal and colonial domination under conditions of cultural dislocation and disruption of Shona gender norms; it is "a defiance through excess, through overcompliance" with domination (Grosz 135), which "(psychically) mutilates" the self to prevent "brutalisation at the hands of others" (138). Hysteria is "the symptomatic acting out of a proposition the hysteric cannot articulate" (134) within bewitching master narratives or the justifying narratives by which the hysteric is mastered.

Dangarembga works to "re-insert" into the histories of Shona "consent" to patriarchal and colonial domination "acts and figures" of resistance[4] under the signs of the hysteric: most spectacularly, anorexia nervosa; more banally, angelic housewifely submission, the horizontal violence of naming women witches, the repression of loss which manifests itself in obsessively repeated justifying myths which entrench colonial rule, and "bad nerves" which accompany playing the part of the "good kaffir" of the colonizer's imagination. These "acts and figures" bespeak principally the manners in which the sexualities of black men and women are contained and mortified by colonialism and by Shona and Western patriarchy respectively, and the nature and scope of masculine and feminine investment in that libidinal continence and mortification.[5] Dangarembga implicitly qualifies Fanon's argument that consent to racial domination is a sign of an inferiority complex, reinforced by the promise of material privilege to an elite which identifies with the colonial power and its values.

The nervous dis/ease in the homestead and mission houses of the extended Sigauke family emblematizes the psychological and epistemic violence of colonial dispossession and cultural dislocation; the conditions of the houses themselves, the patterns of food production and consumption within them, and their domestic relations are indicative of degrees of accommodation to the justificatory myth that colonial mission education and the cultural capital it confers represent progress. Babamukuru and Maiguru, Nyasha's parents and Tambu's uncle and aunt, are the first members of their families to become part of the black colonial elite in Rhodesia through missionary education and tertiary study in South Africa and Britain. The relative comfort, power, and prestige of Babamukuru, headmaster and academic director of the Church's Manicaland Region— and his appropriation of the salary of Maiguru—enable him to fulfil his responsibility, as patriarch of the extended Shona family, to dispel the burden of poverty. His honorific name translates literally as "Great Father" (Chennells 61). The colonial ideology of separate racial development in Rhodesia guarantees minimal interference with his power as Shona patriarch, and his masculine sexuality is affirmed by his ability to capitalize his family within a white Rhodesian economy.

Ironically, this confirmation of masculinity and of his power and prestige as a member of the black colonial elite sustains the spell of Englishness over him and his justificatory myth that an English education and Christianity represent progress. He is dependent on the continuing patronage of his mission employers; a dependency relationship develops between Babamukuru and his brother Jeremiah (Tambu's father), between the mission and homestead branches of the Sigauke family, which encourages Jeremiah's laziness and vitiates his character. Dangarembga comments in an interview that "the men are also in a position of powerlessness" (Interview 345). During her breakdown Nyasha mimics a white Rhodesian accent to say sneeringly of her father, " 'He's a good boy, a good munt. A bloody good kaffir' " (*Nervous* 200). Dangarembga represents the raising of a "new crop of educated Africans" (63) as an investment in a colonial pacification secured by dependency relations.

Helen Tiffin observes:

> Texts, as a number of cultures recognize, actually enter the body, and imperial education systems this century interpellated a colonialist subjectivity not just through syllabus content or the establishment of libraries within which passive colonials might absorb the lessons of the master, but through memorizing the English script, i.e. taking it into the body and re-producing before audiences of fellow colonials that which had been absorbed by heart/mind. (913)

In *Nervous Conditions* the entry of colonialism into the body is represented as ingestion. Jeremiah speaks of Tambu's teacher Mr. Matimba

having "chewed more letters" than he has (24), and of Mukoma (Babamukuru to Tambu) on his return home after his postgraduate education in
England as being "appeased, having devoured English letters with a
ferocious appetite," and "digested" degrees (36). Similarly, Tambu writes
of digesting libraries of books (178). In talking of the dis/ease of the
English-educated Nyasha and her brother Chido, Mainini says that "you
couldn't expect the ancestors to stomach so much Englishness" (203).
In preparation for examinations the children at the mission school are
expected to "recite . . . by rote" in the classroom the "entire syllabus," to
"embed" it in their "memories" (176). Nyasha loses her appetite during
her preparation for examinations, when she nervously overworks herself
"reading and memorising, reading and memorising all the time" (108).
This is a mode of learning that represses her critical intelligence, an
intelligence central to her passion for knowledge. What Tiffin calls the
"reproduction of the English body through colonial subjects" (910) is
also effected by the discipline of school drilling, parades, and inspection
of uniforms, fingernails and lips (*Nervous* 98–99).

Designed for a nuclear family, Babamukuru's and Maiguru's mission
house, the headmaster's house, is provided by their white employers. The
"clinical, antiseptic white" paint (62) is metonymic of the "white masks"
its occupiers are expected to don as "second nature." By Tambu's homestead standards the house is opulently furnished. Babamukuru's tastes are
apparent in the comfortable solidity of the furnishings in the living room
and dining room. Tambu thinks that the large, spacious dining room
table "had a lot to say about the amount, the calorie content, the complement of vitamins and minerals, the relative proportions of fat, carbohy-
drate and protein of the food that would be consumed at it. No one who
ate from such a table could fail to grow fat and healthy" (69). Western
food is eaten there in a Western manner. "Dainty . . . delicate" china and
porcelain tea sets "all covered in roses" shut away in a display cabinet are
Maiguru's most prized possession (69). Roses are stock signifiers of
Englishness. The tea sets imply the upper-middle-class English aesthetic
model of femininity and domesticity to which Maiguru aspires. She herself
is as "dainty" and "delicate" as the tea sets, "so fragile and small she
looked as though a breath of wind would carry her away" (50). She is
consistently represented by Tambu and Nyasha, and most memorably by
Mainini, as a "mother bird" (95); Tambu thinks of her as a "sweet, soft
dove" (101). Her size in relation to the other Shona women in the novel,
her aesthetic of delicacy, and her efforts to overfeed her family and niece
(73, 81) suggest she herself is subanorectic. This state seems also to enact
somatically the self-effacement Babamukuru and Shona culture demand of
her. Maiguru effaces herself "in order to preserve his [Babamukuru's]
sense of identity and value," quite conscious when "collected" of her

libidinal and material investments in self-sacrifice and fatalistic about them (102), despite occasional wistfulness at the wider individualistic opportunities she has foregone, especially in England (101). At mealtimes, with the ritual dishing out of food to the head of the family, Maiguru's subservience and dependency become most overcompliant with patriarchal expectations. She infantilizes herself intellectually and emotionally by using baby talk, calling her husband "Daddy-dear," "Daddy-pie," and "Daddy-d" (80–81); the fussiness draws attention to her presence. The baking of light buns and cakes in the kitchen is always imperilled by a draught from a broken window. That Babamukuru persistently fails to find time to repair the window suggests that he prioritizes delicacy less than does his wife. As the novel progresses, Maiguru's release of anger at sexual domination—articulated as "'I am tired of being nothing in a home I am working myself sick to support'" (172)—relieves some of her nervous symptoms: "She smiled more often and less mechanically, fussed over us less and was more willing or able to talk about sensible things. Although she still called Babamukuru her Daddy-sweet, most of her baby-talk had disappeared" (175).

Babamakuru and Maiguru urge food on their children and niece. To understand Babamukuru and Maiguru one can, I think, reframe Luce Irigaray's analysis of the suffocating mother who overfeeds the child, as elaborated by Elizabeth Grosz: "With no access to social value in her own right, she [the suffocating mother] becomes the mother who has only food (that is, love) to give the child. Unable to give the child language, law and exchange—the phallus—she has only nurturance, and its most tangible manifestations—eating, defecating—through which she may gain social recognition" (121). With little access to social value in white Rhodesian society in their own rights, that is, outside their abilities to play "good kaffirs," Babamukuru and Maiguru become the parents who have Western food and education—the "language, law, and exchange" of white Rhodesia—to give the child as an expression of love, the best that they think they can offer. Babamukuru and Maiguru gain social recognition through this kind of nurturance. Grosz elaborates the potential significance of Irigaray's analysis of the suffocating mother in interpreting eating disorders: "Anorexia and bulimia seem most interestingly interpreted in terms of a mourning or nostalgia for the lost (maternal) object, and either an attempt to devour or consume it (bulimia) or to harden oneself against its loss (in anorexia)" (242). As Nyasha is forced to overconsume English texts—by cramming for examinations—she develops anorexia as a "mourning or nostalgia" not just for the lost mother, but for the lost parents, parents whose individual humanities are submerged in the roles in which they have such strong libidinal investments, and as an attempt to harden herself against the loss.[6]

Babamukuru and Maiguru, Tambu realizes, aspire to an "antiseptic sterility" (*Nervous* 71) in their standards of cleanliness. The apparent "absence of dirt" is proof for her "of the otherworldly nature" of their home. Anne McClintock observes that the "poetics of cleanliness" in the imperial context "is a poetics of social discipline. Purification rituals prepare the body as a terrain of meaning, organizing flows of value across the self and the community and demarcating boundaries between one community and another" (226). Babamukuru and Maiguru are separating themselves from the "matter" integral to Shona living; their "antiseptic" relation to "dirt" becomes a sign of their "class relations" (Ward 8) to socially "lower" Shona people and to more affluent white Rhodesians.[7] Tambu, unused to Western food and eating with a knife and fork, is acutely conscious of the mess she makes at her place during her first meal at the mission, and of the fact that she is the only one at the table eating the sadza her aunt soon orders for her (*Nervous* 82). Maiguru encourages Nyasha and Chido, her son, not to join in Shona dancing on the homestead because they will get dirty (43). Eventually Maiguru, "the senior wife" (134) in the extended family, will refuse to perform her role as caterer and overseer of food preparation for festive gatherings of the family; this is an abject response to the responsibility, the menial role, and the appropriation of her salary to pay for the food.

Mainini realizes that Tambu's reacculturation at the mission makes her think her mother is "dirt" and her "toilet is dirty," and attributes the attitude to the influence of Maiguru's "money and . . . white ways" (140). Mainini's acid comment that Maiguru "could only produce two [children] of her own" (140) links the comparative sterility of the mission home with Maiguru's attitudes towards reproductive sexuality. She fears it in her daughter Nyasha; and Tambu's matter-of-fact homestead acceptance of menarche turns to distress at the mission: "[W]hen it came to washing those rags in Maiguru's white bathroom, to making a mess in the toilet bowl before I flushed it away, the business became nasty and nauseating" (95). In the bathroom the anorexic Nyasha induces vomiting after family meals and flushes away the regurgitated food. It is as if Nyasha is also regurgitating her father's assumptions about her sexuality aired in his demands that she eat: "'Your mother and I are not killing ourselves working just for you to waste your time playing with boys and then come back and turn up your nose at what we offer'" (189).

Thus, the tension between Nyasha and Babamukuru reinforces hysteria: anorexia nervosa in Nyasha; and bad nerves in Babamakuru. If the violent distortion of the body in anorexia nervosa is the last refuge of Nyasha's humanity (vide Sartre), then the physically violent confrontation between the two after the father accuses his daughter of lewd behaviour after a dance is the last refuge of Babamukuru's humanity.

Unchaperoned Nyasha, dressed in a miniskirt, has been talking to a white boy very late at night. Babamakuru blames Nyasha for behavior produced by her dual acculturation in England and Rhodesia, his investment in his and Maiguru's postgraduate education in England, Shona culture's loss of authority under colonial rule, and Maiguru's indirect defiance of his authority through indulging Nyasha's Westernisms (disrespect for elders, clothing indecent by traditional African standards, loss of the Shona language, use of tampons, prizing of daintiness).

What he cannot articulate directly is the reality of the threat to his masculinity posed by what Nyasha's Westernisms represent to him. His masculine authority, like Fanon's, depends upon his ability to "circumscribe black women's sexuality and economic autonomy" (Bergner 81). As a confirmation of his continuing Shona patriarchal authority his daughter must embody Shona ideas about feminine purity, decency, submissiveness, and respect; the gender norms of his culture must be preserved intact. Discussing the traffic in women among men, Bergner notes:

> In addition to a sex-gender economy that organizes men into social groups through the distribution of women, there is an economy regulating the distribution of women so as to construct and perpetuate *racial* groupings. In the colonial context, the operative "law" determining the circulation of women among white men and black men is the miscegenation taboo, which ordains that white men have access to black women but that black men must be denied access to white women. (81)

Babamakuru resists white men's sexual access to his daughter, but reads that access as a sign of Nyasha's Western promiscuity. For Tambu the intricate complexities of the interconnections between colonial and sexual politics among the Shona are made apparent when Babamakuru calls Nyasha a "whore" (*Nervous* 114). She realizes that "victimisation" of "femaleness" is "universal": "It didn't depend on poverty, on lack of education or on tradition. . . . Men took it everywhere with them. Even heroes like Babamakuru did it" (115–116).

Nyasha's anorexia nervosa exposes several intricate layers of that domination and of her alienation. In a 1991 interview Dangarembga suggests that one of the reasons educated Zimbabwean black girls "are so prone" to anorexia nervosa "is that if you live a very intellectual life you do become more divorced from the physical aspects of yourself" ("Between Gender" 346). Nyasha's anorexic body is a parody of a Western ideal of slim, feminine sexual desirability. Nyasha does not want the "heavy, strong hips" prized in Shona culture (*Nervous* 18). Nyasha's anorexic behaviour is a standard "series of caricatures of the various socially validated components of [Western] 'femininity' (especially narcissism, masochism and castration," which ironically reinstates their power (Celermajer 67). Celermajer suggests that the anorexic's

> narcissism can be seen in her obsessive preoccupation with her body, its pleasures, pains and fascinations. Her pride and narcissistic self-control often coupled with disdain towards others not only attests to this self love, but also compensates for the self-degradation and lack of control which her social position dictates. Her masochism is expressed in the gradual destruction of her body and her at times violent self-mutilation. Her castration is manifested in the overwhelming shrinking of her body image, and ironically in her selection of a corporeal symptom that challenges a social ideal by confirming its power over her. (68)

Pleasure in self-sacrifice and disempowerment are certainly also aspects of Shona femininity which Nyasha despises in her mother, and which fuel her matrophobia.

Nyasha's anorexia is, then, a critical and highly ambiguous attempt at self-determination. Her refusal of food at the family table or self-induced vomiting after having to eat there is a response to the sexual and cultural politics enacted at it: the ritualized subservience, baby talk, and fussiness of the mother; the father's reassertions of domestic authority; assimilation into an English colonial modernity enacted through the serving and eating of Western food in an atmosphere of "antiseptic sterility." Anorexia nervosa allows Nyasha to act out the rage symptomatically through the body, which she later articulates during a breakdown:

> "Why do they do it, Tambu," she hissed bitterly, her face contorting with rage, "to me and to you and to him? Do you see what they've done? They've taken us away. Lucia. Takesure. All of us. They've deprived you of you, him of him, ourselves of each other. We're grovelling. Lucia for a job, Jeremiah for money. Daddy grovels to them. We grovel to him." She began to rock, her body quivering tensely. "I won't grovel. Oh no, I won't. I'm not a good girl. I'm evil. I'm not a good girl." I touched her to comfort her and that was the trigger. "I won't grovel, I won't die," she raged and crouched like a cat ready to spring.
>
> The noise brought Babamukuru and Maiguru running. They could do nothing, could only watch. Nyasha was beside herself with fury. She rampaged, shredding her history book between her teeth ("Their history. Fucking liars. Their bloody lies."), breaking mirrors, her clay pots, anything she could lay her hands on and jabbing the fragments viciously into her

flesh, stripping the bedclothes, tearing her clothes from the
wardrobe and trampling them underfoot. "They've trapped
us. They've trapped us. But I won't be trapped. I'm not a
good girl. I won't be trapped." Then as suddenly as it came,
the rage passed. "I don't hate you, Daddy," she said softly.
"They want me to, but I won't." She lay down on her bed.
"I'm very tired," she said in a voice that was recognisably
hers. "But I can't sleep. Mummy will you hold me?" She
curled up in Maiguru's lap looking no more than five years
old. "Look what they've done to us," she said softly. "I'm
not one of them but I'm not one of you." She fell asleep.
(*Nervous* 200–201)

In this scene, Nyasha is neither the good girl of her father's myth of ideal
Shona femininity nor the good compliant kaffir girl of the white Rhodesian imagination. And it is not safe for her to articulate her rage (201),
except through her own body. The making of the clay pots, carefully
ensuring "that they did not crack" (150), had helped Nyasha effect the
libidinal continence demanded by her anorexia. The pots were "smaller
and daintier" than those made before she had gone to England, and
"finished with delicate designs" (149). I have quoted the passage at some
length so as not to compromise the rage by paraphrasing it in critical
prose. Maiguru has said to Tambu that her daughter's "head is full of
loose connections that are always sparking" (74); Nyasha's rage names
the psychologically sustaining connections which have been loosened.
The desire for a conciliatory bonding, a connection, with the parents less
fettered by the interventions of the English symbolic order of white
Rhodesia is signified in her baby talk: "I don't hate you, Daddy. . . .
Mummy will you hold me?"

T. Buchan and L.D. Gregory's "Anorexia Nervosa in a Black Zimbabwean" was published four years after Zimbabwean independence.
The biographical notes on the authors state that Buchan is professor of
psychiatry at the Godfrey Huggins School of Medicine at the University
of Zimbabwe, and Gregory clinical psychologist at the St. Giles Rehabili-
tation Centre in Harare. Buchan and Gregory assert that

the most interesting features of the case were the psychosocial
factors in the aetiology. Firstly she [the patient] was educated
in white boarding schools where she was exposed to the desirability of slimness as a social norm; no such value pertains
in Shona society where a fat wife is traditionally regarded as an
important manifestation of her husband's affluence. Secondly,
her family showed some of the features described as characteristic of anorectic family pathology, such as preoccupation with
outward appearance and success, rigidity, and lack of conflict
resolution. . . . Because of a mistrust of psychiatric treatment,

we were unfortunately unable to investigate the family interactions any further. Middle-class African families commonly
set great store on academic achievement, and overdriven children are by no means rare. . . . (329)

Their ontogenetic understandings of the "social and psychological conflicts
engendered by changes of culture" (326), and of family dynamics over-
look entirely "the colonial situation in which she is living and studying"
(Creamer 360), the institutionalized racism of the Rhodesian state and
its legacies, racialized genderings of embodiment, and the import of
colonial education and Englishness.[8] Dangarembga's sociodiagnostic
approach is immeasurably sharper.

Tambu ostensibly writes her story and the stories of several women
in her extended family after recognizing that her largely uncritical ingestion of Englishness and its myths of racial progress has brought about a
brainwashing, a contraction, not an expansion of her cultural horizons,
self-awareness, and sustaining ties with her community. English mission
education seduces Tambu in part because she does not question
Babamakuru's justifying myth of capitalization which vindicates her desire for education (*Nervous* 57), in part because the class privileges it
accords women like her aunt Maiguru lighten the self-sacrificing "weight
of womanhood" her peasant mother stoically accepts (33), and in part
because in the imaginative worlds of English culture—in English textuality,
"everything from Enid Blyton to the Brontë sisters"—she is introduced
to "places where reason and inclination were not at odds" (93) and finds
herself validated in these places and dependent on the validation (93).
The "glossy covers" of the books never seem "to get dirty or torn"
(195); the "sheer number of books" makes her feel "deeply ashamed" of
the "ignorance" she associates with the peasant homestead and all it
represents (195). Mainini, Tambu's mother, claims that her daughter
listens to Maiguru as though she wants "to eat the words that come out
of her mouth" (140), suggesting that the rich Maiguru can provide
meat, whereas she can only provide the vegetables she and her daughters
grow and prepare for eating through unremitting labour.

As Tambu acquires a taste for her aunt and uncle's Western food
which "refused to go down [her] throat in large quantities" when she
first arrived at the mission, she develops a cleanliness fetish. She comes
to associate blackness with malnutrition, dirt, disrepair, necessity (rather
than desire), lack of womanly self-respect, and sin. At the mission, water,
soap, and mirror (the last two "commodity fetishes" of empire according
to McClintock [214]) allow Tambu to witness pleasurably her apparent
"destiny" of colonial "metamorphosis" of her peasant self. The "full-length
mirror" at the mission is "so bright and new that it reflected only the
present" (*Nervous* 74). Tambu's libidinal investments in her "purifying"

metamorphosis sap her of the capacity for structural criticism she developed on the homestead. At the mission home of her aunt and uncle and the Young Ladies College of the Sacred Heart to which she wins a scholarship, the energy Tambu uses to lose herself in what English textuality represents and the ways it represents race, to "sort into organised parts" her reactions to the unfamiliar (90), and to avoid the "treacherous mazes" of "self-confrontation" by leaving "tangled thoughts" about systems of patriarchal and colonial domination "knotted, their loose ends hanging" (116), represses her mourning over separation from her mother. That mourning seems to be enacted stylistically in her story by her repeated claiming of her tie with "*my* mother" [my italics].

Tambu's single instance of defying Babamakuru, when he insists that her mother and father go through a Christian wedding ceremony, results from his linking of her and her siblings' origins in her parents' non-Christian marriage and her mother's body with sin. To remedy the family's "misfortunes" Jeremiah had proposed engaging a medium to perform a Shona cleansing ceremony to rid the clan of the influence of evil spirits. The Christian Babamakuru is appalled by the suggestion, and traces the problems instead to Jeremiah's failure to honor his mother's wish that he have a "church wedding" (146–147) and to the impurity of his union with Mainini. Tormented by imagined scenes of the wedding Babamakuru demands—images of her mother "immaculate in virginal white satin or (horror of horrors)" herself "as the sweet, simpering maid"—Tambu suffers "a horrible crawling" over her skin, her chest contracts "to a breathless tension," and her bowels threaten her with "their opinion" (149). Making clay pots with Nyasha temporarily keeps her "guilty anger at bay" (150). She runs away briefly, foregoing supper, experiences a perception of her body shrinking to "only a very small spot on the floor" (165), and develops a temporary hysterical paralysis which splits her corporeal schema. Her "mobile, alert" self (166) separates from and watches the inert and speechless body on the bed which refuses to attend the wedding. This dislocation is comparable to the effect of the racist gaze of the white French child at Fanon in *Black Skin, White Masks*. Fanon writes, "I took myself far off from my own presence, far indeed, and made myself an object." He experiences this moment as "an amputation, an excision, a hemorrhage that spattered my whole body with black blood," with the "details, anecdotes, stories" which fabricate racial stereotype; metaphorically the moment is a castration (111–112). The split within Tambu marks a refusal to swallow the antiseptic relation to dirt and sin integral to the class relations between the mission and homestead branches of the family, and Babamukuru's fixation on symbols of female purity. Tambu's "psychological splitting," Neil ten Kortenaar observes, "marks the birth of the sensibility that makes of Tambu a writer. . . . Tambu learns to see herself as well as others from the outside. She then slips back into her body and recovers her voice. . . . She can see from outside and speak from inside" (28).

Tambu's out-of-body experience as a technique of coping with "traumas and stressful situations" is similar to the "process of splitting or dissociation" which Thompson has identified as potentially formative of anorexic or bulimic eating patterns. Dissociation, she writes, "begins as a way to protect oneself from trauma, a way of removing oneself from the location of pain. Initially, it is possible to dissociate at will, but to maintain dissociation over time, it is necessary to use a substance such as food or alcohol" (62).

At one point even Mainini, Tambu's mother, experiences a loss of appetite; it is one aspect of her response to the homestead family's dependency on Babamukuru's patronage and her consequent powerlessness to halt his "dividing" of her from her children, and his "ruling" of her life and the lives of her immediate family (*Nervous* 184). The response, brought to crisis by Babamukuru's decision to allow Tambu to take up her scholarship at Sacred Heart and by her awareness of the cultural and language gap this will create between them, is one of impassive mourning and fatalistic depression. Supriya Nair reads this as a "protest, expressed by a complete withdrawal from domestic functions," which "marks the threat to the domestic work structure, since she will lose not just a daughter but a companion and helper" (135). Tambu describes her aunt Lucia's nursing of her sister Mainini as "a sort of shock treatment" (*Nervous* 185). Her "good medicine" (185) entails emotionally coercing Mainini to take responsibility for her son Dambudzo, offering her company and conversation, sitting in the sun with her, involving her in talk with women of the neighborhood, and feeding her meat and milk to build up her physical strength. This treatment—which reenmeshes Mainini in community—contrasts sharply with the psychiatric treatment of Nyasha. One white psychiatrist denies Nyasha's illness, because "Africans did not suffer in the way . . . described. She was making a scene. We [Babamukuru, Maiguru, and Tambu] should take her home and be firm with her" (201). A more "human" white psychiatrist orders rest in a clinic and doses of Largactil, a brand of chlorpromazine, an antipsychotic and antiemetic drug.

In *Nervous Conditions* the "hysterias" of black Rhodesian people are figured as effects of the ingestion of local patriarchal and colonial English assumptions about gender, race, class, sexuality, and desire in oral and chirographic discursive economies. The desire for, assimilation, refusal, or regurgitation of particular types of food and education (figured as digestion of words and books) are always already marked by cultural hierarchies and the material conditions that enable their consumption, and by a poetics of cleanliness. Dangarembga's sociodiagnostic rewriting of the lives of "hysterical" women and girls, like Fanon's analysis of racial subjectivity, does not confine the "crucial moments in the formation" of their identities "to the oedipal dynamic, the psychoanalytic scene of sexual differentiation and language acquisition" (Bergner 76). Like other "hysterical" women, Dangarembga's traumatized women and girls "embody precisely what is pathological in the scripts written for them" as women (Evans 241), and as racial and class subjects in their late-1960s Rhodesian historical context. Dangarembga rewrites the case history to early adolescence of the patient discussed by Buchan and Gregory. Anorexia nervosa is for her the most extreme embodiment of the trauma produced by the psychological and epistemic violence inherent in the cultural reproduction of gendered black colonial identity and Shona gender norms in a period of cultural dislocation.

NOTES

An earlier version of my discussion of Nyasha's anorexia nervosa was presented as part of a paper on "Feminist Literary Theory and Post-colonial Discourse" at the Australian Women's Studies Association Conference, University of Melbourne, December 25–27, 1990.

1. In *Black Skin, White Masks* Fanon makes a distinction between the "ontogenetic perspective" of twentieth-century psychoanalysis and the "sociodiagnostic" approach necessary to account for "the black man's alienation" (13). While he ostensibly uses "man" in a generic sense, he "takes the male . . . as the exemplary colonized subject," describing "these colonized subjects as studying in Paris, lusting after white women, and competing with white men for intellectual recognition" (Bergner 76).

2. The patient's date of birth (February 1959), her parents' occupations, her father's study abroad, her English experience (beginning at age two, and including the temporary lodging of her and a brother with a foster mother, and consequent forgetting of Shona language), her pattern of education, the dates of her entry to Cambridge University and return to Zimbabwe, and courses of tertiary study accord with information Dangarembga has given interviewers (see especially Wilkinson 188–198). The family dynamic is similar to that Dangarembga represents in the interrelations between Babamukuru, Maiguru, and Nyasha. The patient "won a scholarship to a private, multi-racial boarding school" (Buchan and Gregory 327); Tambu wins such a scholarship in *Nervous Conditions*. The patient develops anorexia nervosa at twenty. Nyasha's date of birth is several years earlier than the patient's and Nyasha becomes anorexic in early adolescence. It is crucial to Dangarembga's engagement with Fanon that Nyasha's anorexia develops in the early stages of a war of independence from a colonial power.

3. Interviewed by George and Scott, Dangarembga speaks about colonial cultural policy and the restrictiveness of the "cognitive map" it allowed nonwhite people in Rhodesia to construct (312).

4. My proposition is based on a formulation of Slemon's (11).

5. The terms "libidinal continence" and "mortification" are Irigaray's (127).

6. Nyasha's refusal of food on a visit to the homestead shortly after the Sigaukes have returned from England anticipates her later anorexic behaviour. Mainini asks Nyasha whether she wants milk or vegetables for lunch. She chooses milk, but "tuck[s] into the vegetables" with the rest of the extended family. Nyasha apparently desires to be part of the family eating vegetables, rather than be separated from them by her choice of milk. When Mainini "offer[s] her the sour milk she had asked for," she becomes "very morose." She copes with the stress of Mainini's isolation of her and her own conflicted desires by "refus[ing] to eat anything, although by this time everybody was very concerned and sympathetic and saying she could have whatever she wanted" (52).

7. Veit-Wild offers a different and ontogenetic interpretation, arguing that the "dirt fixation can be read as a symptom of the generally neurotic condition of the educated African; it finds extreme expression in the state of anorexia. In psychoanalytic terms, the process of civilisation is equated to the process of weaning, of becoming clean; it leads to a compulsory repression of anything dirty and physical as belonging to the anal phase in an individual's development" (336).

8. Creamer criticises their diagnosis at more length (359–360, n. 8).

WORKS CITED

Bergner, Gwen. "Who Is That Masked Woman? or, The Role of Gender in Fanon's *Black Skin, White Masks*." *PMLA* 110 (1995): 75–88.

Buchan, T., and L. D. Gregory. "Anorexia Nervosa in a Black Zimbabwean." *British Journal of Psychiatry* 145 (1984): 326–330.

Celermajer, Danielle. "Anorexia and a Feminism of the Body." *Australian Feminist Studies* 5 (1987): 57–69.

Chennells, Anthony. "Authorizing Women, Women's Authoring: Tsitsi Dangarembga's *Nervous Conditions*." *New Writing from Southern Africa: Authors Who Have Become Prominent Since 1980*. Ed. Emmanuel Ngara. London: Currey, 1996. 59–75.

Creamer, Heidi. "An Apple for the Teacher? Femininity, Coloniality, and Food in *Nervous Conditions*." *Kunapipi* 16. 1 (1994): 349–60.

Dangarembga, Tsitsi. "Between Gender, Race and History." Interview with Kirsten Holst Petersen. *Kunapipi* 16. 1 (1994): 345–48.

———. Interview with Rosemary Marangoly George and Helen Scott. *Novel* 26 (1993): 309–19.

———. *Nervous Conditions*. London: Women's Press, 1988.

Evans, Martha Noel. *Fits and Starts: A Genealogy of Hysteria in Modern France.* Ithaca: Cornell UP, 1991.

Fanon, Frantz. *Black Skin, White Masks.* Trans. Charles Lam Markman. London: Pluto, 1986.

———. *The Wretched of the Earth.* Trans. Constance Farrington. Harmondsworth, England: Penguin, 1967.

Grosz, Elizabeth. *Sexual Subversions: Three French Feminists.* Sydney: Allen, 1989.

Irigaray, Luce. *Speculum of the Other Woman.* Trans. Gillian C. Gill. Ithaca: Cornell UP, 1985.

McClintock, Anne. *Imperial Leather: Race, Gender and Sexuality in the Colonial Context.* New York: Routledge, 1995.

Nair, Supriya. "Melancholic Women: The Intellectual Hysteric(s) in *Nervous Conditions.*" *Research in African Literatures* 26. 2 (Summer 1995): 130–39.

Rose, Jacqueline. *States of Fantasy.* London: Clarendon, 1996.

Sartre, Jean-Paul. Preface. *The Wretched of the Earth.* By Frantz Fanon. Trans. Constance Farrington. Harmondsworth, England: Penguin, 1967.

Slemon, Stephen. "Modernism's Last Post." *Ariel* 20. 4 (October 1989): 3–17.

ten Kortenaar, Neil. "Doubles and Others in Two Zimbabwean Novels." *Contemporary African Fiction.* Ed. Derek Wright. Bayreuth: Bayreuth UP, 1997. 19–41.

Thompson, Becky W. *A Hunger So Wide and So Deep: American Women Speak Out on Eating Problems.* Minneapolis: U of Minnesota P, 1994.

Tiffin, Helen. "Cold Hearts and (Foreign) Tongues: Recitation and the Reclamation of the Female Body in the Works of Erna Brodber and Jamaica Kincaid." *Callaloo* 16 (1993): 909–21.

Vaughn, Megan. *Curing Their Ills: Colonial Power and African Illness.* Cambridge: Polity, 1990.

Veit-Wild, Flora. *Teachers, Preachers, Non-Believers: A Social History of Zimbabwean Literature.* London: Zell, 1992.

Ward, Frazer. "Foreign and Familiar Bodies." *Dirt and Domesticity: Constructions of the Feminine.* Ed. Jesus Fuenmayor, Kate Haug, and Frazer Ward. New York: Whitney Museum of American Art, 1992. 8–37.

Wilkinson, Jane. *Talking with African Writers: Interviews with African Poets, Playwrights and Novelists.* London: Currey, 1992.

10

Latin American Women Writers' Novel Recipes and Laura Esquivel's *Like Water for Chocolate*

Janice A. Jaffe

The women of this city are somewhat light in their carriage, and have learned from the Devil many enticing lessons and baits to draw poor souls to sin and damnation; and if they cannot have their wills, they will surely work revenge either by chocolate or conserves, or some fair present, which shall surely carry death along with it.

—Seventeenth-century Dominican friar, explaining that the women of Chiapas, Mexico eliminated an autocratic bishop by poisoning his chocolate; quoted in Thomas Gage, *The English-American: A New Survey of the West Indies*, 1648

During the same era that inspired the suspicion of women's activities in the kitchen cited in my epigraph, the Mexican nun Sor Juana Inés de la Cruz boldly celebrates the phenomena of the kitchen as worthy of philosophical observation:

> And what shall I tell you, lady, of the natural secrets I have discovered while cooking? I see that an egg holds together and fries in butter or in oil, but, on the contrary, in syrup shrivels into shreds; observe that to keep sugar in a liquid state one need only add a drop or two of water in which a quince or other bitter fruit has been soaked; observe that the yolk and the white of one egg are so dissimilar that each with sugar produces a result not obtainable with both together. I do not wish to weary you with such inconsequential matters, and make mention of them only to give you full notice of my nature, for I believe they will be occasion for laughter. But, lady, as women, what wisdom may be ours if not the philosophies of the kitchen? Lupercio Leonardo spoke well when he said: how well one may philosophize when preparing dinner. And I often say, when observing these trivial details: had Aristotle prepared vituals, he would have written more. (*Woman of Genius* 62)

While Sor Juana's ironized self-mockery for commenting on "these trivial details" reflects her frustration both at the confinement of women to this domestic sphere and at others' belittling of life in the kitchen, her culinary literary analogy at the end offers a tantalizing invitation. I begin with Sor Juana because the recent novel couplings of culinary and literary creation which are the subject of this chapter echo, at times deliberately, Sor Juana's words.

Three centuries after Sor Juana decried the forced relegation of women to the domestic sphere, represented by the kitchen, Rosario Castellanos denounced more emphatically the assumption that women's domain is the kitchen. In her story "Cooking Lesson," the narrator, an educated newlywed woman untrained in cooking announces sarcastically, "My place is here. I've been here from the beginning of time. In the German proverb woman is synonymous with Küche, Kinder, Kirche" (207). That Rosario Castellanos' (Cooking, Children, Church) feminist messages to Mexican women have taken root finds affirmation in Jean Franco's conclusion in *Plotting Women* that the goal of rejecting patriarchal domination has compelled "contemporary women novelists not only in Mexico but all over Latin America to move beyond the confines of domesticity" (186). Yet, surprisingly, a number of Latin American and Latina women writers seem to be reclaiming the kitchen, perhaps affirming seriously the declaration which Castellanos's new bride offers sarcastically.[1] A taste of this veritable buffet of recipes for writing by Latin American and Latina women may reassure concerned readers; none of this plethora of new works advocates a return to the proverbial state of "barefoot, pregnant and in the kitchen," or "la mujer honrada, la pierna quebrada y en casa."

In 1984 the organizers of a conference dedicated to the writings of Latin American and Latina women proclaimed the importance of the kitchen for women writers when they published the conference proceedings under the title *La sartén por el mango (The Frying Pan by the Handle)*. Editor Patricia Elena González summarizes their discussions of women's writing with a metaphoric call to take up their pots and pans: "Diríamos que a medida que cortábamos la cebolla, llorábamos; pero al pelar las capas artificialmente superpuestas sobre nuestra identidad como mujer latinoamericana, encontrábamos un centro. Orale, a tomar la sartén por el mango y a guisar." ("We could say that as we cut the onion, we cried; but upon peeling off the layers superimposed artificially over our identity as Latin American women, we found a center. Alright now, time to take the frying pan by the handle and start cooking," 17). Pointing to the correspondences between cooking and writing, at this conference the Puerto Rican Rosario Ferré described her development as a writer in terms of the kitchen in an essay entitled "La cocina de la escritura" ("The Kitchen of Writing"; 13–33). Sor Juana's assertion that, had he cooked, Aristotle would have written more, appears as the epigraph to this essay. Another work by Ferré, the story "El collar de camándulas" ("The Rosary Chain"), begins and ends with the whispered recitation of a family recipe for poundcake that evolves as a sign of the bond between the story's two female characters and, implicitly, a female reader. At the conclusion of the story the surviving, silenced female character employs the recipe to liberate herself from her male oppressors (122–33). When women writers of color in the United States, including several Latina writers, founded the Kitchen Table Press in 1981, providing a liberating voice for themselves, the name was chosen "because the kitchen is the center of the home, the place where women in particular work and communicate with each other" (Smith 11). Sharing this vision, the Latina writer, Helena María Viramontes entitles her essayistic testimonial about her commitment to writing "'Nopalitos': The Making of Fiction" and likens her own creative process to that of her mother preparing *nopalitos*. Humbly, she acknowledges, "I have never been able to match her *nopales*, but I have inherited her capacity for invention," and, hence, learned to find "my space on the kitchen table" for writing (192).[2] Each of these writers' kitchens or milieux as well as their cooking methods are unique and warrant individual study. Nonetheless, what links the works of all of these women writing after Rosario Castellanos is their reclaiming of the kitchen as a space of creative power rather than merely confinement, in literature which, as *Like Water for Chocolate*, seems to address itself primarily to a complicit female audience. Specifically, I see in Esquivel's narrative a particularly liberating and timely revival of Sor Juana's analogy.

In Laura Esquivel's *Like Water for Chocolate (Novel of monthly installments with recipes, loves and home remedies)*, the recipes for twelve sumptuous Mexican dishes form the narrative frame, and the protagonist learns and teaches "los secretos de la vida" ("the secrets of life") in the kitchen (13). The popularity of Esquivel's 1989 novel—into its eighth printing by October of 1991—seems to have resuscitated heirs to the Dominican friar's wariness of women in the kitchen, such as a critic who, dismissing *Like Water for Chocolate* and its peculiar use of recipes as entirely lacking in literary merit, declares that, "no tiene otra aspiración que ser novedosa" ("it has no aspiration but to be novel," Marquet 58). However, the novelty of Esquivel's enterprise, bringing together two supposedly incompatible companions for women today, the kitchen and writing, does have its ancestry, as does a certain skeptical response it evokes. Admittedly, Esquivel's concoction, which unabashedly mimics the form of a highly popular and melodramatic romance genre directed primarily at women and published in serial form in newspapers or magazines, the *folletín*, while also doubling as a cookbook, may incur criticism for uniting two literary forms notoriously and pejoratively associated with Cortazarian *lectores-hembra* or "female-readers.[3] Yet I find enormously suggestive the popular appeal of this recent lighthearted blending of ingredients from the kitchen and the *folletín*, far transcending the "female-reader" audience of serial fiction and popular romances.

"Like water for chocolate" is a Mexican expression which means "extremely agitated" referring to water sizzling enough to add chocolate to. The English equivalent would be boiling mad, and in Esquivel's novel the expression alludes to women's rage at being confined to the domestic sphere (Santamaría 37). At the same time, this title's culinary origin hints that to truly appreciate its meaning requires not only reading the novel but also preparing its recipe for chocolate. Similarly, from beginning to end, *Like Water for Chocolate* foregrounds parallels between culinary and literary creation. This liaison is implicit on the novel's first page when the protagonist, Tita de la Garza, is born prematurely onto the kitchen table amid the ingredients of her art: ("among the aromas of a noodle soup that was cooking, of the thyme, the bay leaf, the cilantro, the boiled milk, the garlic and, of course, the onion," 13). A prototypical domestic literary form, Tita's diary-cum-recipe book, edited by her grand-niece, comprises the serialized novel we read. Briefly, her story, the serial romance surrounding Tita's recipes, is this. As the youngest daughter of the tyrannical Mamá Elena, a widowed ranch owner living somewhere near the Mexican/U.S. border on the eve of the Mexican revolution, a mysterious family tradition dictates that marriage is forbidden her; instead she must remain at home to feed and care for her mother until the latter's death. The expression *like water for chocolate,* then, describes Tita's anger at her confinement to the kitchen as she endeavors to surmount the obstacles to her happiness. The rage she experiences is also that of women in traditional Mexican society, who were encouraged to repress their feelings, including anger and sexual desire. Tita's fate, which motivates the plot, rivals the most contrived of *folletín* stories, and her obedient intentions in the face of her mother's cruel domination reflect the polarized characterization typical of serialized fiction.[4] However, in *Like Water for Chocolate* the formulae of the *folletín*, including its episodic romantic plot and its melodramatic effects, are adapted to highlight the novel's recipes and the life of the kitchen.

Each chapter's title is that of the recipe to be recounted in it, a mouth-watering list of ingredients serves almost as a table of contents for each chapter, and the narrative begins with appetite-whetting instructions for preparing the recipe which Tita is engaged in making. Of course, because Tita is besieged with interruptions, like the women writers Virginia Woolf describes in *A Room of One's Own*, each recipe's narration is inevitably suspended to incorporate the incidents which intrude upon her cooking (Woolf 66–67). Likewise, the anticipated meal necessarily returns to preempt other activities and their narration. These competing but complementary narratives reinforce one another in postponing the final dénouement of the *folletín*, but the recipes and events narrated are also meant to mirror one another in eliciting nostalgic or erotic responses from their audience. Exemplifying this symbiosis, every chapter concludes, in folletinesque fashion, with a crisis resolved and a meal completed only to precipitate another unforeseen occurrence and accompanying dish, to be taken up in the following chapter. Consequently, a cliff-hanging ellipsis and the promise ("to be continued") closes every chapter, followed by the name of the upcoming recipe, as if the recipe itself were part of the cataclysmic event whose narrative we anxiously awaited. And, in a sense this is so, because in this novelistic world the unique manner of preparing a recipe can unleash untold euphoria or despair. These unexpected reactions suggest that the most authentic recipes are those which also release their consumers to express their passions, whether rage or desire.

Tita's unintentional modification of the recipe for "Quails in rose petals," for instance, provokes such unbridled passion in her sister Gertrudis that she abandons the family and is catapulted into an erotic encounter on horseback with an unidentified villista. Similarly, when, true to *folletín* plotting, Tita's sister Rosaura betrays her by marrying Tita's true love, Pedro, and, to make matters worse, Tita has to prepare the wedding cake, Tita's tears in the resulting cake inspire a disastrous explosion of nostalgic tears and vomiting among the guests. No longer trivial or incidental, here the art of recipe making determines the peripeties of plot. Furthermore, the narration of recipes itself works to define the relationship between reader, narrator, and protagonist.

With a knowing wink to readers who enjoy the arts of recipe sharing and kitchen talk, the narrator initiates a conversation in the novel's first paragraph, on the significant topic of onions. Like Patricia Elena González, whose words in *La sartén por el mango* I repeated earlier, Tita's grand-niece strays from the metaphoric image of an onion's layers to recall the more literal tear-jerking activity of chopping them. The narrator and Tita seem to unite in this gesture, as if to entice those who love the smell of onions and know the almost cathartic experience of chopping and sob-bing. In addition, with the revelation of her own sensitivity to onions and of a family secret to avoid that inevitable flood of tears, the narrator exposes parallels between recipe sharing and narrative:

> The onion must be finely minced. I suggest you place a little piece of onion on your forehead to avoid the annoying tears that come when you're chopping it. The bad thing about crying when you chop onions isn't the simple fact of crying, but that sometimes you begin, as they say, you get an itch and you can't stop scratching. I don't know if this has happened to you, but to me, the simple truth is it has. Hundreds of times. Mom used to say that it was because I'm just as sen-sitive to onions as Tita, my great aunt.

The narrator, with her colloquial language and tone, simultaneously introduces three generations of women who have shared recipes, and invites the implied readers into the kitchen to participate in this activity. What makes a recipe especially appealing for a listener, she knows, is an accompanying story, in this case, as the narrator's admission of her and Tita's enormous sensitivity to onions suggests, a tear-jerking tale. The narrator is alluding to Tita's plight, and we are perhaps also meant to read in this an allusion to the norms of the *folletín* romance, comically adapted by Esquivel. More significant than the *folletín* here, however, is the "embedded discourse" of the recipe, which Susan J. Leonardi has explored as a predominantly feminine narrative strategy that, like *recipe's* root in Latin, *recipere*, "implies an exchange, a giver, and a receiver" (340). Her illustration, from cookbooks and novels incorporating recipes, of recipe exchange as a contract of trust or understanding between giver and re-ceiver, narrator and listener aptly characterizes Laura Esquivel's culinary narrative. When the narrator in *Like Water for Chocolate* introduces herself, her mother, and Tita in the opening paragraph she begins to construct the community described by Leonardi, "a loose community of women that crosses the social barriers of class, race, and generation" (342).

Ignoring Mexican norms that prescribe familial allegiance while implicitly proscribing alliances across class and racial lines, this recipe-sharing community relies on different codes of female solidarity, read through characters' responses to recipes and the kitchen. Bonds of friendship form among characters who appreciate what Sor Juana calls the "natural secrets" of the kitchen, the artistry in creating and preparing recipes, and also their restorative powers. The ranch's Indian cook Nacha, Tita, the maid Chencha, the family doctor's Kickapoo grandmother, and, peripherally, Tita's sister Gertrudis, compose this female community. In this regard, Esquivel's "Novel of monthly installments" can be seen both to mirror the format of serialized fiction and to allude to a specifically female creative community, temporally oriented around a monthly menstrual cycle. In this community, from which Mamá Elena, as will be discussed later, remains notably absent, the members construct mother-daughter bonds, parallel to patterns Marianne Hirsch observes in what she calls the feminist family romance of the 1970's, which foregrounds "the retreat to the pre-oedipal as basis for adult personality, the concentration on mother-daughter bonding and struggle, and the celebration of female relationships of mutual nurturance. . . ." (133).

Tita, born on the kitchen table into such a world, learns the secrets of life in the kitchen from Nacha, who feeds her as an infant and entertains her through childhood by inventing games related to cooking. Tita's childhood in the kitchen, including her play and conversation with Nacha, constitutes both mother-daugther relationship and an apprenticeship in an artist's studio, which Tita directs after Nacha's death: "Tita was the last link in a chain of cooks who since prehispanic times had been transmitting the secrets of the kitchen from generation to generation and was considered the finest practitioner of this marvellous art, culinary art" (53). The tradition which Tita carries on is an oral one, learned experientially; however, with the death of Nacha Tita recognizes the fragility of a dying art, particularly recipes which Tita herself only vaguely recalls. These recipes, at the opportune moment for their use, are whispered by Nacha to Tita from beyond the grave. Gertrudis, perhaps the most devoted fan of Tita's recipes, fears that when her sister dies, "the family's past would die along with her" (182). Understanding both their evanescence in the absence of Nacha and their restorative function in Tita's daily life, Tita records the recipes, together with their accompanying story, because the situation of the recipe, such as Gertrudis's euphoria after tasting "Quails in rose petals," is inseparable in Tita's mind from the instructions for preparing the dish itself. Implicit in Tita's salvaging of Nacha's recipes in their context is a sense of the art of recipe narration as "embedded discourse": "Like a story, a recipe needs a recommendation, a context, a point, a reason to be" (Leonardi 340).

That reason to be, for Tita, resides especially in the effects of recipes on their audience. Nacha's recipes are life sustaining for Tita; they inspire her to write her life to preserve the recipes, and, more literally, Nacha's soups restore Tita to health. Following a nervous breakdown, Tita yearns to remember any recipe, because this would mean "volver a la vida" ("returning to life"; 131). Significantly, the word *recetas* in Spanish refers not only to recipes for food but to prescriptions for medicine. Likewise, the phrase *home remedies* in the novel's subtitle describes various home remedies interspersed throughout the narrative, but is also suggestive of the therapeutic character of the kitchen, specifically its recipes and accompanying conversation. Although the conversation centered on recipe sharing and cooking in this kitchen falls short of that which the African American writer Paule Marshall heard as a child among "the poets in the kitchen," Marshall's description of these women's talk reflects its restorative quality: "There was no way for me to understand it at the time, but the talk that filled the kitchen those afternoons was highly functional. It served as therapy, the cheapest kind available to my mother and her friends. . . . [I]t restored them to a sense of themselves and reaffirmed their self-worth" (6). In the kitchen with Nacha Tita experiences this therapy which both solaces and entertains.

The description of the kitchen, paradoxically symbolic of both confinement and escape, is suggestive of its dual role. The narrator purports to offer an image of the kitchen as an illustration of how it limits Tita's vision of the world, but the spatial imagery contradicts this message:

> It wasn't easy for a person who knew life by way of the kitchen to understand the outside world. This gigantic world which began from the kitchen door toward the inside of the house, because the one that lay adjacent to the back door of the kitchen and that overlooked the patio, the fruit garden, the vegetable garden, yes, it belonged completely to her; she controlled it. (14-15)

Even though the world denied to Tita is represented as "gigantic" it seems to lead no farther than the inside of the house, while the world of the kitchen also comprehends a vast, open expanse outside the back door. Furthermore, the verbs employed to link this world to Tita, "belonged to her" and "she controlled it," are indicative of the protagonist's need for a space to control her own destiny, as she ultimately does through her recipes which transcend these confines. As the narrator explains, even Mamá Elena cannot entirely repress Tita in the kitchen environment which inspires her creative expression, because "there the flavors, aromas, textures and what these might provoke escaped her rigorous control" (53).

Cruel rigor typifies Mamá Elena's management of Tita's life, in and out of the kitchen. An unexcelled master at any skill concerning "split-

ting open, dismantling, dismembering, desolating, weaning, hamstring-
ing, destroying or separating a child from its mother (demothering),"
one fundamental rule of culinary, or literary, art eludes Mamá Elena: the
need to adapt the rules to one's own creative talent. If Tita strays from
the precise rules for a recipe, as with Rosaura's wedding cake and the
"Quails in Rosepetals," she arouses Mamá Elena's destructive fury. But
Tita's creative spirit and its transformative power remain invincible. "But
she couldn't resist the temptation to transgress such rigid formulas as her
mother wanted to impose on her inside the kitchen . . . and in her life"
(200). And, indeed, it is through the ingredients of her recipes that Tita
is ultimately able to transgress or cross over (*transgredir*) the tyrannical
rules set by her mother.

When Tita convalesces in the home of the family's doctor following
her breakdown, she enjoys her first experience of leisure and an accompanying recognition of the oppression she has lived. Staring fixedly at her
now free hands, which in their idleness she barely recognizes as her own,
Tita recalls how a rigid schedule of work in the kitchen has dominated
all her days:

> At her mother's side, what her hands must do was coldly
> determined, there were no doubts. She had to get up, dress,
> light the fire in the stove, prepare breakfast, feed the animals,
> wash the dishes, make the beds, prepare dinner, wash the
> dishes, iron the clothes, prepare supper, wash the dishes, day
> after day, year after year. (114)

Although in spite of this recognition Tita later bows to familial obligation and returns home to care for her infirm mother, when Rosaura
announces that her daughter Esperanza will carry on the family tradition,
Tita takes up the cause of her niece's freedom with the zeal of a crusader.
The aunt willingly instructs Esperanza in culinary artistry, but also takes
advantage of their hours together to provide Esperanza with "other
kinds of knowledge than what her mother offered her" (238). It is
significant that while she nurtures Esperanza, Tita is aunt, not mother,
and she identifies with Esperanza through her own experience as Mamá
Elena's daughter. As Marianne Hirsch explains with regard to the feminist family romance of the 1970s, "It is the woman as *daughter* who
occupies the center of the global reconstruction of subjectivity and sub-
ject-object relation. The woman as *mother* remains in the position of
other . . ." (136). Therefore, recalling her own experience as the youngest daughter, Tita encourages her niece's intellectual curiosity and her
right to decide her own destiny, and ensures that she attends school.
Under Tita's dominion, then, the kitchen evolves as a space not only of
domestic activity but of feminist rebellion. Esperanza comes to value the

community and the creativity which the kitchen can foster, but as a result of Tita's rebellion, as an adult the niece enters the kitchen only when she chooses. Esperanza, in turn, passes on to her daughter, the narrator, the legacy of Tita's embedded recipes but not the oppressive familial law.

In the last monthly installment, faithful to the norms of the *folletín* romance, Tita and Pedro are finally united, although contrary to most Catholic-oriented serial endings, not in wedlock (Erhart 95–96). Instead, they find themselves "alone at last" when Tita's mother and Pedro's wife Rosaura die, victims of their own rejection of the social codes of the kitchen. Mamá Elena perishes from a poisonous overdose of the emetic she takes to counteract the effects of the poison-laced food she believes Tita is preparing for her. Only after her death does Tita discover Mamá Elena's letters from a forbidden romance with a mulatto. The man was murdered for their affair, during which Tita's sister Gertrudis was conceived. We can read Mamá Elena's butcherlike mastery of the kitchen, then, as her own angry response to the brutal imposition on her of societal conventions that forbade relations across racial and class lines. It is her bowing to antiquated social conventions that excludes her from the female recipe-sharing community of the kitchen, a community which continually upsets such norms. Adrienne Rich writes in "When We Dead Awaken: Writing as Re-Vision," that feminists' purpose is "not to pass on a tradition but to break its hold over us" (90). What condemns Mamá Elena, then, is that despite her own youthful rebellion, she ultimately elects to pass on a patriarchal tradition. The same is true for Rosaura, who has rejected the society of the kitchen out of a desire for acceptance by those who perpetuate the repressive norms of the past, "the cream of Piedras Negras society" (239). Her death, of obesity and flatulence, therefore, is an act of poetic justice. Following Mamá Elena and Rosaura's deaths, with all obstacles removed, Tita and Pedro abandon themselves to the erotic euphoria induced by the wedding banquet Tita prepares for Esperanza. Their flames of passion not only engulf the lovers but burn the entire ranch. Magically, Tita's culinary literary creation survives intact amid the rubble.

On the novel's last page the narrator, who, significantly, appears to be speaking to us from the kitchen as she prepares the novel's first recipe, informs readers that we have been reading her great aunt's recipe book-cum-autobiography. The narrator's conclusion, that Tita will continue to live on as long as there is someone to prepare her recipes, constitutes an invitation to turn back, like the narrator, to the first chapter to read and prepare its recipe. In the process, Tita's story has revealed, the heirs of her recipes should make them their own, with the addition of their own stories. This ending offers an invitation to create, highlighting the recipe-sharing community in the folletinesque love story.

If Esquivel delights in imitating the contemporary serial romance, her pleasure derives in part from subverting its conventions, including the norm of ending with an opulent Catholic wedding, an exaggerated fascination with appearances measured in material abundance and a tendency to segregate characters according to race and class (Erhart 96–101). However, this novel hardly represents a denunciation of the *folletín* romance. More probably Esquivel chooses to mimic this fictional form, typical of women's magazines, which generally include recipes, because of her greater fascination with the creative possibilities of the discourse of recipes. In the process of inventing this recipe-sharing community, Esquivel's work displays its sharpest divergence from serialized fiction, where "what is crucially missing . . . is any form of female solidarity" (Franco, "Incorporation" 137).

The female community of the kitchen in *Como agua para chocolate* may reflect women's propensity to define their identity more relationally than men, as suggested by Nancy Chodorow (205–209). Yet, solidarity among Mexican women has historically been very difficult, and the continuing obstacles to female alliances and community are represented in the novel by Mamá Elena and Rosaura. Cherríe Moraga points to the perpetuation of the myth of la Malinche, the Indian woman accused of betraying her people by becoming Cortés's lover, to illustrate how women are encouraged to abandon one another in their search for male approval (173–89). This tendency is all the more pervasive in popular Latin American fictional forms like the serial romance and the *novela rosa*, akin to the Harlequin romance genre. Therefore, although *Like Water for Chocolate* remains undeniably and unapologetically a romance, the creation in it of a community of women that defies these norms is of particular significance. Moreover, as has been observed reprovingly by the reviewer who criticized in Esquivel's novel an aspiration to novelty, "The female characters occupy the foreground in the novel," and "In *Like Water for Chocolate* the masculine presence is secondary" (Marquet 65–66). This is consistent with Marianne Hirsch's observation that in the feminist family romance, with its emphasis on the pre-oedipal and its highlighting of mutually nurturing female relationships, the father tends to be eliminated, and men are in a secondary position (129, 133). By locating the centric space of the novel in the kitchen, a primarily female setting, Esquivel has created an environment which promotes creative female community.

This is not to suggest that the novel supports a return of Mexican women to this domestic sphere, or that it should remain an exclusively female domain. The novel's title refers to a woman's anger at domestic imprisonment. Also, on repeated occasions in the novel men seem enticed to work in the kitchen. More tellingly, the fact that Tita's diary with her recipes emerges whole from the rubble of the ranch symbolizes both the liberation of the female artist from the oblivion of domesticity and the elimination of the patriarchal codes imaged by the ranch under the repressed and repressive dominion of Mamá Elena. Key to the novelty of *Like water for chocolate* is that the protagonist steps outside the kitchen without renouncing the creative force it embodies.

Yet this work also indicates that only after a woman is no longer confined to the space of the kitchen can she publicly celebrate its life. Tita, writing during the mythical time of the Mexican Revolution, records her recipes in her diary, but it remains in that private form until her grand-niece, the narrator, rewrites the diary and recipes as a novel. Sor Juana, an exception among women in the seventeenth century, can indulge in the pleasures of kitchen phenomena, because, as she proudly reminds an admiring poet in a *romance*, she is not forced to work there.[5]

> Gracias a Dios, que ya no
> he de moler Chocolate,
> ni me ha de moler a mí
> quien viniere a visitarme. (*Obras* 67)
> Thanks be to God, that no longer
> do I have to beat Chocolate,
> nor must I be harassed by
> anyone who might visit me.

Writing in 1971, Rosario Castellanos felt compelled to denounce the perception that women's domain is the kitchen, because at that time under twenty percent of women worked in the paid labor force in Mexico and most who did performed jobs which they also performed at home (Elmendorf 146-47). Furthermore, official recognition of literature by women in Latin America remained an anomaly. As the contributions of both female and male authors in the world of Latin American fiction today become more equally appreciated, the challenge to speak to the great diversity of female experience opens the doors for new recipes for writing.

In answer to this appeal, Esquivel offers a liberating vision of a denigrated experience of "dailiness" in many women's lives (Juhasz 223–24). In *Like water for Chocolate*, although repressive societal traditions appear to dominate Tita's life, the specific manner of preparing a recipe actually determines the lives and destinies of the characters. Perhaps the suspicions of the seventeenth-century Dominican friar about the subversive goals of women in the kitchen were justified. By bestowing such transformative power on the creativity of the artist in the kitchen and by converting the creative metaphors of the kitchen into a narrative method, Esquivel answers Patricia Elena González's metaphoric call to take up the weapons of the kitchen and start cooking, with a novel recipe for writing. Her work also suggests that the number and variety of possible recipes is infinite. The ingredients for this recipe include a recipe-sharing community, like Tita and her grand-niece whose voices unite to create the work we read; a kitchen, like the room for creative expression described long ago by Virginia Woolf; and the capacity for invention, which Helena María Viramontes finds in her mother's *nopalitos*. The invitation to readers to share recipes is also an invitation to continue the struggle to overcome the obstacles to creative female community. As for the "Manera de hacerse" ("Method of preparation"), as Rosario Ferré expresses it:

> The important thing is to apply that fundamental lesson that we learned from our mothers, the first, after all, to teach us how to deal with fire; the secret of writing, like that of good cooking, has absolutely nothing to do with sex, but with the wisdom with which one mixes the ingredients. (33)

NOTES

Unless otherwise noted, translations of Spanish passages into English are my own.

1. I use the term Latin American to refer to writers from Mexico, Central and South America or the Hispanic Caribbean. Latina refers to women writers of Hispanic origin living and writing in the United States. It is a political and linguistic term that these writers use in identifying themselves. As Earl Shorris explains in *Latinos: A Biography of the People*, "Politically, *Hispanic* belongs to the right and some of the center, while *Latino* belongs to the left and the center" (xvii). He goes on to note the linguistic reasons for using *Latino/Latina* instead of Hispanic. "Latino has gender, which is Spanish, as opposed to Hispanic, which follows English rules" (xvii).

2. *Nopalitos or nopales* (Cactus paddles), made by slicing and cooling the paddles from the Prickly Pear cactus, are a classic element in Mexican cuisine.

3. In his novel *Hopscotch*, Julio Cortázar opposes the naive *lector-hembra* or "female-reader" who seeks pleasing plots and happy endings to the sophisticated "reader-accomplice" (397–98).

4. For a highly critical description of the *folletín* romance genre popular especially among female readers in Mexico, see Rosario Castellanos, "Corín Tellado: Un caso típico" (142-43).

5. That Sor Juana enjoyed the creative community of the kitchen, however, is attested to by the little-known fact that she authored the first cookbook known in New Spain (Muriel 478).

WORKS CITED

Castellanos, Rosario. "Cooking Lesson." *A Rosario Castellanos Reader*. Ed. Maureen Ahern. Austin: U of Texas P, 1988. 207–215.

———. "Corín Tellado: Un caso típico." *Mujer que sabe latín*. México: Fondo de Cultura Económica, 1984. 138–143.

Chodorow, Nancy. *The Reproduction of Mothering*. Berkeley: U of California P, 1978.

Cortázar, Julio. *Hopscotch*. New York: Random, 1966.

de la Cruz, Sor Juana Inés. *Obras completas*. México: Porrúa, 1985.

———. *A Woman of Genius: The Intellectual Autobiography of Sor Juana Inés de la Cruz*. Trans. Margaret Sayers Peden. Salisbury, CT: Lime Rock Press, 1987.

Elmendorf, Mary. "Mexico: The Many Worlds of Women." *Women: Roles and Status in Eight Countries*. Ed. Janet Zollinger Giele and Audrey Chapman Smock. New York: Wiley, 1977.

Erhart, Virginia. "Amor, ideología y enmascaramiento en Corín Tellado." *Casa de las Américas* 77 (1973): 95–96.

Esquivel, Laura. *Como agua para chocolate (Novela de entregas mensuales con recetas, amores y remedios caseros)*. México: Planeta, 1989.

Ferré, Rosario. "El collar de camándulas." *Papeles de Pandora*. México: Joaquín Mortiz, 1979. 122–133.

———. "La cocina de la escritura." *Sitio a Eros*. México: Joaquín Mortiz. 1986, 13–33.

Franco, Jean. "The Incorporation of Women: A Comparison of North American and Mexican Popular Narrative." *Studies in Entertainment*. Ed. Tania Modleski. Bloomington: Indiana UP, 1986, 119–138.

———. *Plotting Women*. New York: Columbia UP, 1989.

Gage, Thomas. *The English-American: A New Survey of the West Indies, 1648*. London: Routledge, 1946.

González, Patricia Elena, and Eliana Ortega, eds. *La sartén por el mango*. Río Piedras, P.R.: Huracán, 1985.

Hirsch, Marianne. *The Mother/Daughter Plot*. Bloomington: Indiana UP, 1989.

Juhasz, Susanne. "Towards a Theory of Form in Feminist Autobiography: Kate Millett's *Flying* and *Sita;* Maxine Hong Kingston's *The Woman Warrior*." *International Journal of Women's Studies* 2 (1979): 62–75.

Leonardi, Susan J. "Recipes for Reading: Summer Pasta, Lobster à la Riseholme, and Key Lime Pie." *PMLA* 104 (1989): 340–347.

Marquet, Antonio. "La receta de Laura Esquivel." *Plural* 237 (1991): 58–67.

Marshall, Paule. "From the Poets in the Kitchen." *Reena and Other Stories.* Old Westbury: Feminist P, 1983.

Moraga, Cherríe. "From a Long Line of Vendidas: Chicanas and Feminism." *Feminist Studies/Critical Studies.* Ed. Teresa de Lauretis. Bloomington: Indiana UP, 1986. 173–89.

Muriel, Josefina. *Cultura femenina novohispana.* México: UNAM, 1982. 478.

Rich, Adrienne. "When We Dead Awaken: Writing as Re-Vision," *Adrienne Rich's Poetry.* Eds. Albert Gelpi and Barbara Gelpi. New York: Norton, 1975. 90–98.

Santamaría, Francisco J. *Diccionario de mejicanismos.* 2nd ed. México: Porrúa, 1974.

Shorris, Earl. *Latinos: A Biography of the People.* New York: Norton, 1992.

Smith, Barbara. "A Press of Our Own: Kitchen Table: Women of Color Press." *Frontiers: A Journal of Women's Studies* 10 (1989): 11–13.

Viramontes, Helena María. "'Nopalitos': The Making of Fiction." *Making Face, Making Soul/Haciendo caras.* Ed. Gloria Anzaldúa. San Francisco: Aunt Lute, 1990.

Woolf, Virginia. *A Room of One's Own.* New York: Harcourt Brace, 1989.

11

"A Sinkside, Stoveside, Personal Perspective": Female Authority and Kitchen Space in Contemporary Women's Writing

Patricia Moran

[W]hen from a long-distant past nothing subsists . . .
taste and smell alone, more fragile but more enduring,
more unsubstantial, more persistent, more faithful,
remain poised a long time, like souls, remembering,
waiting, hoping, amid the ruins of all the rest; and
bear unflinchingly, in the tiny and almost impalpable
drop of their essence, the vast structure of recollection.

—Marcel Proust, *Remembrance of Things Past*

Memories come back to you in your mouth.

—Judith Moore, *Never Eat Your Heart Out*

The most famous passage in culinary memoir remains its originary moment, when Marcel Proust tasted a tea-soaked crumb of madeleine and the village of Combray suddenly took "shape and solidity" in his memory, as if it "sprang into being . . . from my cup of tea" (51). Whereas for Proust this single "taste memory" became a means of accessing the "vast structure of recollection," for a number of contemporary women writers the link between memory and food has itself assumed extraordinary significance, giving rise to a distinct subgenre of autobiography that locates female subjects in relation to food and cooking, kin and kitchen, appetite and desire.[1] These memoirs make a compelling case for Barbara Haber's contention that "the interpretation of attitudes and customs about food can be a shortcut to understanding the deepest or most hidden truths of people and groups" (69). In this chapter I want to explore the implications of an anxiety that emerges repeatedly in some recent women's autobiographical writing—an anxiety that American women's entrance into the workforce has left the kitchen empty and the home without a hearth. A number of women insist that essential and irreplaceable elements of cultural and ethnic tradition reside in childhood memories of someone's (typically Mother's or Grandmother's) cooking; in a single generation, they claim, as an inadvertent result of the success of second-wave feminism, these elements and the traditions that they embody and transmit are in danger of disappearing. These writers demonstrate, in differing ways, how the sense of community and family identity facilitated by some cooking women worked to transmit interpersonal, relational "ways of knowing" that served as alternatives to the values of consumerist America.[2] Yet while these writers make a good case for the necessity of preserving cultural and ethnic traditions, they assume that it is women who must preserve these cultural and ethnic traditions, an equation of the kitchen with the cooking mother that suggests some nostalgia for American postwar domesticity and for a maternal and feminine identity based upon secure and socially sanctioned domestic roles. Yet I do not agree with feminists such as Judith Stacey and Katha Pollit that this longing for a female "kitchen culture" is only reactionary and nostalgic; this dismissal overlooks the very real losses these writers identify in the contemporary exodus from the kitchen.[3] In this chapter I want to look carefully at a group of texts—Paule Marshall's essay "From the Poets in the Kitchen," the essays collected by Arlene Voski Avakian in *Through the Kitchen Window: Women Writers Explore the Intimate Meanings of Food and Culture,* and Elizabeth Ehrlich's *Miriam's Kitchen: A Memoir*—to sort out a number of issues. First, I want to identify the values writers associate with the kitchen and with cooking women. Then, by reading through Ehrlich's book-length account of her conversion to keeping kosher, I want to identify the pressures and contradictions that might encourage a professional woman to turn away from the public sphere and embrace a seemingly retrogressive domestic role. Finally, I want to suggest some ways feminists can move beyond what now seems a stalled debate about the kitchen and women's relationships to it.

The importance of the kitchen as a space in which women can promote "ways of knowing" antithetical to the values of a patriarchal, racist, and capitalist culture has been argued with particular passion and eloquence by women of color (and memorialized in Barbara Smith's and Audre Lorde's naming their press Kitchen Table). In "From the Poets in the Kitchen," Paule Marshall writes that the women who gathered in her mother's kitchen at the end of long days spent providing domestic labor for white women sought a form of therapy there: "[I]t restored them to a sense of themselves and reaffirmed their self-worth" (6). Here, they found their own authority and voice: "Those late afternoon conversations on a wide range of topics were a way for them to feel they exercised some measure of control over their lives and the events that shaped them. . . . They were in control, if only verbally and if only for the two hours or so that they remained in our house" (7). Given the limitations of her education—Marshall describes the absence of literatures and histories of people of color in her school and local library—these women daily enacted for Marshall the paradigm of verbal artistry and racial heritage:

> [T]hat freewheeling, wide-ranging, exuberant talk functioned as an outlet for the tremendous creative energy they possessed. They were women in whom the need for self-expression was strong, and since language was the only vehicle readily available to them they made of it an art form that—in keeping with the African tradition in which art and life are one—was an integral part of their lives. (6)

Their creative use of English exemplifies Gilles Deleuze's and Felix Guattari's description of a revolutionary minor literature as one that tears it "away from its own language, allowing it to challenge the language and making it follow a sober revolutionary path" (170); the speaker acts as "a sort of stranger *within* his own language" (172). Marshall details the deliberate interventions her mother and her friends worked upon English thus:

> They had taken the standard English taught them in the primary schools of Barbados and transformed it into an idiom, an instrument that more adequately described them—changing around the syntax and imposing their own rhythm and accent so that the sentences were more pleasing to their ears. They added the few African sounds and words that had survived. . . .

> And to make it more vivid, more in keeping with their expres-
> sive quality, they brought to bear a raft of metaphors, parables,
> Biblical quotations, sayings, and the like. . . . (8)

Hence they become for Marshall a "set of giants" more important than the "usual literary giants," and it is to them that she attributes her best work: "[I]t stands as testimony to the rich legacy of language and culture they so freely passed on to me in the wordshop of the kitchen" (12).

Like Marshall, Gloria Wade-Gayles points to the authority and sense of community black women experienced in the kitchen; indeed, the title of her essay, " 'Laying on Hands' through Cooking: Black Women's Majesty and Mystery in Their Own Kitchens," assigns not just authority but a queenly spirituality to her mother and other women in the community. Their kitchens became "temples in which they prepared sacraments for family rituals" (96), and their sense of community with other women had cooking as the "centerpiece of their bonding" (97). Wade-Gayles's description of what women found in the kitchen resonates with Marshall's: "Women . . . went to the kitchen to work, to serve, to think, to meditate, and to bond with one another. . . . In their kitchens, the women experienced influence, authority, achievement, and healing" (97). Her mother's passion for books and ideas, while denied a public and cultural outlet, found expression at the kitchen table; Wade-Gayles writes, "We never simply ate her cooking; we feasted on her love for polemics" (100). And, like Marshall, Wade-Gayles sees enacted in this kitchen culture a set of values not available elsewhere, for the ritual of meal taking keeps black history and self-affirmation alive: "It was a ritual that began during slavery when my ancestors gathered to testify, to bond, to gain strength from one another, to imagine themselves free and empowered. It traveled through time to the housing project of my youth and to Mama's kitchen" (100). To envision her mother as unfulfilled simply because she did not have the same opportunities as her academic daughter did is to be guilty of dismissing those alternative, relational, interpersonal ways of knowing: "In an era that has forgotten the joy of service and the patience of love, it is easy to forget our mothers and minimize the mastery of their art in their own kitchen" (99).

For a number of these writers, the mother's kitchen stands as a repository for values antithetical to consumer culture, a culture typically imaged in the excess and poor nutrition of fast food. For Wade-Gayles, her mother's cooking exemplified black spiritual practices: "It is like the 'laying on of hands' we talk about and testify to and about in the black community; the healing hands touch us through the food they prepare" (98–99). Hence she fears the "spiritual malnutrition" that could result from the loss of her mother's kitchen culture:

>Perhaps in this world of microwave and frozen meals, of caf-
>eteria and fast foods, those kitchens are rarely open and might,
>in fact, be disappearing, along with cast-iron skillets that held
>memory and the weight of character. Without them, how do
>we as mothers lay hands on future generations? How do we
>feed them and what do we feed them in this world of spiritual
>malnutrition? (101)

As Wade-Gayles makes clear, it is not just the mother's cooking, but the
cultural and spiritual messages embodied in that cooking that she mourns,
the cast-iron skillets that held "memory and weight of character." Her
claims resonate with those of Marie Smyth, a poet who grew up in
Ireland, for whom food embodies national identity: "[P]atriotism is the
memory of foods eaten in childhood," she writes (92). For Elizabeth
Ehrlich, the kosher kitchen becomes a space that "sets limits on
appetite . . . not a bad thing . . . in a society bloated with excess" (16).
Like Wade-Gayles, Ehrlich envisions the kitchen as a spiritual locus where
she resists assimilation and transmits Jewish identity and history to her
children. Almost all of these writers, moreover, implicitly connect the
mother's cooking with an important oral tradition; the kitchen is a
"wordshop" (Marshall 12), a place of "practical, mystical teachings, spiraling back through time" and "dished out with soup" (Ehrlich xi). Thus
the replacement of family meals with what Smyth calls "a submerging
tide of a fast-food monoculture" threatens not only to bury "our diverse
food histories and cultures" (94), it threatens matrilineal narratives: "And
what stories will the mothers of this generation tell their children? Will
the knowledge I was given by my mother be lost? How will today's
mothers feed their children's sense of belonging, of nurturing and being
nurtured?" (93).

It would be easy to charge these writers with idealizing the mother's
or grandmother's kitchen. Cultural historian Stephanie Coontz claims
that "many of our 'memories' of traditional family life [are] myths. Families have always been in flux and often in crisis; they have never lived up
to nostalgic notions about 'the way things used to be'" (2). John R.
Gillis similarly argues that Americans create "symbolic families" that
represent "ourselves to ourselves as we would like to think we are" (xv).
The transformation of the vexed and conflicted families of past decades
into static and stable "golden ages" is part of that myth-making process:

>In projecting a static image of family onto a particular past
>time and place, we immediately begin to describe change in
>terms of "decline" or "loss." Ironically, we are also in the
>habit of updating the traditional community and family peri-
>odically so that the location of the golden age is constantly

> changing. For the Victorians, the traditional family, imagined
> to be rooted and extended, was located sometime before in-
> dustrialization and urbanization, but for those who came of
> age during the First World War, tradition was associated with
> the Victorians themselves; today we think of the 1950s and
> 1960s as the location of the family and community we imag-
> ine we have lost. (4–5)

Such images are families we live by rather than live with, Gillis argues;
that is, they are symbolic families that say more about our efforts to
stabilize ourselves than they do about the real lived conditions of families
in the past: "Constituted through myth, ritual, and image, [symbolic
families] must be forever nurturing and protective, and we will go to any
lengths to ensure that they are so, even if it means mystifying the realities
of family life" (xv).

Certainly it is true that Wade-Gayles, Smyth, and Ehrlich write about
yesterday's kitchens and cooking women in a way that idealizes feminine
self-sacrifice; as Marjorie De Vault has shown, the "caring work" involved
in feeding families still falls primarily on women and still requires them
to subordinate their own needs and desires to other family members.[4]
Women have viewed—and continue to view—this kind of "caring work"
as burdensome and oppressive. Accounts such as those by Wade-Gayles
and Ehrlich tend to elide or play down aspects of oppression and subordination. These memoirs, moreover, seem permeated by a sense of
loss, as if the memory of the cooking mother reflects the child's perspective of comfort in the mother's nurturing; when Wade-Gayles remembers,
"We had everything we needed in our mothers' kitchens" (101), the
mother's kitchen becomes a lost childhood Eden, a perfect plenitude.
Elizabeth Kamarck Minnich has commented on the complex emotional
valence surrounding the cooking mother; she identifies her own attach-
ment to the idea of "the mother who cooks" as one derived from childhood memory and need: "Of course I want to think of myself as a
woman who cooks. A cooking woman is strong, fragrant, capable unto
magical, loving and very much in charge in a world my child's memories
hold, still, as more real and more important than the world outside the
house was then" (135). She notes that her attitudes about cooking were
formed by an early identification of cooking with the effective and com-
petent women in her life: "Cooking was rather like being part of the
mystery of being grown-up; fried chicken and shrimp De Jonghe were
the things the women who made safe houses knew how to do" (140).
Yet Minnich herself draws a clear distinction between cooking and "pro-
ducing meals" (143), a distinction she guards as a way of carving out a
nondomestic role for herself. Even as an adolescent, she chooses to learn
"special" cooking, "the making of fancy desserts" (143); somewhat older,

she takes over her mother's dinner parties: "My cooking . . . stayed separate from hers: I did the Special Events and the desserts" (143). Later, married and the step-mother to three boys, Minnich refuses what she terms "the role of feeding women": "I have never tried to inhabit that role: I made Nanny's and Grammy's and Mother's art into something both more private and more social, skirting the familial. I cooked because I loved to cook, and I gave my cooking to friends. Meals? I took my turn at preparing them, not investing in them" (144). It is only when her step-sons are grown and gone that Minnich returns to cooking; she observes that the men in her family, like her, practice cooking as a social act, "a special gift for a special occasion, as a kind of enactment of mutuality. Perhaps we are all still avoiding the sinkhole of need for a Feeding Mother, while we practice artfully creating our own cultured homes" (145).

But is the need for a Feeding Mother merely nostalgic, merely regressive? Or have, in fact, writers like Smyth, Wade-Gayles, and Marshall identified aspects of kitchen culture too easily overlooked when the kitchen is characterized as a domestic ghetto for women not permitted access to educations, careers, or lives outside the home? The feminist critique of the 1950s cult of domesticity held that housewives wasted their lives on trivia; popular representations of housewives depicted them as infantilized, exploited, and even crazy. And it is certainly true that many women felt frustrated with their economic dependence and lack of status; many conveyed their anger and frustration to their daughters only too clearly. Yet domestic work in and of itself is not inherently demeaning; it is when it is characterized as low status and relegated to a subordinate class of people that it becomes demeaning. Arlene Voski Avakian notes, "Because cooking has been conceptualized as part of our oppression, 'liberation' has often meant freedom from being connected to food" (5). It is interesting, for example, that Minnich wanted a doctorate because of the respect accorded her grandfather's study; while it was off-limits to the other women in her family, she was allowed in: "I wanted to have such a place as my own, and my grandfather, by allowing me and only me in while he was working, gave me permission" (138).[5] She describes her grandmother and mother, on the other hand, "as self-conscious about being 'uneducated'" (141). Her decision to avoid "meals" and prepare only "desserts and special events" thus speaks to her desire to avoid being relegated to the domestic, implicitly female realm of the uneducated; her essay points to her family's privileging of the work of the mind over that of the body. Wade-Gayles's portrait of her mother's kitchen, by contrast, suggests that her mother's work in the kitchen was a source of power and authority for her, not just in the family, but in the black community as well.

It is here that we would do well to heed Avakian's claim that food preparation, like other "kin work," forms "part of the invisible labor of women":

> Though absolutely central to our survival, it is what is taken for granted. If we delve into the relationship between women and food we will discover the ways in which women have forged spaces within that oppression. Cooking becomes a vehicle for artistic expression, a source of sensual pleasure, an opportunity for resistance and even power. (6)

Many of the contributors to Avakian's anthology echo this claim. Margaret Randall argues that "Our creativity deserves a monument":

> In contemporary women's struggle to live our feminism, we have consistently been made to feel ashamed of loving to cook; just as prefeminist pressures shamed the women who did not enjoy this activity. And yet—each in our own milieu and according to our circumstance and need—we are most often the artists, organizers, and drudges of what passes the palates and fills the bellies of those we love. (122)

Barbara Haber, the curator of Radcliffe's Schlesinger Library, decries the way in which kitchens and cooking have become "symbols of subservience" to contemporary feminists. Even when feminists do study food, she charges, their intellectual frameworks construct food preparation as a site "fraught with conflict, coercion, and frustration" (68). Feminists have also inadvertently participated in the denigration of kitchen culture: an emphasis on public accomplishment has meant that "women's domestic roles, which preoccupy most women most of the time, have been seen as impediments to women's success, ignoring the possibility that domestic life can be acknowledged and even celebrated without buying into an oppressive value system" (68). She urges feminist scholars to rethink their relationship to the kitchen: "[A]n interest in scholarship is not incompatible with an interest in cooking," she writes (74).

REMEMBERING THE FEEDING MOTHER

That food writing can be an index of contemporary women's efforts to carve out a sense of femininity is exemplified in Elizabeth Ehrlich's autobiographical account of her gradual shift to keeping a kosher kitchen and observing Jewish rituals more attentively. Ehrlich examines multiple strands of kitchen culture: she writes about the connection between kitchen practices and the memories of childhood, her sense of domesticity as artistry, her anxiety about cultural and ethnic loss, and her desire to reclaim the prerogatives of the cooking mother. Ehrlich's memoir speaks to a number of different genres within autobiographical practice: as a conversion narrative, it traces Ehrlich's path from the "diaspora" (her term) of her childhood to her embrace of more Orthodox practices; as a Holocaust testimonial, it recounts the growing intimacy between Ehrlich and her mother-in-law Miriam, a Holocaust survivor; as an autobiography, it traces Ehrlich's search for a stable maternal and feminine role, a search that ends in her transformation of herself into Minnich's Feeding Mother. Her story is congruent with other such accounts of professional women who came of age in the 1960s and 1970s: well-educated, even feminist, these women leave the work force, often after having children, to devote themselves to what seems a nostalgic recreation of the fifties housewife.[6] Ehrlich's story is particularly interesting because she records in detail the kinds of conflicts—and the kinds of justifications—that accompany this path. Initially she worries about how she can balance the demands of her job as a magazine reporter with what she's trying to accomplish at home: "I long drew from observant households a metaphor never written in the Book: the symbolic sacrifice not of Isaac but the Mother. The mother who bends the course of life to have everything ready for that Friday night, who brings in the Sabbath but never rests" (24). Yet by the end of the book she has quit her job, had another baby, and moved from New York to the suburbs; she speaks of gardening, cooking, raising her children, but she only alludes occasionally to the actual writing of *Miriam's Kitchen*—and, significantly, when she does refer to her writing, it is only to her recording of recipes. In fact, while her skills as a reporter are evident in the eloquence, detail, and organization of the book, Ehrlich consistently dismisses her professional life as an irrelevance compared to what she is trying to establish at home. She acknowledges the conflict in a section in which she discusses Passover preparations: "I can either write about it or do it, but not both. I'm not doing Passover this year," she declares (193). Then, drawn in little by little, each concession to having a simple Seder compelling her to add yet another aspect of ritual, she finds herself asking, "Why would I want any life to live other than a Passover week with my family?" (195).

The answer to this question begins in Ehrlich's search for a stable Jewish identity in her Detroit childhood, where she feels herself "an onion roll amongst cupcakes" (34). Her parents, themselves raised in observant families and kosher homes, lived kosher-style: they kept "the taste but not the blessing" (178). The result is a childhood that Ehrlich terms a "diaspora," an exile from Jewish roots and practices. Ehrlich longs for more recognizable marks of her cultural heritage; significantly, she early on equates Jewish identity with keeping kosher: "I wanted something recognizable to wear as an I.D. badge. . . . [W]e children clamored for . . . a kitchen arsenal to objectify our leanings, to tether us to a solid post" (183). The kitchen serves already as the stable foundation, the anchor that can weight Ehrlich's feelings of rootlessness. Indeed, the very basis of the stable identity revolves around kosher practices so ingrained that they have become internalized and can be drawn upon almost reflexively. Out of long-standing custom, for example, her mother makes ready the Sabbath, cooking chicken soup, cleaning the house, and lighting candles on Friday night. Because her mother grew up "secure within that *perfection*" (my emphasis) of a kosher, observant household, she can afford to pick and choose: "[I]nto that pot went sentiment, homeland and yearning, the ten commandments, and the right to decide yourself what you want to do" (149, 150). While her mother tells Ehrlich she merely did what she knew how to do, Ehrlich perceives her mother's cooking soup as "keeping the flame alive" (151).

In fact, this kind of customary, reflexive behavior is what Ehrlich wants for herself and her children. As she sees it, ritual actions embody and convey spiritual meaning; form becomes one with content. The performance actualizes the latent spiritual meaning: "The doing . . . brings back all I saw and felt and knew. It is not the same without the doing" (214); "Drawn to ritual, I may perhaps draw nearer to meaning. First principles are becoming interwoven in the fabric of daily life" (315). But as a latecomer to ritual, Ehrlich feels herself inevitably more distanced from the perfect meshing of form and content than those who internalize the rituals in childhood. She thus never wavers from the rules, whereas people like her parents and her husband are more comfortable with an occasional lapse. She will not stop for fast-food chicken, for example, whereas she imagines her husband could: "Here is the difference between those returning to tradition (me) and those securely rooted but not absolutist in life" (260). Similarly, when she converts her kitchen to kosher, her mother teasingly refers to her as a *rebetsin*, a "rabbi's wife," a "gentle put-down" for a woman of zealous and newfound virtue; Ehrlich ruefully reflects that her mother's "soul was kosher even if the food was *treyf* [not kosher]. I sometimes think that I am the opposite" (298). Hence it is Ehrlich's hope that her children will develop "kosher souls." In a passage near the close of the book, Ehrlich describes her daughter's singing of a *Shabbas* after-meal grace on a walk home from a Chinese restaurant: "She did not know that the words remind us there is a universe out there, beyond one's own sated contentment," Ehrlich remarks "She recited by rote. . . . [B]ut someday she will understand the words. The form is hers and the form holds content" (359). The emphasis on content points toward both meanings: form promises meaning and meaning promises fulfillment

The birth of this daughter, in fact, spurs Ehrlich to develop a kind of kitchen culture that will transmit familial—implicitly Jewish—values.

Ehrlich reflects, "Even a small baby somehow moves life into the kitchen" (123); once in that kitchen, "cooking took on other values. . . . I was finding a regular way in the kitchen as I was finding my way as a mother—fertile ground for dormant Jewish roots" (124). As her language suggests, Ehrlich views the need to cook for and to feed children as an inherently organic and natural maternal desire specific to women. At the same time, she uses images of foundations and buildings to depict the kind of stable identity and family structure she wants to construct for her children. In a repeated phrase, Ehrlich writes that she "wanted to build a floor under my children, something very strong and solid" (xii): "I didn't worry about spiritual pollution, only about building a floor under my children. A basic floor that would hold them as they grew and went their way" (126). Later, after she has successfully converted her kitchen to kosher and herself to the cooking and feeding mother, Ehrlich will recall with satisfaction an evening when she refuses to get fried chicken at a fast-food restaurant despite her son's demands:

> We came home and fixed dinner, the children helped or had to wait longer, and at last we ate, looking at one another around our own kitchen table. I knew what went into our bodies that evening, and I could feel good about it. . . .
>   . . . we also cemented one more brick into the rising edifice of our life as a family. We eat at home, mostly, and less and less often dine out. We don't make spur-of-the-moment decisions. We pick and choose and have a certain consciousness about it. We don't have a fast-food life. (261)

Deliberate, planned, orchestrated, the family meal enables the stable family to coalesce around the kitchen table, where the mother can feel good about the food—and herself. As in the well-known fairytale, the cement and bricks that form the family edifice withstand the wolf of American consumer culture.

Creating the brick house is not an easy task, however, in part because the tradition that Ehrlich has inherited from her parents is so dilute that it is in danger of disappearing altogether. *Miriam's Kitchen* is rife with accounts of familial Jewish cooking and ritual that has vanished irrevocably: Ehrlich's maternal grandmother's recipes; the recipe for Aunt Dora's honey cake; even her paternal grandmother's Passover celebration: "[W]ithout my grandmother to hold things together, its Jewish essence also dispersed. . . . Our reliable reunion became Christmas" (99). These losses Ehrlich associates with what the American chef James Beard called "taste memory." Hence Aunt Dora's honey cake contained something more than strudel "stretched to transparent perfection": "In the package [which Aunt Dora sent annually to her father] were history, family, culture, tradition, heart" (18); the cake speaks of "[t]he religion of persecution and wandering, of Sabbath and synagogue, of ambition and obligation" (337). "When tasted, this cake could stop the passage of time," Ehrlich observes (336). Yet this cake that could stop the passage of time itself dies with Aunt Dora.

Ehrlich eventually recognizes remnants of her heritage embedded within American (that is, Christian) acts of assimilation: many of the dishes her Aunt Selina cooks for Christmas, for example, have been taken from a traditional Hanukkah menu. Nonetheless, she fears that her children will grow up with memories of an alien tradition:

> [T]ime was running out on us, the second generation. Our ecumenical center could not hold. In a few years there would be children with no memory of my grandmother's Passover to balance Selina's Christmas. We would have to create new Jewish memories for them, or find the text of their later longings to be scalloped potatoes, tinsel, and ham. (103)

The allusion to Yeats's "Second Coming" underscores the apocalyptic urgency Ehrlich brings to reclaiming Jewish traditions; with its images of events spinning out of control, the poem suggests the fragmentation and rootlessness of those who have no center to hold them in orbit. And when Ehrlich turns to her mother-in-law for cooking lessons, she discovers yet another reason for keeping kosher. For Miriam is a Holocaust survivor whose cooking is a form of testimony to all those Jewish families and traditions destroyed in the camps; she "cooks through a repertoire the rest of the world has nearly forgotten" (6). Ehrlich's mission takes on added urgency when she begins to see herself as the sole heir of Miriam's legacy[7]: "[I]t has come down to this: Miriam, an only child, who came out of the war with a mother, two aunts, and an uncle, showing me on behalf of a single grand-daughter. . . . What else might I have done today, on this balmy Friday, simply cannot exist. The pronoun 'I' does not exist" (265). Eventually, like the biblical Ruth, Ehrlich takes direction from her intimate connection with her mother-in-law: "Whither thou goest I will go," she quotes (236).

Miriam's Kitchen is at its most moving when Ehrlich lovingly documents the growing intimacy she and Miriam develop during these lessons. The kind of story telling and oral history that essayists in *Through the Kitchen Window* associate with the cooking mother is literalized in the chapters in which Miriam's stories about the Holocaust emerge in between steps of a recipe. Miriam cooks as a way to counter the nightmare of the past (xii); survival for her is cooking, "creat[ing] the world again, by memory" (44). Ehrlich is attracted to Miriam's kitchen, moreover, because Miriam seems to know exactly what her role is as a woman:

she embodies for Ehrlich the kind of internalized knowledge that promises stability and serenity. Ehrlich's images for Miriam reflect this equation, for she consistently likens Miriam's cooking to a natural, organic process. Miriam cooks "to a fine internal clockwork" (154); her baking has a rhythm like the inevitable and eternal movement of the sun and the seasons: "The year ebbs and flows. Miriam's cakes work, form, swell, and subside, and the universe is good to us: another cake already on horizon's rim" (155). At other moments Ehrlich pictures Miriam as a domestic artist whose repertoire resembles a set of musical compositions played in an orderly seasonal rhythm:

> Miriam's repertoire is a dependable selection. It is Bach, Brahms, and Beethoven, with a little Chopin, Dvořák, and Irving Berlin added in over the years.
>   Life, with such constancy to the classics, can be managed. . . .
>   . . . Keeping kosher, I think, must also be simpler, less of a headache, if one is rendering the same symphonies, sonatas, and songs each year. Keeping kosher is hard in my house, when my cooking style resembles a long, undisciplined riff: madrigal fading to muzak, the Mexican Hat Dance, the overture to *Carmen*, and for the children, endless variations on "The Cat and the Fiddle." (63–64)

Ehrlich finds the structure of Miriam's "classical" cooking a calm, orderly, deeply ingrained pattern, a pattern both deeply soothing and deeply satisfying; by contrast, her comic, self-deprecating images of herself point to her sense of inner fragmentation and family chaos.

What Ehrlich perceives as Miriam's more "grounded" sense of female identity, moreover, reminds Ehrlich of her own grandmothers, immigrants whose "truest sphere" was the kitchen: "I forgot the practical, mystical teachings, spiraling back through time, that the grandmothers had dished out with their soup. I forgot the dignity my immigrants had, that comes with the connection to something larger than everyday life, even when you are doing nothing more than stirring soup" (xi). In these kitchens Ehrlich experiences the atmosphere of intimacy and story telling that she later values with Miriam. Her paternal grandmother sat before her stove, stirring soup, "dishing out salty perceptions of life": "she chopped, grated, salted, peppered. There she handed on traditions brought from the Old World and translated amidst the exigencies of the New. Much of my valuable learning took place in that kitchen" (xi). Her maternal grandmother also recalls Miriam: "[S]he never seemed rushed or frazzled, she was elegant and deliberate in her kitchen. This was her life and she was consistent in it. Kitchen work was not something apart from life or distinct from what counted, not something to get through in order to get to the life you preferred" (241–242).[8] What Miriam and the grandmothers practice is something Ehrlich will eventually identify as "female religion," a mode of housekeeping and cooking that endows the mundane with meaning:

> It has always been the religion of the home that compelled me, not that of the public sphere. My felt heritage was kitchen, and holiday, and attitude, the atmosphere that my grandmothers were able to protect and transmit, against odds, through time. You could have that heritage . . . and still live in the world. Whether husbands went to synagogue or not, and what they did there, always seemed somewhat beside the point. (342)

Instead, these women "hallow the everyday" (318); their traditions encompass birth and death, and while some of those traditions come from the Torah and generations of teachers, others, "the most mysterious," are "passed from one *bubbe* [grandmother] to another" (342). For Ehrlich, the women who practice this kind of female religion remain connected to an intuitive female wisdom. Hence of all the women who predicted the sex of her first child, "only my Ivy League-trained obstetrician predicted a boy":

> Any other woman in any way connected to a folk tradition, anywhere in the world—the West Indian checkout clerk at the supermarket, the Harlem-reared secretary at work, the Chinatown peddler, the Hispanic woman on the bus, and of course, Miriam—these women unanimously appraised my complexion and the configuration of the weight I was gaining, and stated definitively, "It's a girl." (199)

Ehrlich increasingly prizes this female wisdom of the home and family above the professional and educational knowledge of the public, implicitly masculine sphere; admitting that her maternal grandmother could read Hebrew but would not have been educated in the Texts, Ehrlich remarks, "We can fan our complaints into great flames, but one truth is fireproof: those girls knew what they knew" (198). Later, she writes that the *bubbe* knew the traditions "in a way that is beyond knowing: so ingrained was the tradition, it had become, for her, pure expression" (319). Just as those trained in Judaic ritual from childhood on have kosher souls, so those women trained in domestic artistry from childhood on have an almost instinctive or intuitive grasp of this female religion.

Two events in the memoir—one having to do with birth, the other with death—bear witness to the way in which Ehrlich finds female religion "hallowing the everyday." The first, the ceremony to name Ehrlich's

daughter, acquaints her with a distinctly female tradition within traditional Judaism: whereas the *bris*, the ceremony of male circumcision, is
an obligation, the "baby naming for a girl is pure tradition . . . one of
those distinctions that makes a girl seem less valued than a boy" (197).
Ehrlich initially suspects, in fact, that celebrations for daughters are modern
inventions, only to learn from her mother that her grandmother "assured
that a delicate thread of female connection was worked into the generations' embroidery, on my behalf. . . . She stood at the handlettered parch-
ment scroll and stitched her mother's name, Libe Beyle, into her prayers
for me" (197). The imagery of stitchery and weaving, of needlework and
embroidery, provides a feminine complement to the implicitly masculine
scrolls. The thread also images the generational link that Ehrlich finds so
attractive: "[G]iven names in a family reach endlessly back through time.
We live with our legacies . . . and life is made dimensional thereby" (199).
When she is called away from home to participate in the ceremony,
however, she is chagrined to find that she would rather remain at home:
"Ice cubes had to be cracked out of freezer trays, fresh towels had to be
hung at the last minute—female religion" (203). Suddenly caught up in
the confusions of gender, Ehrlich wonders what model of femininity she
will provide for her daughter: "Her name was about to be threaded into
the tradition. What was her place in that fabric to be? What was mine?
Was it only about duty, obedience? Was it only about being a woman in
the kitchen?" (203). Decidedly ambivalent, she does indeed attend the
ceremony, but she remains acutely aware of who steps in at home to
replace her: "While I took my baby to the *bima* [temple platform] on
that thrilling journey, infused with the power of what we might become,
my sister and my brother's wife stayed home. The rabbi was right, the
service was beautiful. The baby girl's aunts, however, missed the entire
thing" (204). The conflict between access to the public sphere and the
demands of the private sphere colors the whole episode.

The baby naming occurs early on in *Miriam's Kitchen*, and it is a
mark of how Ehrlich's values change that her ruminations on her
grandmother's funeral display more certainty about the inherent value of
female religion. Ehrlich places this account, chronologically anterior to
her daughter's birth, near the close of the book; this account demonstrates how motherhood and interactions with Miriam have revived for
Ehrlich the "practical, mystical teachings" of her grandmothers. Ehrlich
no longer seems deeply divided about women's unequal access to the
public sphere: noting that the ten-man quorum, the *minyan*, does not
count women, Ehrlich writes,

> I have never yet been to a *shiva* where women were counted
> in the *minyan*. I am unlearned; were I counted, I would not
> know what to do. In other settings, this worries and offends

> me, but not in this one. *Shiva*, for me, still is about that old-time female web, the embroidery with which women build and embellish. (320)

The pattern for her, she recalls, was set at her first *shiva*, one held in honor of her *bubbe* in "the old-fashioned style familiar to [her]" (320). What Ehrlich remembers is a female pattern of comfort and nurture, of care for others: "My impulse, on a *shiva* call, is to draw close, hold a lonely hand, fix a chopped liver sandwich for a grieving friend, that is all" (320). As in the baby-naming ceremony, women forego the public events in order to enact kitchen culture and female religion by tending to the needs of others:

> Inside, the table would have been laid for a meal by women, who came straight here from the service at the funeral home, letting their men drive to the ceremony and witness the emotional farewell. The women would have boiled the eggs and peeled and rinsed them, found tablecloths and dishes and cups and knives tucked in unfamiliar cupboards, and set out food they had prepared. (319)

Throughout the seven days of sitting *shiva*, in fact, women remain busy, "clearing, setting, washing, wrapping and unwrapping, making coffee, making tea" (320). But Ehrlich no longer wonders whether women are missing out on something important. Women's work for her now sustains the fabric of life and provides her with the satisfying stability she had hungered for: "If I lose my footing, I have the woven web of centuries, with all its compromises, even banalities, to fall into" (321). Indeed, by the end of the book, Ehrlich will speculate that women do the most essential work of all, for their domestic labor brings the Sabbath into being: "When you wash your floor, dust, cook, and set the table on Friday... you 'make' Sabbath. . . . Are women God?" she wonders (355). Sabbath reminds her of the "artist's paradox": just as the laws of perspective shape our impression of the painting's flat canvas, so the preparations shape the experience of the Sabbath, for the "*Shabbas* feeling cannot be attained from a color-by-numbers kit" (355). These claims for the artistry and value of female religion conclude Ehrlich's pilgrimage, her journey complete as she comes full circle and returns to her grandmothers' rituals and the female wisdom of kitchen culture.

DEALING WITH—OR DUCKING OUT OF—THE STALLED REVOLUTION

Ehrlich's account is eloquent in its depiction of the importance and centrality of kitchen practices in the transmission of cultural traditions and religious beliefs; her deep intimacy with Miriam and her celebration of multigenerational bonds between women recall Virginia Woolf's famous line that "we think back through our mothers if we are women" (the cover photograph, supplied by Ehrlich, shows a little girl—Ehrlich?—running up to hug her mother, who stands next to a dining room table and waits with open arms; in the background hovers the grandmother, at the threshold of the kitchen, wearing an apron). Yet a feminist reader may come away with a deep sense of uneasiness and a number of unanswered questions. Ehrlich's revival of her grandmothers' kitchen culture elides the 1950s, a decade when many women were deeply unhappy about being relegated to the domestic sphere, where they felt unappreciated and infantilized. (Ehrlich's mother rejected a full-time domestic role in the 1950s, electing instead to study literature and work.) Ehrlich's own decision to leave work, handled in a very muted way in the memoir, suggests that she was in effect holding down two jobs: a paid job at work, an unpaid job at home. Despite a supposed egalitarian marriage in which both parents worked, for example, Ehrlich found herself more and more responsible for organizing family life: "[T]his sort of thing must become a priority mission for someone in the household, and that person would have to be me," she explains. But Ehrlich does not explain why that person would have to be her. Tellingly, when she draws up a list of what needs to be done in order to prepare for the Sabbath, she automatically assigns her husband a secondary role and assumes his inability to take on more of the domestic tasks:

> I can't cook on Friday, I'm working on Friday. I can cook on Thursday night after the children are in bed if I'm not too tired, or I can cook at five in the morning on Friday. My husband could cook, but he can't cook. If I have the money, I'll have the house cleaned.
>
> I have to shop before cooking, and when will I do it? I will shop on Thursday evening, if I have the strength. Or my husband could shop, if I made up the list on Wednesday. (291)

Ehrlich portrays herself as the primary manager and organizer, while her husband helps her, as if in fact the domestic jobs are hers in the first place. Ehrlich apparently never considers her husband a potential equal partner in the kitchen or in the sharing of domestic tasks: she repeatedly states that keeping kosher exacts a heavy toll from women, as if men cannot be expected to share the burdens (24). No wonder, then, that she constantly refers to her exhaustion as she tries to juggle the demands of work and family; no wonder, since she seems to be able to afford to leave her job, that she becomes a full-time homemaker.

Yet it is also clear that Ehrlich is herself deeply conflicted about her attempt to combine work and family; she struggles and finally fails to quash powerful conventional definitions of appropriate maternal and feminine behavior. She notes, for example, her sensitivity to Miriam's disapproval: instead of "a daughter-in-law who didn't work, one with perfect nails and a house to match," Ehrlich writes, "she got me, a mad circus juggler keeping too many plates aloft, while which ones were crashing I didn't know" (300). Again, Ehrlich's sense of chaotic inner fragmentation is at odds with the calm, orderly, stable image she wishes to project. This more conventional role is what she wishes to model for her daughter, moreover, and one of the most disconcerting aspects of the memoir is Ehrlich's profound investment in her daughter's initiation into the practices of kitchen culture. Whereas she barely mentions her two sons in conjunction with cooking, she repeatedly dwells upon the—to her pleasing—prospect of her daughter's learning the grandmothers' ways. Setting out the recipe for a form of dumpling which contains a bit of chicken skin, a morsel Ehrlich's grandmother had referred to as the dumpling's soul, Ehrlich exults, "My daughter calling my mother for the recipe? My mother who approximated her mother's recipe? Her motherless mother who reinvented her mother's recipe? The ancient and timeless matzo ball? Yes, that's my religion" (218). The sight of her daughter's cooking with Miriam recurs throughout the book; so important is it to Ehrlich that she even recalls such sights years later: "I close my eyes and I see: that six-year-old girl on the screened front porch . . . making . . . dumplings with her grandmother" (308). In fact, when Ehrlich lists Miriam's possible heirs, she lists only herself and her daughter, omitting her husband (Miriam's son!) as well as her sons: "[I]t has come down to this: Miriam, an only child . . . showing me on behalf of a single granddaughter" (265). Apparently Ehrlich never considers passing this heritage on to her sons: the kitchen for her is an entirely female realm.

Ehrlich's journey toward keeping kosher, then, is a complex one. It is also one that resonates with an increased media emphasis on women's return to the home. While statistical studies suggest that this return has been grossly exaggerated—these stories actually dwell upon and thereby inflate a small percentage of well-off professional women with the economic wherewithal to leave paid work—Ehrlich's memoir still raises important and troubling issues for feminists. Women's movement into the work force has not freed them from primary responsibility for housework and child-rearing; instead, women perform "double duty"—a paid job and a second shift at home.[9] The failure of men to contribute their fair share of housework and childcare has resulted in what Arlie Hochschild has called a "stalled revolution." "For many women," write Elliott Currie, Robert Dunn, and David Fogarty, "entering the labor force to keep the family standard of living intact has meant more work, less leisure, and a more harried family life" (324). Judith Stacey notes that women's increased participation in paid work has produced a "portentous social effect through the drastic decline in the potential pool of female volunteers . . . who have sustained much of family and community life in the United States since the nineteenth century" ("Sexism" 341). The "general deterioration of domesticity and social housekeeping . . . in turn is fueling reactionary nostalgia for traditional family life among leftists and feminists as well as among right-wing forces," she charges (341). Yet it is easy to see why. With the visible unhappiness of dependent, exploited, and infantilized housewives no longer in front of us, the image of the Feeding Mother becomes ever more seductive, a marker of a time when (some) women performed one job instead of two. Ehrlich's repeated references to her own sense of chaos and inner fragmentation bear vivid witness to the toll the "stalled revolution" exacts, even from feminists like herself who might have expected to work out more equitable marital arrangements.

Furthermore, and perhaps even more important, Ehrlich's account suggests how deeply divided some women may be about the loss of traditional female culture and the kind of female bonding fostered in the intimate space of the kitchen. As I indicate above, food scholars and historians believe feminists have been far too cavalier in dismissing these aspects of kitchen culture. The testimony of writers like Gloria Wade-Gayles and Paule Marshall bears vivid witness to the fact that kitchen culture can be a vibrant source of a powerful female voice, a vital female authority. The women they memorialize have been successful in carving out a space of expression and resistance within the kitchen. At the same time, the hostility many feminists express toward domesticity has an equally valid source—the knowledge that women's "kin work" exacts enormous individual costs: the more women are naturally associated with domesticity and cooking, the harder it becomes to restart the "stalled revolution" and institute more equitable arrangements within the home and within the culture at large. Ehrlich tends to reinstitute a traditional definition of femininity while at the same time eliding the class privilege that underpins it. For, as Katha Pollit notes, motherhood and domesticity have become class privileges: "For the well-off, running the house becomes a holy task, than which nothing of which the human spirit is capable could possibly be more important," she writes (10). Yet poor women are demonized for not being able to combine domestic labor with working: "At the bottom of the social scale family life is invisible; all that matters is paid work, never mind if slogging long hours for low pay means your kids suffer" (10). These are contradictions feminists must continue to call attention to and work to overcome, even as we learn to recognize and yes, even celebrate, women's kitchen culture.

I want to end, however, with a cautionary note. Ehrlich speaks of how her mother "kept the flame alive" by celebrating the Sabbath in a traditional way. What Ehrlich overlooks is how other women keep the flame alive by keeping the doors to the kitchen open, into the world of public accomplishment, education, paid work. In an eerie way, Ehrlich's memoir suggests that she does in fact equate femininity with public exclusion. Ehrlich recalls how, when she first menstruated, her grandmother slapped her face, a custom Ehrlich believes enacts punishment in advance for sexual sins (205). Another traditional explanation for this practice, however, holds that the slap symbolically initiates women into the pain of subordination.[10] Near the end of the memoir, Ehrlich relates another painful anecdote: her daughter, having learned to read Hebrew, is refused the right to read in her grandfather's temple: "This is an unhappy first for my daughter. The impersonal exclusion arrives like a slap. . . . [S]he *is* capable of participating, contributing" (344). Ehrlich's text points to a compelling reality that she herself seems to play down: if we celebrate the kitchen and kin work as an exclusive domain for women, we risk exclusion from the public sphere and punishment for daring to transgress. Painful as it might be, then, the notion of an exclusive matrilineal kitchen culture must be sacrificed: sons, not just daughters, should learn these culinary ways of knowing; the jealous guarding of a compensatory alternative authority must give way to the hope that "many hands make light work."

NOTES

1. For a discussion of the recent emergence of the "culinary memoir," see Traci Marie Kelly, " 'If I Were a Voodoo Priestess': Women's Culinary Autobiographies." Kelly considers the unusual formal aspects of the culinary memoir as well as its source in a female oral tradition. While she discusses Elizabeth Ehrlich's memoir within these parameters, she does not explore the questions of female authority and kitchen space that I raise here.

2. See the two studies by Mary Field Belenky et al., *Women's Ways of Knowing: The Development of Self, Voice, and Mind*; and *Knowledge, Difference, and Power: Essays Inspired by* Women's Ways of Knowing. As the authors point out, their work has often been attacked as essentialist, but in fact it is not: they never claim these modes of acquiring knowledge are singularly feminine, although they do argue that these modes have developed as strategies for dealing with disempowerment, silencing, and the devaluation of knowledge acquired in unconventional ways (*Knowledge* 7).

3. The term "kitchen culture" comes from the anthology of the same name, *Kitchen Culture in America*, ed. Sherrie A. Inness.

4. In addition to Marjorie L. De Vault, *Feeding the Family: The Social Organization of Caring as Gendered Work*, see Arlie Hochschild and Anne Machung, *The Second Shift: Working Parents and the Revolution at Home.*

5. Minnich's account recalls the passage in Virginia Woolf's *To the Lighthouse* in which Cam remembers wandering from the garden into her father's study (189–190); the study serves as a marker of male privilege and the respect accorded male activities and the life of the mind.

6. These well-publicized accounts obscure the actual number of women who leave the workforce to devote themselves full-time to childcare and home-making. In fact, according to recent U.S. Census data, mothers with small children are increasingly entering the work force ("Helping Working Families"). Women who do leave work to become full-time homemakers tend to come from the higher, more affluent income brackets. For a discussion of the gap between media accounts and the actual data on working women, see Bianchi and Spain, 42. For some representative articles celebrating the "personal"—never economic—reasons for becoming a full-time wife and mother, see pieces by Sarah Evans, "Mothers Making Themselves More at Home"; Evan Gahr and Richard Miniter, "Is Going Home Possible?"; Linda S. Lichter, "Home Truths"; Liz McCloskey, "Feminist Homemaker Confesses"; Mark Singer, "Mom Overboard!"; and Angela Ward, "A Feminist Mystique." For an early discussion of media backlash to feminism, see Deborah Rosenfelt and Judith Stacey, "Second Thoughts on the Second Wave."

7. It is a mark of Ehrlich's unquestioned sense of gender division that she never perceives her husband, Miriam's son, as the appropriate inheritor of Miriam's legacy.

8. Miriam's assumption of the role of grandmother is complete when she masters the recipe for Ehrlich's grandmother's chocolate cake: "Three children now, three birthdays each year, and never a birthday has passed since then without 'Grandma's chocolate cake'" (133). The name of the recipe—and the role embedded in that name—subsume the individuals who make it. Miriam has even intuited the original form of the cake, baking it in a bundt pan, as Ehrlich's grandmother did, instead of in round pans, as Aunt Selina did when she served it to Miriam.

9. For discussions of this phenomenon, see Arlie Hochschild and Anne Machung, *The Second Shift*; and Stephanie Coontz, *The Way We Really Are* 262–81.

10. See, for example, Carol Lee Flinders, *At the Root of this Longing: Reconciling a Spiritual Hunger and a Feminist Thirst*, 147.

WORKS CITED

Avakian, Arlene Voski. *Through the Kitchen Window: Women Writers Explore the Intimate Meanings of Food and Culture*. Boston: Beacon, 1977.

Bartky, Sandra Lee. *Femininity and Domination: Studies in the Phenomenology of Oppression*. New York: Routledge, 1990.

Belenky, Mary Field, *et al. Knowledge, Difference, and Power: Essays Inspired by* Women's Ways of Knowing. New York: Basic, 1996.

―――. *Women's Ways of Knowing: The Development of Self, Voice, and Mind.* New York: Basic, 1986.

Bianchi, Suzanne M., and Daphne Spain. "Women, Work, and Family in America." *Population Bulletin* 51.3 (December 1996): 2–45.

Coontz, Stephanie. *The Way We Really Are: Coming to Terms with America's Changing Families.* New York: Basic, 1997.

Currie, Elliott, Robert Dunn, and David Fogarty. "The Fading Dream: Economic Crisis and the New Inequality." *Women, Class, and the Feminist Imagination: A Socialist-Feminist Reader.* Ed. Karen V. Hansen and Ilene J. Philipson. Philadelphia: Temple UP, 1990. 319–37.

Deleuze, Gilles, and Felix Guattari. "What Is a Minor Literature?" *Narrative/ Theory.* Ed. David H. Richter. New York: Longman, 1996. 273–80.

De Vault, Marjorie L. *Feeding the Family: The Social Organization of Caring as Gendered Work.* Chicago: U of Chicago P, 1991.

Ehrlich, Elizabeth. *Miriam's Kitchen: A Memoir.* New York: Penguin, 1997.

Evans, Sandra. "Mothers Making Themselves More at Home: Many Women Forgo Return to Working World Despite Pressures." *Washington Post* October 2, 1989: A1+.

Flinders, Carol Lee. *At the Root of This Longing: Reconciling a Spiritual Hunger and a Feminist Thirst.* San Francisco: Harper, 1998.

Gahr, Evan, and Richard Miniter. "Is Going Home Possible? (Entrepreneurs, Career Women Return to the Home)." *American Enterprise* 9.3 (May–June, 1998): 50. *California Digital Library Magazine and Journal Articles.* Online. University of California Library. August 4, 1999.

Gillis, John R. *A World of Their Own Making: Myth, Ritual, and the Quest for Family Values.* Cambridge: Harvard UP, 1996.

Haber, Barbara. "Follow the Food." Avakian 65–74.

"Helping Working Families." *San Francisco Chronicle.* October 30, 2000: A20.

Hochschild, Arlie, and Anne Machung. *The Second Shift: Working Parents and the Revolution at Home.* New York: Viking, 1989.

Inness, Sherrie A., ed. *Kitchen Culture in America.* Philadelphia: U of Pennsylvania P, 2001.

Kelly, Traci Marie. " 'If I Were a Voodoo Priestess': Women's Culinary Autobiographies." Inness 251–69.

Lichter, Linda S. "Home Truths." *Commentary* 97. 6 (June 1994): 49–52.

Marshall, Paule. "From the Poets in the Kitchen." *Reena and other Stories, Including the Novella "Merle" and Commentary by the Author.* New York: Feminist Press, 1982.

McCloskey, Liz. "Feminist Homemaker Confesses: Taking the Irony out of Housework." *Commonweal* 123.12 (June 14, 1996): 6. *California Digital Library Magazine and Journal Articles.* Online. University of California Library. August 4, 1999.

Minnich, Elizabeth Kamarck. "But Really, There Are No Recipes . . ." Avakian 134–47.

Moore, Judith. *Never Eat Your Heart Out.* New York: North Point, 1997.

Pollitt, Katha. "Home Discomforts." *The Nation* January 24, 2000: 10.

Proust, Marcel. *Remembrance of Things Past.* 1934. Trans. C. K. Scott Moncrieff and Terence Kilmartin. Vol. 1. New York: Random, 1981.

Randall, Margaret. "That's What My Tongue Knows." Avakian 117–33.

Rosenfelt, Deborah, and Judith Stacey. "Second Thoughts on the Second Wave." *Feminist Studies* 13.2 (Summer 1987): 341–61.

Singer, Mark. "Mom Overboard! What Do Power Women Who Decide to Quit the Fast Track Do with Themselves All Day?" *New Yorker* 72.2: 62–74.

Smyth, Marie. "Hedge Nutrition, Hunger, and Irish Identity." Avakian 89–94.

Stacey, Judith. "Are Feminists Afraid to Leave Home? The Challenge of Conservative Pro-family Feminism." *What is Feminism?* Ed. Juliet Mitchell and Ann Oakley. New York: Pantheon, 1986. 208–37.

———. "Sexism by a Subtler Name? Postindustrial Conditions and Postfeminist Consciousness in Silicon Valley." *Women, Class, and the Feminist Imagination.* Ed. Karen V. Hansen and Ilene J. Philipson. Philadelphia: Temple UP, 1990. 338–56.

Wade-Gayles, Gloria. " 'Laying on Hands' through Cooking: Black Women's Majesty and Mystery in Their Own Kitchen." Avakian 95–103.

Ward, Angela. "A Feminist Mystique (Those Who Ask When I'm Going Back to Work Make It Clear that Homemaking Is Not a Real Job." *Newsweek* 112. 11 (September 12, 1988): 8–9.

Woolf, Virginia. *To the Lighthouse.* New York: Harcourt, 1928.

Yeats, William Butler. "The Second Coming." *The Poems.* 1921. *The Collected Works of W. B. Yeats.* Ed. Richard J. Finneran. Vol. 1. New York: Scribner, 1997. 189.

Contributors

Debra Beilke is associate professor of English at Concordia University-St. Paul, where she teaches courses in writing, American literature, and world literature. She has published articles on southern humor and writers such as Zora Neale Hurston, Frances Newman, Julia Peterkin, and T. S. Stribling. She is currently working on a book-length manuscript on literary humor in the Southern Renaissance.

Chris Foss teaches at Mary Washington College. He has previously published on Ford Madox Ford, Henry James, Julia Kristeva, Percy Bysshe Shelley, Robert Louis Stevenson, Algernon Charles Swinburne, and the film version of Valerie Martin's *Mary Reilly*.

Pamela K. Gilbert is associate professor of English at the University of Florida. Her work has appeared in journals such as *Nineteenth Century Studies, Nineteenth Century Prose, Women and Performance, English, LIT: Literature/Interpretation/Theory, Essays in Art and Sciences, Essays in Literature, Victorian Newsletter*, and others. She is also the author of *Disease, Desire and the Body in Victorian Women's Popular Novels* (Cambridge University Press, 1997), and coeditor, with Marlene Tromp and Aeron Haynie, of *Beyond Sensation: Mary Elizabeth Braddon in Context* (State University of New York Press, 2000). Another edited collection, *Imagined Londons*, has been published by State University of New York Press, 2002. She is currently finishing a book which traces the construction of the social body and public health in England, especially London, from 1832 to 1866.

Tamar Heller, assistant professor of English at the University of Cincinnati and assistant editor at *Victorian Literature and Culture*, is the author of *Dead Secrets: Wilkie Collins and the Female Gothic* (Yale University Press, 1992) and of essays on such topics as women writers (Charlotte Brontë, Margaret Oliphant, Edith Wharton), romance novels, and Victorian pornography. She is also coeditor, with Diane Long Hoeveler, of *Approaches to Teaching Gothic Fiction* (New York: MLA Press, forthcoming 2003) in the MLA Series on *Approaches to Teaching World Literature*.

Janice A. Jaffe's research focuses on the politics of translation and on food in Latin American literature. In addition to studies on literary translation, she has published on Latin American women writers from the colonial period to the present, including Sor Juana Ines de la Cruz, Rosario Ferre, and Laura Esquivel. She is an associate professor of Spanish at Bowdoin College.

Suzanne Keen, professor of English at Washington and Lee University, is the author of *Victorian Renovations of the Novel: Narrative Annexes and the Boundaries of Representation* (Cambridge University Press, 1998) and *Romances of the Archive in Contemporary British Fiction* (University of Toronto Press, 2001). Her current projects include a textbook on narrative form and a book-length study, *Empathy and the Novel*.

Patricia Moran is associate professor of English at the University of California, Davis. In addition to articles on women writers, psychoanalytic theory, and female sexuality, she is the author of *Word of Mouth: Body Language in Katherine Mansfield and Virginia Woolf* (University of Virginia Press, 1996). She is currently completing a study of modernist women writers and the female body, *The Flaw in the Centre: Women, Modernism, and the Aesthetics of Damage*.

Adrienne Munich is professor of English and Women's Studies at the State University of New York, Stonybrook. She is the author of books and articles on Victorian literature and culture, among them *Andromeda's Chains* (Columbia UP, 1989) and *Queen Victoria's Secrets* (Columbia UP, 1996), and is the coeditor of the journal *Victorian Literature and Culture*. Most recently, she coedited the selected poems of Amy Lowell (Rutgers, 2002) and a forthcoming collection of critical essays about Amy Lowell (Rutgers, forthcoming 2003).

Linda Schlossberg received her Ph.D. in English from Harvard University in 1998. She lives and writes in San Francisco. She is the coeditor (with Maria C. Sanchez) of *Passing: Identity and Interpretation in Sexuality, Race, and Religion* (New York University Press, 2001).

Ann Folwell Stanford is associate professor at the School for New Learning, DePaul University. She has published articles in *American Literature, African American Review, MELUS, Literature and Medicine, NWSA Journal*, and others. She has recently completed a study on women novelists of color and the politics of medicine. Drawing on her creative writing workshops for the last five years with women in Cook County Jail, she is currently writing about women, writing, and incarceration.

Sue Thomas is reader in English and coordinator of the English program in the School of Communication, Arts and Critical Enquiry at La Trobe University, Melbourne. She is the author of *The Worlding of Jean Rhys* (Greenwood, 1999), coauthor (with Ann Blake and Leela Gandhi) of *England through Colonial Eyes in Twentieth-Century Fiction* (Palgrave, 2001) and compiler of *Elizabeth Robins (1862–1952): A Bibliography* (University of Queensland, 1994) and many other titles in the Victorian Fiction Research Guides Series. She has published extensively on nineteenth- and twentieth-century women's writing and decolonising literatures.

Index